UTAH

OFF THE BEATEN PATH®

OFF THE BEATEN PATH® SERIES

SIXTH EDITION

UTAH

OFF THE BEATEN PATH®

DISCOVER YOUR FUN

MICHAEL RUTTER

Globe
Pequot
Guilford, Connecticut

To my wife, Shari, for all the miles we've traveled.

All the information in this guidebook is subject to change. We recommend that you call ahead to obtain current information before traveling.

Globe
Pequot

An imprint of The Rowman & Littlefield Publishing Group, Inc.
4501 Forbes Blvd., Ste. 200
Lanham, MD 20706
www.rowman.com

Distributed by NATIONAL BOOK NETWORK

British Library Cataloguing in Publication Information available

Library of Congress Cataloging-in-Publication Data available

ISBN 978-1-4930-4414-6 (paperback)
ISBN 978-1-4930-4415-3 (e-book)

♾™ The paper used in this publication meets the minimum requirements of American National Standard for Information Sciences—Permanence of Paper for Printed Library Materials, ANSI/NISO Z39.48-1992.

Contents

NORTHERN
UTAH

Salt Lake City ★

Provo ■

WEST–CENTRAL
UTAH

NORTHEASTERN
UTAH

Price ■

Delta ■

CENTRAL
UTAH

Moab ■

SOUTHEASTERN
UTAH

Cedar City ■

SOUTHWESTERN
UTAH

Introduction

Your experience will center around the landscape because Utah is a panorama of extremes. The land itself is a character, along with the other players, the climate and the folks who call the Beehive State home. The word *Utah* means "high up" or "people of the mountains." "Life Elevated" is proudly displayed on our license plates. Indeed, the average elevation is over 6,000 feet. We have the "greatest snow" on earth—quite a claim for one of the most arid states in the Union.

The Rocky Mountains, the Great Basin, the Colorado Plateau, and the Mojave Desert form one of the most unique regions on earth. Again, think extremes, the lush, lofty peaks of the Uinta Mountains; the crusty Bonneville Salt Flats, a terror to overland travelers trying to reach the gold fields; the sculpted entrada sandstone rock bridges of Arches National Park; or the Joshua Tree National Natural Landmark, a botanical gem that averages five inches of rain per year. The terrain, the climate, and the colors are what you would expect to find stretched across a continent—not blended into a state casually referred to as "the crossroads of the west."

Rain, snow, ice, wind, and water have sculpted Utah. The sandstone monoliths of Zion Canyon, the limestone hoodoos of Red Canyon, and the granite cliffs of Little Cottonwood Canyon show that Mother Nature is not only a creator but an artist. As an added bonus, there are 800 varieties of wildflowers, abundant big game, and 462 species of birds.

Around the next corner you will discover something totally unexpected, maybe a small grand canyon, a limestone pinnacle, a bighorn sheep, or a mountain peak over 13,000 feet. Simultaneous beautiful can be breathtaking—almost frightening. It challenges your aesthetics and enhances your senses: look for something intriguing in a labyrinth of rock that pokes out of the ground at Needles or investigate the poignant solitude of an abandoned homesteader's cabin weathering in dusty ruin at Brown's Park.

This is also a land of heritages. Stare as long as you dare at the Holy Ghosts hovering on the sandstone walls, stunning and shapeless, but life-sized and real. The Ghosts were painted about 2,000 years ago and are part of The Great Gallery in Horseshoe Canyon. It is a splendid 200 feet long and 15 feet high, perhaps the most significant rock art in North America. There has been human activity in this canyon for over 10,000 years. Mammoth hunting Paleo-Indians were followed by the Desert Archaic, Fremont, and Ancestral Puebloans cultures. Consider, too, the other natives, the Goshutes, Utes, Paiutes, Shoshoni, and Navajos. The bold Spanish priests Dominguez and Escalante wandered the region in 1776 looking for an overland route. The mountain men searched for beaver pelts and then the pioneers settled this dry but colorful land.

Brigham Young chose Utah as "the right place" for the Mormons. Seeking respite from intense religious persecution, the Saints sought refuge in their Great Basin Kingdom as their mountain home. They found what they were looking for in the Salt Lake Valley in 1847. Brigham Young's prophecy that the desert would blossom like a rose came to fruition. The Mormons, indeed, created a home in a relentless wilderness. But isolation for the Mormons couldn't last. Making its appearance in 1869, the intercontinental railroad changed everything. Not only did it signal the end of the pioneer era, it ended the Mormons' brief period of sanctuary. With the railroad came industry and mining. Gold and silver, among other minerals, sent prospectors hollering "Eureka!" Mining camps turned into boomtowns. Gamblers, prostitutes, and drifters followed, locating themselves uncomfortably close to austere Mormon farmers and ranchers. Some of the West's most infamous outlaws were here. This included the wily and beloved Butch Cassidy, a Utah native. Along with the Sundance Kid, Kid Curry, and Matt Warner, the Wild Bunch followed the Outlaw Trail. Cassidy was the most successful outlaw in the West. He had grassroots support and was a meticulous planner. Was he killed in South American or did he come back to Utah?

As fate would have it, boom and bust was the way of many Western towns, including towns in Utah. There are ghost towns, to be sure, but many communities still retained their frontier flavor. Utahans embrace and appreciate their heritage and enjoy long retrospective looks back at the olden days. There are a host of small-town museums which introduce travelers to our history. Many are focused on particular towns, valleys, and counties. Scores of historic homes

State of Utah Fast Facts

Area: 84,916 square miles

Population: 2.8 million

Capital: Salt Lake City (largest city)

Statehood: January 4, 1896

Highest Point: Kings Peak, 13,528 feet

Lowest Point: Beaver Dam Creek, 2,000 feet

Nickname: Beehive State

Motto: Industry

State Bird: Seagull

State Flower: Sego Lily

State Tree: Blue Spruce

have been converted into bed-and-breakfast inns, allowing you an intimate glimpse at the domestic livelihood of early inhabitants.

Utah has so much to offer. Please help preserve it by adhering to zero- or low-impact land ethics, which include packing out what you pack in. The beauty we have to offer is often fragile, keep to the roads and two-tracks, and stay on established trails. Indian ruins, artifacts, and rock art demand the same respect. In Utah you see many archaeological finds as they were originally discovered, not sheltered and secured in a museum. Witnessing these treasures in a pristine state is a privilege, a legacy for future generations.

And, while we have economic and luxurious accommodations, there are many places that allow you to get completely off the grid. Enjoy "no service" on your phone in the backcountry. Listen to the real sounds of the desert, the forest, or the canyons. Most of the state's population lives within twenty miles of the Wasatch front so you can get away from it all. Remember to book ahead when you make travel plans. Seasonal rates can vary widely, so it pays to look carefully.

Indulge yourself and escape to Utah.

Northern Utah

Northern Utah probably wouldn't be the most populated region in the state if it weren't for its most striking feature, the **Wasatch Mountains**. Thrusting out of the barren floor of the Great Basin, the Wasatch Range nurtures the cities strung along its foot, sending down the all-too-precious water that allowed civilization to blossom from the desert. Sculpted by ancient glaciers and rising to incredible heights, the mountains also serve as a dynamic backdrop.

In addition to the Wasatch Mountains, you can count the **Great Salt Lake** as another unique, if not bizarre, geographical feature in Northern Utah. While exploring the area in 1824, **Jim Bridger** happened upon what he believed to be the Pacific Ocean. Tasting the salty water, he was astounded to find "the ocean" practically at the foot of the Rockies and such a short distance from Cache Valley. Little did he know, he was possibly the first white man to behold the Great Salt Lake, and maybe the first in a long line of pioneers to be befuddled by it.

The rest of the country is finally waking up to the beauty of Northern Utah, making it one of the fastest growing regions in America, much to the chagrin of many of its natives. The

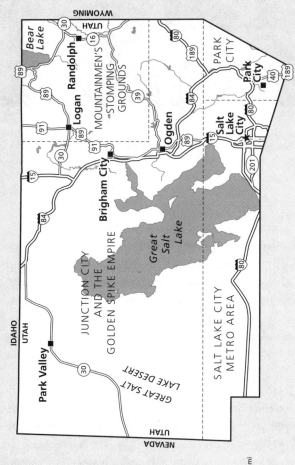

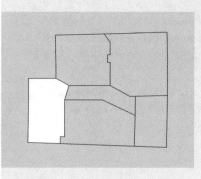

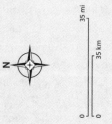

International Olympic Committee also took notice, hosting the 2002 Winter Olympic Games in Salt Lake City and surrounding sites.

Salt Lake City Metro Area

The capital of Utah, **Salt Lake City**, is also the headquarters and spiritual center of the Church of Jesus Christ of Latter-day Saints (LDS, Mormons). Seeking deliverance from religious persecution, **Brigham Young** led 143 men, 3 women, and 2 children to the Salt Lake Valley in 1847. Upon first sighting the barren desert valley, Young uttered the most famous five words in Utah's history: "This is the right place." If Young had isolation in mind, he had certainly said the appropriate thing. Months after Brigham Young's party landed in Salt Lake City, nearly 2,000 other Mormons followed.

Only the most fervent of people could have raised a city 1,000 miles from the nearest civilization. Mormon ingenuity and sacrifice paid off, but not without the help of what the Mormons consider a miracle. In 1848 the city was plagued by crickets that would have devoured the crops if it hadn't been for the miraculous appearance of seagulls. As if the incident had been rendered in the Bible, the seagulls ate the crickets and spared Salt Lake City from devastation.

Today, Salt Lake City presents an unexpected host of cultural, historical, and culinary features that are often overlooked in the mad dash to the ski resorts. The heart of the city is, of course, **Temple Square**, where the six spires of the granite Salt Lake Temple poke through the skyline. Each year twenty-four million people visit Utah, making it a likely stop for the off-the-beaten-path traveler.

So, what better place to start in Salt Lake City than downtown at the **Salt Lake City and County Building**? One of Utah's most impressive pieces of

AUTHOR'S FAVORITES IN NORTHERN UTAH

Temple Square	Bonneville Salt Flats
Antelope Island	Fly fishing the Weber River
Downtown Park City	Bear River Bird Refuge
Downtown Salt Lake City	This is the Place Heritage Park
Browning Firearms Museum	Transcontinental Railroad National Back Country Byway
The Logan Temple	

architecture, the City and County Building was built on a plot of land that was originally the campsite for newly arrived pioneers in 1847. Over the years the plot became the nucleus of the city, acquiring the name Washington Square. Medicine shows, carnivals, and circuses all took place here before the Romanesque sandstone building was erected.

The building was completed just in time to serve as Utah's capitol building, which it did for nineteen years after Utah gained statehood. Restored in 1989, the City and County Building, open Mon through Fri 8 a.m. to 5 p.m., has a small exhibit of photographs that document the history of the structure. The Utah Heritage Foundation gives free one-hour tours of the building from May to October on Tues at noon and 1 p.m., and Saturday by appointment. Call the foundation at (801) 533-0858 to confirm times. Washington Square is between 400 and 500 South on State Street.

The Church of Jesus Christ of Latter-day Saints Conference Center is the newest addition to Temple Square. It is currently the largest religious auditorium in the United States. Every six months, members from around the world attend the General Conference. They fill the historical tabernacle, of course, and the new Conference Center. This building boasts many levels, including a spectacular waterfall beginning on the roof. It flows down the side, creating a pool at the bottom. Trees and plants can be found inside and outside on every level.

If you're looking for accommodations downtown, you could visit the **Peery Hotel** (801-521-4300 or 800-331-0073; peeryhotel.com) at 110 West Broadway (Third South), Salt Lake City. Established in 1910, the Peery went through years of degradation as a fleabag hotel until it was restored in 1985. Today it lives up to its previous grandeur, offering seventy-seven individually

Sunrise on the High Desert

If you collect sunrises as part of your human journey, consider the Northern Utah deserts. Once you're away from the city and the smog, you can't pick a bad spot. The rise of the sun will be glorious and worth crawling out of bed early for.

Etched against the razor-edged peaks, the eastern sun, in all its fury, creeps slowly into morning, sending rays of light in a hundred different colors to tease the land. And then, almost at once, the giant orb explodes across the barren land, washing the landscape in daylight. The brilliant colors start to fade as the sun rises, and you're better for seeing the dawn.

Sunrise lovers love the rugged, desert regions on the west side of the Great Salt Lake, on the marshes near Grantsville, or near the Bonneville Salt Flats. Pull your car off the road, brew a cup of hot chocolate, and wait for the show.

decorated rooms with a nice array of antiques. Continental breakfast, room service, shoeshine, and airport shuttle are some of the amenities included.

Discreetly tucked away in the mouth of City Creek Canyon, **Memory Grove Park** is footsteps from downtown Salt Lake City but seems a world away. Rushing creek water, grassy banks, and tall pines create a wonderfully sedate atmosphere. Spotted with Greek-columned memorials, a Vietnam-era tank, and a meditation chapel, the park is home to the Utah Veteran's Memorial, dedicated to the Utahans who served and died in wars going back to World War I. A foot trail, frequented by joggers and mountain bikers, continues for 6 miles up City Creek Canyon. From North Temple/Second Avenue, head north on 135 East, about a half-block east of State Street. Or take the trail down from Capitol Hill, beginning just east of the capitol building.

Just a few blocks from Memory Grove Park, at 67 East South Temple, Salt Lake City, **The Beehive House** (801-240-2681) was built in 1854 for Brigham Young and his family. The name comes from the bees and beehives, representing industry, found throughout the building's architecture. The house is now a museum, displaying artifacts and original pioneer furnishings in a number of rooms. Part of the museum, a dry goods store that was also part of the house, sells horehound. It is open from 9:30 a.m. to 4:30 p.m. Mon through Sat (until 6:30 p.m. during the summer), and Sun and holidays 10 a.m. to 1 p.m.

After a day of skiing, hiking, or mountain biking, you may be in the mood to pursue city life. Many enjoy relaxing at the **Red Iguana** (801-322-1489) at 736 West North Temple. It serves some of the most authentic Mexican food in Utah in an upbeat and unpretentious setting. The restaurant is casual and fills up nightly with folks enjoying what is really the most important matter at hand—the food. Unfortunately, reservations are not accepted, so expect to wait for a table. Open daily 11 a.m. to 9 p.m. (until 10 p.m. on Fri and Sat) and Sun from noon to 9 p.m.

The **Utah State Historical Society Museum** (801-533-3500) is housed in the restored Rio Grande railroad station at 300 South Rio Grande (450 West). Its many rotating exhibits often focus on the ethnic groups that helped to settle Utah. It also has research and photograph libraries that display more about Utah's history. While you're there, drop by the **Rio Grande Café** (801-364-3302) for an excellent meal that won't exhaust your budget.

Above the **University of Utah** in the foothills of the Wasatch Mountains, **Red Butte Garden and Arboretum** (801-581-0556; redbuttegarden.org), at 300 Wakara Way, bills itself as the West's premier botanical gardens. Red Butte covers 150 acres, upon which leisurely trails lead past trees, shrubs, floral displays, ponds, natural waterfalls, meadows, and a historic sandstone quarry. Red Butte also has summer outdoor concerts. The easiest way to get to Red Butte is

Worshipping Architecture

There are many religious architectural wonders in Salt Lake City. *The LDS Salt Lake Temple* (801-240-2534) is located at the heart of the city, featuring pioneer craftsmanship and beautiful grounds. *The Holy Trinity Cathedral* (801-328-9681) at 279 South 300 West, stands out in the Greek Orthodox community and houses a Hellenic museum. *St. Mark's Cathedral* (801-322-3400), at 231 East 100 South, is built of sandstone walls and heavy wood ceiling trusses. It contains an 1859 Scottish pipe organ, possibly the oldest pipe organ in Utah. *The Cathedral of the Madeleine* (801-328-8941), at 331 E. South Temple, is one of the finest cathedrals in the West. Its two front towers soar 220 feet high, and inside are intricate carvings in oak and marble, as well as Venetian mosaics. While you are admiring the artwork, you may also enjoy one of their frequent free organ concerts.

by following 400 South up the mountain and past the University of Utah. When the road veers to the south, look for the sign.

In the heart of Salt Lake City, **Liberty Park** (between 1300 and 900 South and west of 700 East) contains tennis courts, a swimming pool, a carousel, and a pond on which you can paddleboat—to name just a few of the park's enticements. In the southwest corner of the park, you'll find **Tracy Aviary**, home to birds from around the world, many of them endangered. Here you'll find two of the eight Andean condors bred in captivity. With a 10-foot wingspan, these ominous creatures are not only the largest bird of prey but also the largest bird of flight. Strolling through the aviary's tree-canopied grounds, you might also spot East African crowned cranes, blue-crowned motmots, Hawaiian geese (the rarest of geese), and our own bald eagles, along with scores of other species you've probably never seen or heard of. Open 9 a.m. to 5 p.m. year round. In June, July, and August there are late Mondays: it's open until 8:00 p.m. For details about special events at the aviary, call (801) 322-2473 or visit their site at tracyaviary.org.

To the north of the aviary and past the little amusement park, be sure to stop in at the **Chase Home Museum of Utah Folk Art** (801-533-5760), housed in the 1854 Chase Home. The adobe brick home, which also belonged to Brigham Young, is truly an appropriate place to display Utah's best folk art. On the ground floor the museum shows changing exhibitions on specific artisan crafts. Upstairs you'll find the **State Collection of Utah Folk Arts**, a wonderfully diverse and multicultural amalgamation of works created by Utah residents. Navajo baskets, Bulgarian pottery, and a Hmong storycloth fit among Armenian needlework, Mexican piñatas, and American duck decoys. The curators, who post black-and-white pictures and short biographies of the

Salty Ol' Salt Lake: The Old Lake Bonneville

The **Great Salt Lake** is impressive—something every visitor should see on a trip to Utah. Nevertheless, it's nothing like it used to be. In the old days, long before the Mormons and locusts, the lake was much larger and it wasn't known as the Great Salt Lake. In fact, it wasn't that salty at all.

It used to be known as **Lake Bonneville**. Back in the olden days—the Pleistocene to be exact—it covered about a third of the state (and part of Nevada and Idaho). The climate was quite a bit cooler then and much wetter.

Bonneville was a pluvial lake, created by abundant rainfall (it was even larger than the pluvial lake that produced Death Valley). At one time it covered more than 35,000 square miles and was several miles deep. Lake Bonneville started to shrink 10,000 years ago, when the climate changed and feeder streams and rivers began to dry up. There was no outlet for the salt, and the land and lake became salty. The Great Salt Lake is four times saltier than any ocean. Salt flats, technically called playas, are common occurrences in this part of the world. The largest playa, known as the Bonneville Salt Flats, can be found in the northwestern corner of the state on I–80 near Wendover, where many land speed records have been set. This alkaline wonder is 4,000 square miles of salt. It's about the flattest place on earth and was referred to as the "dreaded salt flat" by early travelers.

artists next to the respective works, seem dedicated not only to the collection but also to the artists. Certainly the museum is something to make the locals proud. The museum is open Wed 11 a.m. to 8 p.m., and Thurs through Sat 11 a.m. to 4 p.m.

Wildflowers, A Bed and Breakfast (801-466-0600 or 800-569-0009; wild flowersbb.com), at 936 East 1700 South, epitomizes the Victorian architecture that graces the streets of Salt Lake City. With purple trim, blue siding, and a redbrick foundation, the house is almost as colorful as the garden, where columbines, wild geraniums, and quaking aspens (among other things) grow. In the parlor you'll find paintings by the innkeeper, who managed to get a Ph.D. in English on top of becoming a talented painter. Although a little on the small side, the four rooms are nicely furnished and come with their own baths. The suite, appropriately called the Bird's Nest, roosts on the third floor with a patio affording a terrific view of the city and surrounding mountains. They serve a hearty vegetarian breakfast.

Two ski resorts and a host of hiking, biking, and cross-country trails make **Big Cottonwood Canyon** an excellent but well-traveled destination. From downtown Salt Lake City head east on Interstate 80, south on Interstate 215,

A Unique Retail Experience

Gardner Village, located at 1100 West 7800 South, West Jordan, is composed of twenty-two historic buildings from around the valley. Redbrick paths weave between the buildings, decked out to fit the season, and the duck pond. The original building at this site was the Gardner flour mill, built in 1877 and now on the National Register of Historic Places, which houses both the largest country furniture store west of the Mississippi and *Archibald's Restaurant*, located in the silo. The other buildings have plaques telling their history and contain stores unique in Salt Lake Valley, which sell antiques, dolls, home furnishings, candy, art, and much more. One of the stores has the distinction of being one of the largest lace retailers in the West. Other stores include a day spa, a bakery, and a gardening shop with its own in-store floral designer. For more information or a list of retailers, call (801) 566-8903 or visit gardner village.com.

and then follow the signs. A good option for hiking in Big Cottonwood is the **Brighton Lakes Trail**, starting behind the lodge at the **Brighton Ski Resort**. This moderately strenuous trail meanders through stands of aspens and evergreens and leads past three placid lakes—Lake Mary, Lake Martha, and, after 2.5 miles, Lake Catherine. If the scenery has you hooked, then continue for ½ mile to the summit of Catherine Pass (elevation 10,200 feet), where the view is no less than mind-boggling.

With shorter lift lines and cheaper lift tickets, Brighton (801-532-4731 or 800-873-5512), at Star Route, Brighton, and Solitude (800-748-4754 or 801-534-1400), at 12000 Big Cottonwood Canyon, Solitude, are less commercial, less pretentious alternatives to other ski resorts in the Salt Lake area. You can ski both the adjoining resorts the same day by buying a "Big Cottonwood Ski Pass," which accesses you to each of the resorts' seven lifts and sixty-plus runs. If downhill skiing isn't your bag, you may be interested in Solitude's Nordic Center, which rents equipment and offers more than 20 kilometers of cross-country ski trails groomed for both classical and skating styles.

Just before you come to Brighton, you'll see a turnoff for Guardsman Pass. The dirt road, manageable for regular passenger cars, crosses over the crest of the Wasatch Range and drops down into either Park City or Midway (depending on which fork you take on the east side of the mountains). This is the best possible route from Salt Lake City to either of these places from late June to mid-October, or whenever there's no snow blocking the road.

At the southern tip of the Great Salt Lake west of Salt Lake City is the illustrious **Saltair**, "The Grand Lady of the Lake." The Saltair legacy, unfortunate as it has been, goes back more than one hundred years, when the first pavilion was erected on the lake's shore. A special express train ran from Salt Lake City to Saltair, facilitating the amazing popularity of this place. Young folks from all around Utah gravitated to Saltair to float on the water, eat saltwater taffy, and boogie on the biggest outdoor dance floor in the world to the live sounds of America's biggest acts, such as Glenn Miller, Tommy Dorsey, and Louis Armstrong.

In 1925 Saltair burned to the ground, and from the ashes an even more splendid structure was raised. More attractions were added, including the alligator pit, the "Wild Man of Borneo," and the Siamese twins, who were said to have once gotten into a fist fight. After World War II, Saltair lost its novel charm, and by 1959 it was closed and left to rot. Another fire burned the pavilion down in 1970. In the 1980s Saltair was once again resurrected. It did well for a short eight months, after which flood waters seeped into the pavilion and destroyed much of the brand-new structure. For ten years it sat as a mystery to those traveling by it on Interstate 80. The owners, given an ultimatum by the state to either rebuild or destroy it, decided to go for it once again. In 1993 a new building was dedicated on the one-hundredth anniversary of Saltair.

Today Saltair is mainly used as a concert hall, generally for rock acts. You can't miss the pavilion as you're traveling 17 miles west of downtown Salt Lake City on Interstate 80.

Park City

Park City hardly needs any introduction these days. What started out as a rough-and-tumble mining town has exploded into a skiing mecca. Besides **Park City Ski Area**, there are two other ski resorts minutes from town: Deer Valley and The Canyons.

To get some idea of what the town used to be like, stop in at the **Park City Museum** (435-649-7457) at 528 Main Street, which also serves as an information center for the town and area. The museum offers interactive exhibits, artifacts, and the city's original basement jail. Housed in the old City Hall, its design is typical of the Victorian structures lining Park City's Historic Main Street. Beginning in 1868, when the first claim was staked at Park City, prospectors blasted a total of 1,000 miles of tunnels throughout the surrounding mountains. Twenty-three men made more than $1 million on the mines. One of those millionaires was George Hearst, father of newspaper publisher William Randolph Hearst. People came from all over the globe to work in the mines. The town evolved into a multicultural village and took on a character completely different from Salt Lake. The museum also tells the story of Park City's

The Olympic Parks

Now that the 2002 Winter Olympics have come and gone, the Olympic venues have become Utah playgrounds. *Soldier Hollow* (435-654-2002), near Midway, offers cross-country skiing, tubing, and snowshoeing. Those who would like to try their marksmanship skills can receive instruction on the biathlon course year-round. Summer activities include horseback riding, hiking, biking, ATVs, and golf. If speed is your addiction, try the **Utah Olympic Park** in Park City (435-658-4200), which offers ski jumping instruction and bobsled rides year round. Or you can skate on "The Fastest Ice on Earth" at the **Utah Olympic Oval** (801-968-6825) off of 5400 South in Salt Lake City. They offer year-round skating, drop-in hockey, and instruction on everything from speed and figure skating to hockey and curling. For more information about any of these sites, visit olyparks.com.

skiing—the town's saving grace after the mines went bust in the 1930s. The museum is open Mon through Sat, 10 a.m. to 7 p.m., and Sun noon to 6 p.m.

Besides all the shops, bars, and galleries that line Historic Main Street, there is a huge concentration of restaurants, many of which are superb. Located at 151 Main Street, Park City, *Grappa Italian Restaurant* (435-645-0636) has you hooked before the food is set down before you. When you enter, an incredible aroma of herbs and spices arrests your sense of smell. You then see hand-painted tiles, custom-carved chairs, and a bevy of baskets. After so much wonderful foreplay, you have to wonder if the food matches up. Well, it does. To start out, try one of Grappa's excellent designer pizzas, baked in a wood-burning oven. Although the menu changes every two to three months, you can expect something as great as Romano-crusted shrimp, fricassee of poussin (spring chicken), or game hen roasted on an open spit. Be sure to reserve a table, especially during the ski season. The restaurant opens at 5 p.m. during the winter, and at 5:30 p.m. during the summer. To see sample menus, visit grapparestaurant.com.

The Kimball Art Center (1401 Kearns Blvd.; 435-649-8882) has changed quite a bit during its eighty-year history. Originally built as a livery stable, it became a garage and service station before finally becoming an arts center in 1976. It features local and professional artists, hosts many community events, and conducts art classes and workshops. Open Mon through Fri from 10 a.m. to 5 p.m., and Sat and Sun from noon to 5 p.m.

The Kimball Art Center also sponsors the *Park City Arts Festival*, closing down all of historic Main Street for the first weekend in August. It is the largest arts festival in Utah, so it draws a wide variety of visual and sculptural artists. Many of the local restaurants sell sample wares, and music groups from around the world perform. For more details, call (435) 649-8882 or visit kimball artcenter.org.

Nature photography galleries have become almost commonplace in Utah. But there is one gallery that sets the standard for all others, and that's ***Mangelsen Images of Nature Gallery*** (364 Main St.; 435-649-7598 or 888-238-0233). The gallery is a showcase for the work of ***Thomas Mangelsen***, chosen wildlife photographer of the year in 1994 by the BBC. National Geographic, Smithsonian, and Audubon (among others) have all published Mangelsen's pictures. He's also worked as a cinematographer on films such as *National Geographic's Flight of the Whooping Crane* and PBS's *Cranes of the Grey Wind*. The photo of a spawning salmon flying into the mouth of a grizzly bear is perhaps his trademark shot and is indicative of the remarkable forbearance Tom exercises out in the field—the wilds of North America and Africa. In addition to grizzlies, Tom has captured polar bears, bald eagles, moose, lions, and tigers in their most casual behavior. The gallery is open Mon through Thurs 10 a.m. to 8 p.m., Fri and Sat 10 a.m. to 10 p.m.

If you don't want to fight lift lines, an alternative is ***White Pine Nordic Center*** (435-649-6249; whitepinetouring.com) located at 1541 Thaynes Canyon Drive in Park City. Charging modest prices for a trail pass, White Pine has 18 kilometers of tracks groomed on flat and hilly terrain. If you're new to Nordic skiing, you can take a class from the ski school. The Nordic center also rents all the necessary cross-country gear, as well as snowshoes. ***White Pine Touring*** (1790 Bonanza Dr.; 435-649-8710) has bike rentals, guided tours, and lessons available. They are generally open from 9 a.m. to 6 p.m.

If you are looking for more of a wilderness experience on cross-country skis or snowshoes, contact Patton Massengill at the ***Norwegian Outdoor Exploration Center*** (333 Main Street Mall, Second Fl.; 435-649-5322). The school takes you out into surrounding mountains, where you can spend the night in an ice cave or yurt. Or try adventure yurt dining—spend the day exploring, then head to the yurt for a dinner provided by Grappa.

Another alternative to the slopes is a ride in a hot-air balloon. Operating year-round you can soar high above town to get a panoramic look at

You Never Know Who You'll Meet

It's not out of the ordinary to bump into a number of famous folk in Utah—especially on the ski slopes. If you ski at Sundance, you might run into—literally—veteran actor Robert Redford. It's his resort. On other runs you might stargaze at any number of famous actor/director types, since many have cabins in the vicinity.

surrounding mountains. ***Park City Balloon Adventures*** (7436 Brook Hollow Loop Rd.; 435-645-8787 or 800-396-8787).

Each January, Park City receives national attention when the ***Sundance Film Festival*** comes to town. Brainchild of Utah resident ***Robert Redford***, this ten-day event is the country's premier showcase for independently produced narrative and documentary films. Showings are held at different theaters around town, in Salt Lake City, and at Redford's own resort, Sundance. Despite all the Hollywood hoopla that has surrounded the event in recent years, you can still have a great time cruising around town to catch film after film, many of which will probably never make it to a theater near you. The festival also gives you the opportunity to issue compliments or fling insults at the filmmakers or actors, who are usually on hand for after-screening discussions. It's always best to buy tickets as far in advance as possible by calling (801) 328-3456 or online at sundance.org.

One of the key factors that went into the selection of Salt Lake City as the host of the 2002 Olympic Winter Games was the ***Utah Winter Sports Park***, located four miles north of Park City at 3000 Bear Hollow Drive, Park City (off Highway 224). After the Olympics were held, the name was changed to Utah Olympic Park. A training center for the US Nordic Ski Team, the park is also the site for the Olympic Nordic ski jump, freestyle jump, bobsled, and luge competitions. The public is invited to watch the athletes in action year-round. Yes, the jumping continues in the summer thanks to the park's unique features. One of these is the ceramic tile in-run and plastic landing, making the 90-meter jump possible even if there is no snow. The other neat feature of the park is the 755,000-gallon pool of water in which freestyle jumpers land after performing their aerial stunts.

Spectatorship isn't the only thing visitors can do at the Utah Olympic Park. If you know how to ski, you, too, can try jumping. For a fee, the park gives you the opportunity to launch off several of the facility's jumps. Starting with an instructor-led orientation and a few practice runs on a tiny snow jump, the Jump Pass advances you first to a 10-meter jump, next to an 18-meter jump, and then, with the approval of your instructor, to a 38-meter jump. Special Nordic ski equipment is not necessary; regular alpine skis are sufficient. Lessons are held Dec through March, Wed through Sun, 10 a.m. to 4 p.m. You can try ski jumping during the summer also on their specially treated jumps. If bobsledding is more your sport, you can try it here year-round too. During the winter for a fee you can go down the icy run; however, during the summer, the wheeled version will be available. Call (435) 658-4200 for more information on the lessons or on special exhibitions. Also at the park, the less adventurous can tour the interactive exhibits at the ***Alf Engen Ski Museum*** (435-658-4240) to learn more about skiing in the intermountain West. The museum is open daily from 9 a.m. to 6 p.m.

Junction City and the Golden Spike Empire

The history of **Ogden** deviates from that of most towns in Utah. Whereas most Utah towns developed as homogeneous Mormon communities, Ogden grew in another direction once the transcontinental railroad was linked at **Promontory Summit** in 1869 and railroad officials decided that Ogden would become their junction point. The town became a hotbed of drinking, gambling, and prostitution as the workers stayed to indulge in the fruits of their labor. More and more Gentiles (non-Mormons) moved in, and the town boomed. Much to the chagrin of the Mormons, who came to Utah to isolate themselves from the Gentiles, Ogden evolved into the most cosmopolitan city in Utah, an honor it would keep until the decline of the railroad after World War II.

Standing at the end of Historic Twenty-fifth Street at 2501 Wall Avenue, Ogden, **Union Station** (801-393-9890; theunionstation.org) is a memorial to Ogden's heady days—when it was the railroad hub in the West. The station's heyday climaxed during World War II, when it served as a stop for nearly 200 trains every twenty-four hours. The present station, built in a Spanish Colonial style, is actually the third depot to have been built on the site. The first one was built shortly after the Golden Spike was driven home at Promontory, Utah. To

Where the Buffalo Roam

Utah hosts two wild, roaming buffalo herds: one in the Henry Mountains in Southern Utah, the other on Antelope Island near Salt Lake City. *Antelope Island* is a good place to get a buffalo's-eye view of the shaggy beasts many feel symbolize the Old West.

For many, the annual Bison Roundup in late October signals the official start of autumn. It's family fun, shaggy style. This is an old-fashioned roundup, with modern accoutrements. There are plenty of horses and official-looking cowboys; a few Range Rovers, helicopters, and aspiring cowboys add to the flavor.

The Children's Bison Roundup is held the first week of October, followed by the more formal (if not absolutely official) roundup the last week of October and the first week or so of November. After the big beasts are corralled, visitors can watch as they are inoculated and weighed and blood samples are taken. For more information, call *Antelope Island State Park* (801) 773-2941.

Starry Nights in Utah: A Dark-Sky Park

It's important to see the stars and be able to look into the night. It's something to be cherished and protected—but it's an experience that can't be taken for granted. Even in wide-open Utah, there is light pollution—especially on the Wasatch Front. A dark sky park is a protected location that offers a starry-night experience.

For this reason, Utah has eleven certified Dark-sky locations: Antelope Island State Park, Arches National Park, Canyonlands National Park, Capitol Reef National Park, Cedar Breaks National Monument, Dead Horse Point State Park, Dinosaur National Monument, Goblin Valley State Park, Hovenweep National Monument, Natural Bridges National Monument, and Weber County North Fork Park.

The *International Dark-Sky Association* (IDA) in conjunction with public and private land owners helps preserve "night skies" for present and future generations. An International Dark Sky Park (IDSA) is a location that has a "distinguished quality of starry nights and a nocturnal environment that is specifically protected for its scientific, natural, educational, cultural heritage, and/or public enjoyment."

compensate for the enormous railway traffic flowing through Ogden, a second one, designed with the Victorian ostentation afforded in those days, was raised in 1889. In 1923 it burned down, and a new depot (the present one) opened the following year. Two murals on the walls of the main lobby depict the building of the first transcontinental railroad.

Union Station, completely renovated in 1978, has found new life as the site of a visitor information center, restaurant, theater, and five museums—three of which are wonderfully unique. Cars from the golden age of automobiles are on display. *The Kimball Car Collection* also includes old license plates and other artifacts.

The *Wattis–Dumke Model Railroad* presents a detailed diorama of the *Overland Route* from Weber Canyon (South Ogden) to the Sierra Mountains. Twelve trains run along a scale-model railroad through the diorama, giving you an idea of the geography engineers had to negotiate when building the Overland Route. The exhibit tells the story of the Lucin Cutoff, hailed as one of the biggest engineering feats of its time. This cutoff refers to a trestle built across the Great Salt Lake that shaved 43 miles off the original Overland Route. Also on display are opium pipe bowls, opium bottles, and other artifacts that give testament to the 8,000 to 15,000 Chinese immigrants who worked on the Central Pacific, 500 to 1,000 of whom lost their lives on the job. At the railroad museum you'll also learn about the "Big Boys." Designed to champion the menacingly steep grade of the Wasatch Mountains, the Big Boys were the heaviest, most powerful steam locomotives ever built.

Upstairs from the railroad museum is the *John M. Browning Firearms Museum*, where you'll learn whom to praise or admonish (depending on how you feel about guns) for the evolution of firearms. The museum showcases the work of the foremost designer of firearms the world has ever known—John M. Browning. An Ogden native and son of a polygamist, Browning accrued more than seventy-five patents on his firearm inventions, including the first automatic weapon. On display are hundreds of Browning shotguns, rifles, handguns, and automatic weapons—many of which are originals. All the Union Station museums are open Mon through Sat 10 a.m. to 5 p.m.; closed Sunday.

Railroad workers and, later, soldiers who passed through Ogden during both world wars knew exactly where to go looking for excitement. It was just outside the doors of Union Station on Historic Twenty-fifth Street, which had a reputation of being one of the most sordid couple of blocks in the West and home to just about every vice imaginable at the time. *Electric Alley*, Twenty-fifth Street's red-light district, was Ogden's Gomorrah, replete with brothels, streetwalkers, bars, and opium dens.

When the railroad began taking a nosedive in the 1950s, so did Twenty-fifth Street. What was once the pulsing heart of Ogden turned into a tapped-out vein, a skid row attracting the sort of characters director David Lynch could feel comfortable using in his movies. In recent years, however, Twenty-fifth Street has become Historic Twenty-fifth Street and has made a turnaround from the place your mother always warned you about to the place you might want to take your mother for lunch and maybe a little shopping. Renovation of many of the buildings has uncovered an attractive couple of blocks, now home to restaurants, cafes, and shops that breathe new life into the street that Ogden tried to sweep under the carpet for more than thirty years. You can pick up a self-guided tour of Historic Twenty-fifth Street at the visitor center in Union Station.

Rooster's Brewing (253 Twenty-fifth St.; 801-627-6171) pours different kinds of beer (plus some specials) made on the premises. Salt Lake and Park City have microbreweries, too, but the best Utah-brewed beer is said to be brewed in Ogden. It washes down pizza, burgers, buffalo wings, or barbecue from Rooster's eclectic, changing menu. Floral designs add an organic, not to mention creative, touch to the interior walls. Open Mon through Thurs 11 a.m. to 10 p.m., Fri and Sat 11 a.m. to 11 p.m., and Sun (brunch) 10 a.m. to 9 p.m. The outdoor grill gets cooking at 5 p.m., weather permitting.

One of the most attractive houses in Ogden thankfully happens to be a museum. *Eccles Community Art Center* (2580 Jefferson Ave.; 801-392-6935) is housed in a venerable sandstone mansion built in 1893 in a Richardsonian–Romanesque style. Previously owned by the philanthropic Eccles family, the house was part of the Weber State University campus before the school moved to its present location. Here you'll find the work of local and regional artists working in several different media. Tours of the house are also available by appointment. Open 9 a.m. to 5 p.m. on weekdays and 9 a.m. to 3 p.m. on Saturday.

If you have an interest in classic cars, the Ogden area is certainly the place to be. Unlike the luxury cars for the superrich at the Browning–Kimball Car Museum at Union Station, the *Millstream Classic Car Collection* has twenty-five or so models that average folk (of a certain age) have probably owned at one time or another. With cars such as the Hudson Hornet, several Packards, and three convertible hard-top Ford Fairlanes ('57, '58, and '59), Jack Smith's collection is nostalgic. Admirers of 1950s regalia will rejoice. The museum is located in Willard at 255 E. 1080 N. The museum is open 9 a.m. to 5 p.m. (801-540-8930)

To get off the beaten path head to *Ogden Valley*, east of Ogden on the other side of the Wasatch Front. Here you'll find several bed-and-breakfasts, not to mention three ski areas, a reservoir (popular with boaters and sailboarders), and several trails on which you can hike, mountain bike, or cross-country ski.

There are three ways of getting to Ogden Valley, all equally scenic. The first is over *Trapper's Loop*, the second through *Ogden Canyon*, and third and least-used is over *North Ogden Pass*—accessed by taking Harrison Boulevard to its northern end and then following signs to the pass, which drops you into the northern reaches of the valley. From Ogden you can make a scenic loop by taking any two of these three routes.

To get to Trapper's Loop, head east on Interstate 84 through Weber Canyon. Take the Mountain Green exit (92) at the head of the canyon and follow the signs to Huntsville, reached via Trapper's Loop (Highway 167)—a scenic byway that provides dramatic views of the Wasatch Mountains and Ogden Valley. The byway lets out at the south end of Ogden Valley and at the southern tip of Pine View Reservoir.

The most congested route to Ogden Valley (but a pretty one, nonetheless) is through Ogden Canyon, accessed by taking Twelfth Street to its east end. The scenic byway (Highway 39) begins with a view of a 150-foot waterfall, snakes through the narrow canyon alongside the rushing Ogden River, and arrives at the canyon head 6 miles farther on—where *Pine View Reservoir* and Ogden Valley open up. Inside the canyon, mountains and cliffs soar thousands of feet above, allowing you to get a look at the Wasatch Mountains from deep within.

A good choice for accommodations in Ogden Valley is *Snowberry Inn Bed and Breakfast* (801-745-2634; snowberryinn.com) at 1315 North Highway

Space: Another Frontier

In the nineteenth century pioneers crossed the Western frontier, and the railroad quickly followed. During the twentieth century Utah participated in crossing another frontier: space. Two miles north of Golden Spike National Historic Site on Highway 83, you will find the **Thiokol Rocket** display, where you can see real examples of rocket motors that have sent the astronauts into space. From the display area, you can see part of the Thiokol plant as well as the rocket tests they occasionally perform out here.

If you'd like to see more aerospace technology, stop by the **Hill Aerospace Museum** in Roy, off I-15. Here you can see antique missiles and helicopters and famous warplanes, including the B–17 Flying Fortress and the P–510 Mustang. The museum is open from 9 a.m. to 4:30 p.m. every day.

158, Eden. This log house sits at the foot of the Wasatch Mountains and provides a great view of **Pine View Reservoir**. Tasteful Western decor and cozy surroundings make for perfect après-ski lodging. Each of the five rooms has its own personality and comes with a private bath. Ask for the Alaskan Room, where you can soak in a claw-foot bathtub while taking in a view of the valley and reservoir. See their website for special package deals. You'll find the Snowberry on the west side of the reservoir along Highway 158, about 3 miles from the Highway 39 junction at the head of Ogden Canyon. You'll see the sign on your left just after you pass the Pine View Yacht Club.

As Utah's oldest continually operating saloon, the **Shooting Star Saloon** (801-745-2002), 7350 East 200 South, Huntsville, epitomizes the image that most people have of a saloon. Dark wood, mounted game heads, and a pool table are all part of the picture. But there is one thing that stands out at the saloon: the mounted head of Buck, a St. Bernard that weighed in at 298 pounds when he was alive in the 1950s. Buck was so big that he is listed in the *Guinness Book of World Records* as the largest dog. By the shape of his muzzle, you might wonder if he was part grizzly bear, but Buck only appears that way because the taxidermist had to use a grizzly mount when he prepared Buck for hanging on the wall.

In 1879 a Swede by the name of Hokin Olsen opened up the saloon in his basement, then called Hokin's Hole. He operated the bar throughout Prohibition, for which he was regularly dragged to jail. Whenever he was in jail, his wife kept the bar running and the profits turning. If the locals wanted to take whiskey home, they would purchase a map that led them to a spot where Hokin had buried a jug or two. When things get cooking at the saloon, don't be surprised if the crowd breaks out into the chicken dance. Open Mon through Sat, 11 a.m. to 9 p.m., and 11 a.m. to 8 p.m. on Sun.

Sixty species of birds, many of which are endangered, nest at the **Bear River Migratory Bird Refuge**, a 65,000-acre preserve on the northeast shores of the Great Salt Lake. Avocets, long-billed curlews, willet, killdeers, black-crowned night herons, and scores of other species of birds make this an enchanting place to spend the day. A 12-mile, one-way auto loop built on dikes takes you around one of the refuge impoundments, where you'll see waterfowl in their natural habitats—the marshes, mud flats, and open pools. Besides birds that nest here, an additional 140 species have been spotted at the refuge. Be sure to take along a field guide and pair of binoculars so that you can identify the species. The best time to visit the refuge is in the morning or early evening. From Ogden head north on Interstate 15 to Brigham City. Get off the freeway at exit 368 and then turn right. Take a left onto 2600 West and follow signs to the bird refuge, located about 15 miles west of Brigham City. Visitors are encouraged to ride bicycles through the refuge so that they have a better opportunity to view the birds. Call (435) 723-5887 for more information. The refuge is open from dawn to dusk.

Even though the **Golden Spike National Historic Site** isn't exactly a destination for the off-the-beaten-path traveler, you'll still want to stop here anyway to pick up a map and detailed directions to the **Spiral Jetty**, creation of the late Robert Smithson. Anyone who has taken a modernist art class has probably come across a picture of this strange work of environmental art, constructed on the northern shores of the Great Salt Lake in 1973. Extending from the beach out into the lake, the *Spiral Jetty* is a 1,500-foot-long coil made out of mud, rocks, and salt crystals. Engaged in what would seem more like a construction job than a work of art, Smithson used tractors and dump trucks to unload the thousands of pounds of material that went into shaping this oddity. Depending on the levels of the Great Salt Lake, the *Spiral Jetty* may be submerged beneath the lake's waters. Definitely call the Golden Spike National Historic Site (801-471-2209) for the status of the jetty's appearance before you make a visit. Getting there is extremely tricky, so you will need a map from the Golden Spike visitor center, which is on the way to the *Spiral Jetty*. From I-15 take exit 368 and head west on Highways 13 and 83 through Corinne and past Thiokol, makers of the space shuttle rocket boosters.

If you can't get enough of the railroad history in Northern Utah, take the **Transcontinental Railroad National Back Country Byway**, allowing you to travel along the last 90 miles of grade laid by the Central Pacific before connecting with the Union Pacific at Promontory. The dirt and gravel road, negotiable for high-clearance vehicles only, takes you through rugged and desolate country that has hardly changed since the Central Pacific workers labored across the desert landscape. Not much remains of this segment of the railroad, known as the Promontory Branch. Connecting the towns of Lucin and Corinne, the Promontory Branch became obsolete soon after 1904, when the Lucin Cutoff, a trestle built across the Great Salt Lake, created a more direct route to Ogden. After that, only local trains chugged along these rails. In 1942 the rails were lifted and donated to the war effort.

You can begin the byway either just west of Golden Spike or at Lucin—accessed via Interstate 84 and Highway 30. Don't attempt driving this road in wet weather. Because the road is extremely narrow at parts, vehicles longer than 30 feet are not recommended. Bring plenty of water and a spare tire, just in case. Cyclists find this an excellent ride. There are no services along the byway, so be prepared. For road conditions call ***Golden Spike Visitor Center*** (801-471-2209).

Interpretive signs along the byway point out rail sidings and townsites that have long been abandoned. ***Kelton***, about 36 miles from the east end of the byway, was a burgeoning city with several hotels, stores, saloons, a library, and a peak population of 700. Although the Lucin Cutoff killed Kelton's progress, the town wasn't abandoned until 1934, when it found itself at the epicenter of one of the worst earthquakes ever to shake Utah. A tiny graveyard now marks the town. If you still want to see Kelton but would rather not deal with driving the byway, consider getting there via Highway 30. Exit I–84 just north of Snowville onto Highway 30. Taking the left fork, head about 35 miles southwest until you see the BLM sign to Kelton. The dirt road connects with the byway at the townsite 7 miles south of the Highway 30 junction.

If you visited the *Spiral Jetty*, you might be convinced that there's something to environmental art. Or maybe you think it's all hooey. In that case you probably shouldn't go through the hassle of visiting the **Sun Tunnels**, located near Lucin on the east side of the Great Salt Lake. Nancy Holt, an artist from New York and wife of *Spiral Jetty* creator Robert Smithson, chose one of the loneliest places on earth on which to place her four concrete tunnels. Weighing twenty-two tons each, the tunnels are a sight to behold out here on the sunbaked terrain. Holt aligned the tunnels so that the sun would shine directly through them on the winter and summer solstices. Out of the walls she cut star-shaped patterns that correspond to the constellations Capricorn, Perseus, and Draco.

There are no signs to the *Sun Tunnels*, so getting there is a bit tricky. On Highway 30 head about 80 miles southwest of I–84 and take a left at the Lucin turnoff. Go 5 miles on a dirt road to the old town, past the west end of the Transcontinental Railroad National Back Country Byway. Cross the railroad tracks and drive past a cluster of trees. Take the left fork, posted as the way to the TL Bar Beefmaster Ranch. After about a mile, take the first left you see. From there you should be able to see the tunnels. Continue another mile or so and you're there. Do not attempt going to the *Sun Tunnels* in wet weather; it's easy to get stuck. Remember that the nearest service is 50 miles away.

Mountainmen's Stomping Grounds

Covered by a carpet of lush vegetation rolled out between the Bear River Mountain Range and the Wellsville Mountains, **Cache Valley** has for centuries endeared people to its fertile, pastoral appearance. Shoshoni Indians knew they had come across something special when they wandered into the area around AD 1300 and named it "House of the Great Spirit." Jim Bridger, the most notorious of Western mountainmen and trappers, was also enchanted when he came in search of nondepleted beaver populations.

Then called Willow Valley because of the willow trees growing along the streams, Cache Valley attracted mountainmen from all over the Rocky Mountains, who came here to trap and store their furs in holes dug out of the valley floor. These "caches" inspired a new name for the valley, one that stuck. In 1827 many of the mountainmen, including Bridger, congregated at a site in present-day Logan for the annual summer rendezvous.

Bad relations with the Shoshonis stalled settlement of the valley until 1856, when Peter Maughan received instructions from Brigham Young to build a fort in what is today Wellsville. By 1877 the construction of Logan Temple was under way. In a weird twist of history, the Shoshonis actually helped the Mormons build the structure because they believed the temple would help preserve the sacredness of the site, on which they had performed healing ceremonies long before Anglos had appeared. Hospitable relations ended with the construction of the temple, when settlers began moving in by the hundreds. The ongoing friction between the cultures culminated on the banks of the Bear River near the north end of Cache Valley (in Idaho). It was called the Battle of Bear River and it claimed around 300 Shoshoni lives. It was one of the largest massacres in a single day in history.

With the construction of Logan Temple and the subsequent **Logan Tabernacle** emerged the city of **Logan**. Today Logan is Cache Valley's largest community and one of Utah's most populated towns. Visible throughout the valley, the temple sits at a prominent point just above downtown Logan, no doubt inspiring a certain amount of fervor among church members. Builders of the temple dragged timber and limestone boulders down from Logan Canyon, finally completing the structure after seven years of heavy labor. Only Mormons with a certain standing in the church can enter the temple, but folks can walk around it. People are, however, invited to enter the Logan Tabernacle, located downtown on Main and Center Streets. Completed in 1891 after nearly twenty-five years, the tabernacle required much of the same labor the temple did but received less priority, which is why it took so long to finish.

With its spacious lawns and big trees, the tabernacle adds to the quaintness of Logan's Historic Main Street, a street that's typical of Utah towns born in the late nineteenth century. Main Street and its bisecting streets have retained a fair amount of their late-nineteenth-century charm thanks to the preservation-ist spirit of the Logan people, who have resisted doing what most Utah towns have done in the name of progress—build over the past. To learn about the his-tory of Main Street's buildings, pick up the self-guided walking tour brochure from the Bridgerland Travel Region office (160 North Main St.; 435-752-2161 or 800-882-4433).

One of the buildings the brochure mentions is the ***Bluebird Restaurant*** (19 North Main St.; 435-752-3155). After Utah State University and the Mormon church, the Bluebird is perhaps Logan's oldest institution. The Bluebird began in 1914 as a soda fountain and candy and ice-cream store. Conceding to popu-lar demand for its goods, the business enlarged, erecting a comely building on Main Street in 1923. A marble soda fountain, hand-painted walls, and rich wood fixtures all went into the ostentatious design, which included a ballroom and several meeting rooms. Open 11 a.m. to 9 p.m. on Mon; Tues through Thurs, 11 a.m. to 9:30 p.m.; and Fri and Sat 11 a.m. to 10 p.m.

Another great feature on Main Street and part of the rich performing arts scene in Logan is the ***Ellen Eccles Theater*** at 43 South Main Street, Logan. Built in 1923 and originally called Capitol Theater, it was renovated in 1993, bringing back to life the theater's grandeur. Today, it hosts a variety of plays,

Lights, Action, Roll 'Em

Although Westerns are the predominant movie genre filmed here, Utah has a variety of unique settings.

Indeed, Utah has a movie "climate" to satisfy most every demand. The Beehive State is especially noted for its quiet little towns—towns that are an ideal depiction of small-town, late nineteenth-century Americana. Television series such as Touched by an Angel and Promised Land have taken advantage of our village heritage.

Filming on location is common. For added flavor, native Utahans are frequently employed as extras or for small roles.

Utah Streets Are More Than Clever

As a rule, most of us don't give too much thought to streets. They are, after all, rather commonplace. It's only when we're trying to find an address in an unfamiliar place that we wish there were some system of order.

Gratefully, almost all Utah towns are systematically laid out for your address-finding pleasure. If you know your compass directions, locating an address in a Utah town is not a difficult task.

The Mormon pioneers, under the influence of Brigham Young, designed their cities around a central point such as a church, city hall, or park, in increments of 100. In Salt Lake City, for instance, the town is laid out around Temple Square. Logically, streets are numbered 100 South, 200 East, and so on. Even if the street has another name, it also has a number.

musicals, ballets, and concerts, not to mention operas, performed during the months of July and August by the **Utah Festival Opera and Musical Theatre**. The company attracts nationally acclaimed singers from around the country. During these two months, you can see as many as four operas and musicals in two days. For general scheduling and ticket information at the Ellen Eccles Theater, call the **Cache Valley Center of the Arts** at (435) 752-0026. For information on the Utah Festival Opera and Musical Theatre, call (435) 750-0300 or (800) 262-0074, or see their season offerings at ufoc.org.

The place to go for after-theater conversation or any other time of the day, for that matter, is **Caffe Ibis** (52 Federal Ave.; 435-753-4777; caffeibis.com). Located a block off Main Street, the Caffe Ibis doubles as a market and cafe. In addition to its selection of international coffees roasted on-site, the market sells a hodgepodge of cooking oils, herbs, and spices, as well some other basic food items. The tiny but intimate cafe delivers a good cup of coffee and a variety of espresso-based drinks. There's usually a small selection of cold dishes, not to mention pastries, ice cream, or other goodies. Sidewalk seating makes the cafe popular with college students. Open 6 a.m. to 9 p.m. Mon through Thurs, until 10 p.m. Fri and Sat, and 8 a.m. to 6 p.m. Sun.

If you have a penchant for glorious kitsch, then by no means miss **Anniversary Inn** (169 East Center St.; 435-752-3443). From outside the main house, Anniversary Inn looks like your typical Victorian home. Painter Lorin Humphreys used the main parlor in an attempt (of sorts) to do what Michelangelo did to the ceiling of the Sistine Chapel, except Humphreys's celestial beings look more like comic book figures. Occupying the main house and surrounding buildings, the sixteen rooms are meant to fulfill the kinkiest of fantasies. With names such as Space Odyssey, Jungle Bungalow, and Aphrodite's Court, it isn't too hard to envision what these rooms entail. Jungle Bungalow, for instance, puts you in the deep, dark jungle of Africa with emerald green carpet, waterfalls, and a leopard-skin bed cover. A more telling feature of the room, however, is the heart-shaped Jacuzzi and mirrored canopy. Despite what the rooms may lack in authenticity (or taste, for that matter), they do serve their purpose well for honeymooners. As you would expect, the innkeepers welcome couples only, with the exception of a "tiny infant." Dreams, as you know, don't come free. To see the rooms, go to anniversaryinn.com/logan.html.

The *American West Heritage Center*, located at 4025 S Hwy 89-91 in Wellsville, is the place to find the Cache Valley Mountain Man rendezvous and other events that celebrate the pioneering spirit of the people of Utah. There is a farm that recreates life on a 1917 dairy farm as well as a community museum. Open 9 a.m. to 5 p.m. Call (435) 245-6050 or visit awhc.org for further information on daily and special events.

Even if Logan happens to be your destination, you should still consider staying at the *Old Rock Church Bed and Breakfast* located about 5 miles southeast of Logan in the sleepy town of *Providence*. The fortress-like Mormon church was completed in 1871, thirteen years before the Logan Temple was dedicated. Boulders used to complete the 30-inch-thick walls were quarried and hauled down from the Bear River Mountains. In 1926 a Georgian-style "wing," actually a mansion in itself, was added on to the church.

The innkeeper decided a bed-and-breakfast was the dignified thing to do with the Georgian wing. As for the rock church, transforming it into a place for weddings and receptions seemed logical. Meticulous care went into renovating and refurbishing the building, included hiring an architectural consultant and an interior designer. The result is something to make the locals proud. Each of the sixteen rooms has been carefully decorated with a good measure of sophistication to suit a certain period in design, such as neoclassical or Victorian. Call (435) 752-3432 or visit oldrockchurch.com for more information or to make reservations. From Logan, head south on Main Street. Take a left (east) on Providence Lane (1200 South) and then a right on Main Street in Providence. The Old Rock Church Bed and Breakfast is a block down on 10 South.

Hyrum City Museum (435-245-0208), located at the Civic Center on 50 West Main Street, *Hyrum*, could have one of the most eclectic collections of things you are bound to see in the state of Utah. After seeing everything they have on display, you may wonder if the curators aren't pulling your leg. Anything and everything goes at the museum. Here are just a few items among the hodgepodge: an Egyptian alabaster canopic jar (used to contain a mummy's internal organs), an Etruscan-carved limestone lamp, a chunk of cement from the Berlin wall, volcanic ash from Mt. St. Helens, and a nineteenth-century baritone horn. Check it out on Tues and Thurs 12 p.m. to 6 p.m.; Wed and Sat 10 a.m. to 3 p.m.; Fri and Sun the museum is closed. To get to Hyrum from Logan, head about 13 miles south on Highway 165.

Since 1948, **Hardware Ranch Wildlife Management Area** has been in the business of feeding the elk during the winter. Along with the feedings, the ranch has evolved into an important elk research center, managing more than 700 of them. Wildlife biologists tag the elk so that they can monitor migration patterns and study population characteristics. The research is then considered when establishing regulations for elk hunting.

Besides the research, the ranch now provides an opportunity to get an eyeful of the animal that was designated state mammal of Utah in 1971. A horse-drawn sleigh ride through the ranch enables you to get up close and inspect the details of this second-largest member in the deer family. October is a good time to come, because it is then that bull elk sound their bugle mating calls. Sleigh rides start in December. For more information regarding events at the ranch call (435) 753-6206 or visit wildlife.utah.gov/discover/hardware-ranch .html. Hardware Ranch is located in Blacksmith Fork at the end of Highway 101, 15 miles east of Hyrum. Signs point the way.

Fronting the east side of Cache Valley, Bear River Mountain Range affords a host of recreational possibilities: hiking, rock climbing, skiing (downhill and cross-country), mountain biking, and even spelunking. The road that makes all these things possible is the 40-mile **Logan Canyon Scenic Byway** (Highway 89), crossing over the range from Logan to Bear Lake. The road takes you along the raging Logan River, past a series of interesting geological features, and through a rich growth of trees and shrubs. Autumn is the best time to take the byway. Fall colors in Utah don't get much more stunning than in **Logan Canyon**, where the maples turn a fire-engine red and the aspens a golden yellow. The place to get your bearings on Logan Canyon is at the Logan Ranger District office (435-755-3620), located on Highway 89 at the mouth of Logan Canyon. Here you'll get information on campgrounds, trails, fishing, or any other interests you may have.

climate**fast**facts

Northern Utah's climate:

winter, 10 to 39 degrees

summer, 60 to 95 degrees

about 16 inches of precipitation.

Ten miles from the mouth of the canyon is **Wood Camp Campground** and the **Jardine Juniper Trailhead**. Despite being so close to the highway,

Step Back in Time

People in Utah love learning about their history, and summer is a great time to indulge this passion because of the many living-history events and museums available. Mountain Men rendezvous occur all over the state, educating people about the early trappers, pioneers, and Native Americans who lived here. *Old Deseret Village* (801-582-1847) at the "This is the Place" Heritage Park has reconstructed and relocated pioneer buildings, re-creating life from 1847 to 1869. Buildings include a bank, social hall, schoolhouse, hotel, printing shop, and various stores; and staff dressed in period clothes give demonstrations about pioneer life at each location. Also in Salt Lake City is the *Wheeler Historic Farm* (801-264-2241), which is open year-round. The dairy farm illustrates life at the end of the nineteenth century, using animal and manual labor to manage all seventy-five acres. Visitors who come around 5 p.m. can help collect eggs or milk the cows.

the pine-canopied campground is one of the nicest in the canyon. About .25 miles from the campground on the other side of the river are the trailhead and parking area. The trail extends 5 miles and 2,000 vertical feet up a winter avalanche chute. Forests of aspens, Douglas firs, and junipers shade the way. One of these junipers, called the Jardine Juniper, is more than 3,000 years old. With a height of 44 feet, 6 inches, and a circumference of 26 feet, 8 inches, the tree is thought to be the largest, and oldest, juniper in the world. The tree takes its name from William T. Jardine, a former US Secretary of Agriculture and a Utah State alumnus. Since its discovery in 1923, the tree has become a trademark for newspapers, companies, and organizations in Logan. You'll see the tree about 2 miles from the trailhead.

Fifteen miles from the mouth of the canyon is Temple Fork (Forest Road 007), named such because it was here that builders of the Logan Temple obtained their timber. The unpaved, clay-packed road (good enough for passenger cars when dry) goes past Temple Springs trailhead and accesses *Old Ephraim's Grave*, 7 miles from the highway on Forest Road 056. The grave was the final resting spot of the most infamous grizzly bear to tromp through these parts.

Old Ephraim was the thorn in the side of every rancher and shepherd in the area, and the arch nemesis of Frank Clark, who, in his crusade to rid the area of bears, shot fifty of them. For several years Clark, a shepherd from Idaho, tracked "Old Eph," who was easy to follow because of his deformed, three-toed foot and the several dead sheep he would leave in his wake.

Just beyond the turnoff to *Beaver Mountain Ski Area* on Highway 89 (24 miles from Logan) is the entrance to *Beaver Creek Lodge* (435-946-3400 or

Utah Trivia

There are 991,970 acres of mixed forest in Utah.

Utah has the highest literacy rate in the nation.

About 60 percent of Utah's population are members of The Church of Jesus Christ of Latter-day Saints, better known as Mormons.

By 1900, fifty years after entering the Salt Lake Valley, the Mormons had founded nearly 500 settlements in Utah and surrounding states.

Utah's central location in the western United States has always meant a steady flow of traffic across its expanse, giving the state its nickname "The Crossroads of the West."

Utah became the forty-fifth state on January 4, 1896.

In 1990 Indian rice grass (Oryzopsis hymenoides), a perennial bunch grass, became Utah's state grass.

Utah is home to the following inventors: Philo T. Farnsworth, a television pioneer; Robert Jarvik and Willem Kolff, the artificial heart; Lester Wire, the traffic light.

Professional basketball returned to Salt Lake City when the Jazz moved to Utah in 1979.

The water in the Great Salt Lake is four times as salty as any ocean.

On Antelope Island in the Great Salt Lake, you can find antelope, wild buffalo, range cattle, and rattlesnakes.

800-946-4485; beavercreeklodge.com), which affords its guests attractive stone fireplaces and a fine array of wood furnishings. With the *Cache National Forest* at its back door, the lodge looks out onto a huge meadow and, above that, Beaver Mountain. The cozy rooms come with lodgepole bed frames, quilts, and jetted tubs. The lodge rents snowmobiles in the winter and offers horseback rides in the summer. Skiers, boarders, cross-country skiers, mountain bikers are always welcome.

From the summit the road descends down the eastern slope of the mountains, providing great views of *Bear Lake* below. Situated on the Utah–Idaho border, Bear Lake stretches nearly 20 miles in length and 4 to 8 miles in width. Stop at the *Bear Lake Overlook* to get an aerial view of the lake and the lowdown on the geology and history of the 28,000-year-old body of water. Due to the limestone particles suspended in the lake's water, Bear Lake has a strikingly blue, almost turquoise, sheen. Because of the lake's isolated evolution, four species of fish that live in Bear Lake are found nowhere else in the world. One of these species, the Bonneville cisco, is a tasty catch for anglers, who often come here in the winter to dip their nets through the ice.

Places to Stay in Northern Utah

EDEN

Snowberry Inn Bed and Breakfast
1315 N. Hwy 158
(801) 745-2634 or
(888) 334-3466
snowberryinn.com
Moderate

LOGAN

Anniversary Inn
169 E. Center St.
(435) 752-3443
anniversaryinn.com/logan.html
Deluxe

Best Western Baugh Motel
153 S. Main St.
(435) 752-5220
Moderate

Best Western Weston Inn
250 N. Main St.
(435) 752-5700
Standard

MIDVALE

Days Inn
7251 S. 300 West
(801) 566-6677
Standard

MILLVILLE

Beaver Creek Lodge
P.O. Box 139
(435) 946-3400 or
(800) 946-4485
Moderate

FOR MORE INFORMATION ABOUT NORTHERN UTAH

TRAVEL COUNCILS

Golden Spike Travel Region
2501 Wall Ave.
Union Station
Ogden, 84401
(801) 627-8288 or
(800) 255-8824
Fax: (801) 399-0783

Bridgerland Travel Region
160 North Main St.
Logan 84321-4541
(435) 752-2161 or
(800) 882-4433
Fax: (435) 753-5825

BUS SCHEDULES

Salt Lake City
(801) 743-3882

Ogden
(801) 621-4636

Road Conditions
(800) 492-2400

TOP ANNUAL EVENTS IN NORTHERN UTAH

AUGUST

Bear Lake Raspberry Days
Garden City
(800) 448-BEAR

Box Elder County Fair
Tremonton
(435) 230-0207

Cache County Fair
Logan
(435) 716-7150

Country Fair Days
South Weber City
(801) 479-3177

Davis County Fair
Farmington
(801) 451-4080

Duchesne County Fair
Farmington
(801) 738-1191

Emery County Fair
Castle Dale
(435) 687-2403

Rich County Fair and Rodeo
Randolph
(435) 793-5155

Weber County Fair
Ogden
(801) 399-8711

SEPTEMBER

Bison Roundup
Antelope Island State Park
(801) 773-2941

Mountain Man Rendezvous
Bear Lake State Park, Garden City
(435) 946-3343

Peach Days
Brigham City
(801) 723-3931

Utah State Fair
Salt Lake City
(801) 538-8400

OCTOBER

Oktoberfest
Snowbird
(801) 933-2110

NOVEMBER

Working of the Animals/Bison Roundup
Antelope Island State Park
(801) 773-2941

DECEMBER

Festival of Trees
Salt Lake City
(801) 588-3684

Christmas around the World
Brigham Young University, Provo
(801) 422-7664

The Nutcracker
Ballet West, Salt Lake City
(888) 451-2787

OGDEN

Best Western Inn
1335 W. Twelfth Street
(801) 394-9474
Standard

PARK CITY

Chateau Apres
1299 Norfolk Ave.
(435) 649-9372
chateauapres.com
Deluxe

Park City Marriott Hotel and Conference Center
1895 Sidewinder Dr.
(435) 649-2900
Deluxe

Stein Eriksen Lodge
7700 Stein Way
(435) 649-3700
Deluxe

PROVIDENCE

Providence Inn Bed and Breakfast
10 S. Main St.
(435) 752-3432 or
(800) 480-4943
providenceinn.com
Deluxe

SALT LAKE CITY

Airport Inn Travelodge Hotel
2333 W. North Temple
(801) 539-0438
Standard

Econo Lodge
715 W. North Temple
(801) 363-0062
Standard

Peery Hotel
110 W. Brdwy
(Third South)
(801) 521-4300 or
(800) 331-0073
peeryhotel.com
Deluxe

Super 8 Motel
616 S. 200 West
(801) 534-0808
Standard

Wildflowers, A Bed and Breakfast
936 E. 1700 South
(801) 466-0600 or
(800) 569-0009
wildflowersbb.com
Moderate

SANDY

Comfort Inn
8955 S. 255 West
(801) 255-4919
Standard

WELLSVILLE

Best Western Sherwood Hills Resort
Highway 89–91
(435) 245-5054
Moderate

Places to Eat in Northern Utah

HUNTSVILLE

Shooting Star Saloon
7350 East 200 S
(801) 745-2002
Moderate

LOGAN

Bluebird Restaurant
19 North Main St.
(435) 752-3155
Expensive

Caffe Ibis
52 Federal Ave.
(435) 753-4777
caffeibis.com
Moderate

OGDEN

Prairie Schooner
445 Park Blvd.
(801) 392-2712
Very expensive

Rooster's Brewing
253 Twenty-fifth St.
(801) 627-6171
Moderate

Union Grill
2501 Wall Ave.
(801) 621-2830
Moderate

PARK CITY

Adolph's
1300 Kearns Blvd.
(435) 649-7177
Very expensive

Chimayo
368 Main St.
(435) 649-6222
Very expensive

Grappa Italian Restaurant
151 Main St.
(435) 645-0636
grapparestaurant.com
Very expensive

Grub Steak Restaurant
2093 Sidewinder Dr.
(435) 649-8060
Moderate

Park City Pizza Company
1612 Ute Blvd.
(435) 649-1591
Moderate

SALT LAKE CITY

Lion House Pantry
63 East South Temple
(801) 363-5466
Inexpensive

The Market Street Grill
48 West Market St.
(801) 322-4668
Very expensive

Red Iguana
736 West North Temple
(801) 322-1489
Expensive

Rio Grande Café
270 South Rio Grande St.
(801) 364-3302
Inexpensive

Ruby River Steak House
435 South 700 East
(801) 226-9410
Moderate

Central Utah

Central Utah's landscape mirrors Northern Utah to a great extent, but with the exception of Utah Valley, Central Utah has escaped some of the development that is making Northern Utah a megalopolis. Mountain ranges extend through the central region of Utah. Between them are pastoral valleys nurturing scores of rural towns, many of them founded shortly after the Mormons arrived in the Salt Lake Valley. Several scenic drives extend into the Wasatch Mountains, the Wasatch Plateau, the Tushars, and other mountain ranges in the region, providing a host of possibilities for alpine excursions. Mounts Timpanogos and Nebo crown the region, their glacier-carved peaks thrusting over the valleys below.

Central Utah offers a connection with Utah's heritage. From the Swiss pioneer architecture of Heber Valley to the Scandinavian settlements of Sanpete Valley, Central Utah embraces its past and, at times, still lives it.

Utah Valley and Environs

With backdrops such as Mt. Nebo and Mt. Timpanogos, Utah Valley has no short supply of surrounding beauty. Utah Valley

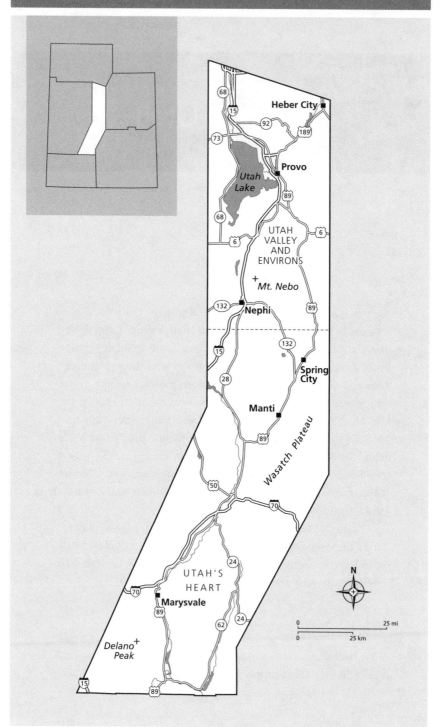

Heber City

68
15
92
189
73

Utah Lake

Provo
89

68
UTAH VALLEY AND ENVIRONS
6
6

+ Mt. Nebo

132
Nephi
89

132
15
Spring City
28

Manti
89

Wasatch Plateau

50

70

24

UTAH'S HEART
70
Marysvale
89
62
24

Delano + Peak

15
89

N

0 — 25 mi
0 — 25 km

supports a number of towns along its benches and out along the shores of Utah Lake. Although a couple of Spanish priests, Dominguez and Escalante, first explored the valley back in 1776, Mormon settlers named the first Utah Valley settlement in honor of Etienne Provost, a French–Canadian trapper who wandered into the valley in 1824 and 1825. The French name wouldn't do, so they anglicized Etienne's surname to Provo.

Today, **Provo** is the valley's largest and most interesting city. Popularly known as the home of **Brigham Young University**, Provo is an attractive town that is laid out much like its neighbor to the north, Salt Lake City. Filled with several historic buildings and a nice array of shops and restaurants, **Provo Town Square** is where you'll get the best taste of what the city has to offer. Having been restored to their original appearance, most of the buildings date from the 1890s, when the square grew into Provo's center of commerce. When you are in **Orem**, eat at my favorite Mexican restaurant, **Mi Ranchito** (1109 S. State St.; 801-225-9195). There are a number of house specials, including the chicken enchilada. The chips and salsa is to die for.

The Hines Mansion Luxury Bed and Breakfast (801-374-8400 or 800-428-5636; hinesmansion.com), 383 West 100 South, Provo, was designed by Richard Karl August, architect of the Utah State Capitol, for R. Spencer Hines, one of the richest men in Provo in 1895. The mansion radiates late nineteenth-century charm, with many of its original wood moldings, brick walls, and stained-glass windows. The nine bedrooms, each with a different theme, are

The Hutchings Museum in Lehi

Located at 55 North and Center in Lehi, the *Hutchings Museum* is a slice of Utah's past. The museum contains an eclectic collection celebrating Utah and its rich history. Simply put, this is a wonderful conglomeration of neat "stuff" you'll never see under any other roof. The bottle collection is superb and many folks' personal favorite. If you're a pushover for glass, this is a must-see. There are also artifacts celebrating the Old West, including Butch Cassidy's rifle, which was damaged when he took a tumble from his mount. It was repaired and a silver coin was used as a sight. There are Ancestral Puebloans and Fremont artifacts and early pioneer tools used for building cabins.

The museum's founder, John Hutchings, loved geology. As a boy he set out to acquire every sort of mineral and rock Utah had to offer. They are all here, along with a number of mining tools. The cased uncut gems are especially interesting. Hours are 11 a.m. to 5 p.m. Tues through Thurs, and 11 a.m. to 9 p.m. Fri and Sat. It is closed on Monday. Admission is $4 for adults and $3 for children. For more information, call (801) 768-7361.

furnished with antique and reproduction furniture by hosts Sandi and Gene Henderson. A free tour of the house is offered each day from 2 to 4 p.m. The Country Garden has ivied walls and overlooks a pond and flower garden. The Library has a secret passageway and a spiral staircase. In the Captain's Quarters, nautical instruments hang on the wall and a saltwater aquarium is imbedded in the wall. Each room has a private bath with whirlpool, and a full breakfast is provided.

About 5 miles south of Provo, *Springville* has long been known as "Art City," mainly because of its claim to fame—the *Springville Museum of Art* (126 East 400 South; 801-489-2727). The building, designed in the style of Spanish colonial revivalism, was erected to house Springville High School's art collection, acquired through private donations and the annual Art Queen beauty contest. The contest, begun around the late nineteenth century, allowed the high school to earn enough money to add a painting each year to its collection. The painting was, of course, unveiled by the new Art Queen.

By the 1930s the high school had acquired the greatest collection of art in Utah. With help from the Work Projects Administration (WPA) and the Mormon Church, the comely Springville Museum of Art was finished in 1937 at a cost of $100,000. Although the high school is no longer involved with the museum, the museum still holds an annual April Show.

The upstairs gallery exhibits 250 pieces from the 1,300-strong collection from more than 250 artists. The museum also has changing exhibitions on its

Not Slimy but Slithery: Snakes and Such

Want to show your kids a good time and see some reptile friends? Or maybe you don't want your kids to inherit the same phobias about serpents that you have? Come handle a snake and get a snake's-eye view of a turtle or a lizard, too. It's great for kids of all ages.

The Monte L. Bean Life Science Museum on the Brigham Young University campus in Provo, a great museum to visit in its own right, has a wonderful reptile show. You'll start off looking at some cleverly stuffed serpents. (This helps those who are uneasy about the live ones to come.) Next you'll visit the turtles, learn the difference between an alligator and a crocodile, and view the lizards on display.

Finally, you get a bunch of snakes to look at—and touch and hold if you feel so inclined. Look one right in the eye and pretend you're not scared. Shows are on Mon at 6:30 p.m. and 7:30 p.m., and on Sat at 1:30 p.m. For a special showing call (801) 378-5051 a week in advance to schedule. The show is free.

AUTHOR'S FAVORITES IN CENTRAL UTAH

Mount Timpanogos	Brigham Young University
Alpine Loop Scenic Backway	Springville Museum of Art
Nebo Loop Scenic Byway	Cascade Springs
The Provo River	American Fork Canyon
Provo Canyon	Fly Fishing the Provo River
Fish Lake	

ground floor. Hours are 10 a.m. to 5 p.m. Tues through Sat (until 9 p.m. on Wed) and closed on Sun.

You can't imagine a quainter place to eat than the *Art City Trolley Restaurant* (256 North Main St.; 801-489-8585). As the name indicates, the restaurant is set within a converted trolley car, decked out with photos and knickknacks from the trolley era. The buffalo wings served here are famous throughout the region. And the barbecue and kama'aina ribs ignite the taste buds like none other in the state. Open 11 a.m. to 9:30 p.m. Mon through Thurs, 11 a.m. to 10:30 p.m. Fri, and noon to 10:30 p.m. Sat. Check out what is definitely the hippest, most happening place in this small town.

Like all major cities along the Wasatch Front, Provo is not without its canyon, providing the backdoor retreat to nature for which Utah has become famous. *Provo Canyon Parkway* (Highway 189) begins at the north end of University Avenue in Provo and cuts eastward through the Wasatch Mountains, following the Provo River to Deer Creek Reservoir and Heber Valley.

Veering off the Provo Parkway and ending up in American Fork Canyon, the 19-mile *Alpine Scenic Backway* (Highway 92) is a jaunt through some of the most incredible scenery in the Wasatch Mountains. This narrow, paved road (not recommended for RVs) twists through towering groves of aspens while ascending the eastern slope of Mt. Timpanogos, providing fantastic views of these 11,750-foot jagged peaks. So incredible is the scenery that you'll feel guilty if you take it all in from the confines of your car. So be sure to plan a hike, a bike ride, a stroll, or anything else that gets you out breathing air that isn't conditioned. The road closes just above Sundance from late October to early June, or whenever snow blocks the way.

First stop on the Alpine Scenic Backway is *Sundance*, about 3 miles above the Provo Parkway (RR3 Box A–1, Sundance 84604). Few ski resorts in

Ever Been Hot Potting?

In an age of space travel, the Internet, and microchips, sometimes the simple, natural pleasures are still the best. A long soak in a natural hot spring is incredibly relaxing and therapeutic.

If you've never been to a hot spring, satiate your curiosity at the **Diamond Fork Hot Pots**, off Highway 6 in Spanish Fork Canyon. (Drive east from Spanish Fork and turn north at the Diamond Fork exit.) Winter is perhaps the most popular "hot potting" season. Picture this: snowy banks, mountain silhouettes, below-freezing temperatures... and you in up to your neck, wisps of steam rising from the hot water.

If you don't mind the mild smell of sulfur oxide and would enjoy a pleasant twenty- to forty-minute hike (or cross-country ski trip), the experience can be memorable. Bring a lunch and spend the day. Or better yet, go at night and stargaze. And don't forget to bring a towel. No fee.

America have nurtured such a symbiotic relationship with the environment. Careful development and eco-minded decisions under the tutelage of owner Robert Redford have turned the resort into what many consider a utopia of sorts. Happily, skiing is not the only thing on the agenda at Sundance. It is also home to some great cultural happenings, such as the **Sundance Institute**, a workshop for independent filmmakers and burgeoning playwrights. Although most of the **Sundance Film Festival** action occurs in Park City, you can still catch screenings of festival films at the institute (call 801-328-3456 or go to sundance.org for festival information). During the summer you can enjoy hiking and biking the trails, then eat a picnic dinner while watching a classic movie on a giant outdoor screen. The Utah Symphony also holds regular concerts on the outdoor stage, surrounded by the wooded mountains. For more information about these events, call (801) 225-4107 or visit sundance resort.com.

Accommodations at Sundance live up to the resort's drop-dead scenery at the foot of **Mt. Timpanogos**. Unlike most resorts, Sundance has no enormous lodge to accommodate as many people as possible. Instead, the resort offers discreet lodging in wood-studded cottages, in which you have the choice of a suite, junior suite, or basic room. The resort also offers its guests entire cabins that are tucked away high above the resort. Whatever accommodations you choose, you can be assured of tasteful Southwest decor and the utmost in coziness. But there's a steep price tag for lodging at a resort that hasn't been overdeveloped. To check on rates and to make reservations call (801) 225-4107 or (800) 892-1600.

Ski Resorts in Summer: Hiking and Mountain Biking

Don't assume that Utah's numerous ski resorts close up shop when the snow has melted and the alpine flowers are blooming in the meadows. The skis and snowboards might be tucked away in a closet, but hiking and mountain biking are in full swing.

Ski resorts have some of the finest hiking and biking trails around, and you can't beat the scenery or the accommodations. There are steep, expert slopes and gentle bunny runs, so everyone can feel comfortable. The view is breathtaking; don't forget your camera. If you didn't pack your bike on this trip, don't worry. Rental bikes, helmets, and other safety equipment are available for a reasonable price at most resorts.

If you love all the breathtaking mountain scenery, but your muscles ache and tighten when you think of a steep, grueling hike or pedal up the slope, fear not. Many Utah ski resorts have just the ticket. You can ride the tram (with your bike) as high as you want, and then hike or bike downhill. You can't go wrong!

Fourteen kilometers of trails at Sundance's Nordic Center provide cross-country skiers with a chance to ski through the silent, snow-covered aspen groves and alpine meadows of **Elk Meadows Preserve**. Located 1½ miles north of the main entrance to Sundance, the Nordic Center offers skating, and telemark rentals and lessons. Call (801) 225-4107 or (800) 892-1600 for more information.

Horseback riding is something else you can do during your stay at Sundance. The Sundance Stables offer rides along the extensive network of trails at the base of Mt. Timpanogos. One-hour, two-hour, three-hour, or all-day rides are available. You'll find the turnoff for the stables 1½ miles past the main Sundance entrance. Reservations are required. Call (801) 225-4107 or (800) 892-1600.

Near the summit of **Alpine Scenic Backway**, another paved road veers down the mountain and ends up at **Cascade Springs**, a surprisingly lush oasis where water bubbles up from limestone caverns deep within the earth and cascades down a series of terraces overgrown with wildflowers, cattails, watercress, maples, scrub oaks, willows, aspens, and so on. From Cascade Springs you can either return to the Alpine Scenic Backway or make your way down to Heber Valley. A dirt road, passable by regular cars, drops into the west side of the valley near Midway, providing excellent views along the way.

On the east side of the Wasatch Mountains and at the east end of **Provo Canyon Parkway** (Highway 189), **Heber Valley** offers more knockout views of Mt. Timpanogos. The valley is a lush, pastoral setting engulfed by mountains. When pioneers settled the valley in the 1860s, Switzerland came to mind, which isn't surprising, considering that many of them were from that country. Along with Ouray, Colorado, Heber Valley has become known as "The Switzerland of America." But in recent years the agrarian appearance of Heber Valley has given way to golf courses, subdivisions, and bedroom communities that now sit on top of what used to be farmland and grazing pastures.

Although Heber Valley is on the developmental fast track, **Heber City** hasn't yet washed itself of its Western, small-town feel.

Train buffs shouldn't miss the opportunity to hop aboard the **Heber Valley Historic Railroad**. Starting out in Heber City at the **Heber Valley Railroad Depot** (450 South 600 West, Heber), the 1904 steam locomotive and the vintage coaches make their way through farmlands, chug along the shores of Deer Creek Reservoir, and then descend into Provo Canyon. The line, originally stretching between Heber and Provo, was built in 1899 as part of the Utah Eastern Railway. For years this train was known as the "Heber Creeper," called such because the train seemed to creep up the Provo Canyon tracks, which were laid on a 2 percent grade.

There are two round-trip excursions available. One is a two-hour ride through Heber Valley and along the shores of **Deer Creek Reservoir**, ending at Deer Creek dam. The other takes about three and one-half hours and continues past the dam into Provo Canyon, following Provo River to Vivian Park. The railroad sometimes offers live bluegrass on its two-hour trips. The Heber Valley Historic Railroad generally runs May through October, but there are special excursions planned at certain times in the winter, most heavily around Christmastime. Call the railroad at (435) 654-5601 or visit hebervalleyrr.org for scheduling and ticket information. It's a good idea to reserve in advance.

Insect, Dinosaur, Basket, Art

What do all of these things have in common? They're all within walking distance of one another at free museums on the campus of **Brigham Young University**. The Monte L. Bean Life Science Museum (801-378-5051) has more than one million preserved insects, 6,000 birds, 200,000 mounted plants, and much more. The **Earth Science Museum** (801-378-3680) has a huge fossil collection, including a *supersaurus* and an *ultrasaurus*. Ancient artifacts and displays from all over the world are in the **Museum of Peoples and Cultures** (801-422-0020), including some that are 50,000 years old. Two art galleries on campus have rotating exhibits. The **B. F. Larsen Gallery** (801-378-2881) features contemporary artists; the **Museum of Art** (801-422-8287) hosts major traveling collections.

The Pig Pied Piper of Snake Canyon

Snake Canyon, not far from Heber and Midway, got its name honestly. Folklore has it that rattlesnakes were so thick, the settlers barely dared to enter. In the craters of Snake Canyon, you could see balls of rattlesnakes. Many children died of snake-bite. Only men with heavy leather boots and stout hearts dared to walk the viperous paths.

Midway settlers had a serious problem. They needed access to the tall stands of timber in the high country but were understandably afraid to go via Snake Canyon. Finally, in desperation, the town fathers called upon a Pied Piper of sorts—a man who said he could get rid of the snakes. The next spring, the Pig Pied Piper brought in a bunch of hogs—apparently pig fat and tough pigskin kept rattler bites from seriously affecting the voracious oinkers.

All spring, summer, and early fall, the hungry pigs munched on the abundant population of snakes. The breeding pigs and piglets grew and rid the canyon of rattlesnakes. Before the snows flew, the man brought his hogs down to market, where the snake-fed porkers sold for a glorious price. Legend has it there were still a few rattlers, but to this day snakes have never again been a problem in Snake Canyon.

The Swiss influence on Heber Valley becomes much more obvious when you enter **Midway**, a town that has gone out of its way to capitalize on its history, which began with a number of Swiss immigrants. Surrounded by pastures and beautiful mountain vistas, the town's orderly streets are graced with Swiss architecture.

The town's odd name comes from an event that led to the creation of the town. Beginning in 1859, two communities were established along Snake Creek some distance from one another. Fearing attack by local Indians who held the Snake Creek area to be sacred, the two communities banded together and agreed to build a fort midway between their two settlements. The fort's walls were actually seventy-five log cabins built side by side, forming a huge square. City blocks were laid out around the square, which became the town's nucleus.

Each September Midway celebrates the town's Alps-like scenery and its Swiss heritage with **Swiss Days**. Artisans, entertainers, and spectators flock to the little town, festooned with Swiss colors for the two-day event. Dancing, food, parades, and people dressed in folk clothing add to the festivities. For exact dates call (435) 654-2580 or visit midwayswissdays.com.

Besides its Swiss heritage, Midway's claim to fame is its "hot pots." Underground water, warmed in the earth's interior, seeps up through cracks in the earth's surface, depositing minerals carried with it on the journey. Over the centuries, the minerals have built up into domes, or hot pots. Long considered

Chasing Pheasants

If your idea of fun is chasing pheasant, shotgun in hand, Central Utah is a great place to visit. While the regular pheasant season is short, and a lot of the property is private, pheasant hunting thrives at hunting clubs.

Such clubs have a six-month season. Shooting starts in September and ends in March. Prices are reasonable, even if you are not a member. For a modest fee, plus the price of the birds you take, you can have a great hunt. Clubs have rental dogs (and shotguns), too.

Earl Sutherland runs the *4-Mile Hunting Club* outside Nephi, a well-run club and a personal favorite with the locals. Earl calls 4-Mile a "working man's" outfit—there are lots of pheasant-saturated fields. The birds at this club fly quickly; the shooting is fast and furious. You can arrange a shooting time by calling Earl at (435) 623-0704.

a medicinal treasure, the hot pots spawned a resort in the tradition of European spas.

More than a hundred years ago, Swiss-born Simon Schneitter was struck with an idea. With so many neighbors constantly calling to bathe in his hot pot, why not go big time and open a resort? Using wood boards, Schneitter built a pool and filled it with water piped in from the hot pots. And with that he had a resort, calling it Schneitter's Hot Pots. Since then the resort with one mineral bath has turned into *The Homestead*, a resort with 148 lodging rooms, a golf course, two tennis courts, two restaurants, in-room massage, sleigh rides, cross-country skiing, horseback riding, two pools (indoor and outdoor), and more. Oh, yeah, and mineral baths.

The Homestead (700 North Homestead Dr.; 435-654-1102 or 800-327-7220) is mainly composed of small cottages. You have a choice of lodgings in a suite (standard to premium prices). If you're thinking about going all-out, you can rent a condominium or a private home. For more details about the rooms, visit homesteadresort.com.

About 20 miles south of Provo in the town of *Payson* (exit 254 on Interstate 15) begins (or ends) another high-country exploration of the Wasatch Mountains. The 37-mile *Nebo Loop Scenic Byway* switchbacks up to the base of Mount Nebo, along the way flashing incredible views of the valleys below. With an altitude of 11,877 feet, *Mt. Nebo* is the highest peak in the Wasatch Range and one of the range's most sublimely beautiful. The paved loop stretches between Payson and Highway 132 (6 miles east of Nephi), making it an excellent alternative to traveling between Payson and Nephi on I–15, which is about as exciting as eating nuts. The road usually opens around mid-June

Nebo Loop Scenic Byway

The Mount Nebo Loop is more than a National Scenic Byway; it's a natural wonder. This designation means the loop is special—there are only thirty such designations in the United States. Utah has two.

The loop is a 37-mile road from Payson to Nephi (only about a thirty-minute drive). Anytime is a wonderful time of the year (although it would take a snow machine to cross in winter), but fall is an all-time favorite. The quaking aspens, maples, and buck brush start to turn, creating a sea of color. Summer and spring are also lovely, when alpine meadows are replete with wildflowers.

Keep an eye out for deer and elk, as well as small game. There are plenty of over-looks and hiking trails. There are fishing waters and campgrounds. When you go, take a lunch, a good pair of field glasses, and a pair of hiking shoes. Make a day of it. For wildlife viewing, mornings and evenings are best. Don't miss the loop.

Several campgrounds, picnic sites, and overlooks line the Nebo Loop Road. And you can access more than one hundred miles of trails, many of which wander through the Mount Nebo wilderness area and ascend Mt. Nebo to its summit. About 16 miles south of Payson, Payson Lakes is a marvelous setting, filled with several placid lakes and campgrounds. Farther south along the loop road is the trailhead for Nebo Bench Trail, taking you through large stands of aspens and conifers until it ascends above the timberline at the base of these glorious peaks. After 8 miles the trail connects with the Mount Nebo Trail, which leads to the summit.

Devil's Kitchen, about 28 miles south of Payson along Nebo Loop Road, is a geo-logical feature you would expect to find in Southern Utah. Red spires composed of river gravel and silt stand erect on the steep, eroded mountainside. A ½ mile trail takes you to an overlook of Devil's Kitchen, where some interpretive signs give you the lowdown on this "Mini Bryce Canyon."

For more information on camping and trails along the Nebo Scenic Loop contact the Spanish Fork Ranger District office (801) 798-3571 at 44 West 400 North in Spanish Fork. If you're coming from the south, stop in at the Nephi Ranger District office (435) 623-2735 at 740 South Main Street in Nephi.

and closes once the snow builds up (usually around late Oct). Autumn is, of course, the best time to make your pilgrimage, when a blaze of gold, maroon, and orange colors the mountainsides.

The Young Living Family Farm (435-623-8006) is 40 miles south of Provo just off I–15 in the small community of *Mona*. Here you will find an exotic zoo with a rare white buffalo, Goliath horses, miniature ponies, yaks, camels, llamas, zedonks (a mix between zebras and donkeys), and wild Watusi goats. There is also a duck pond with paddleboats to ride, a Western village with a child-sized Wells Fargo stagecoach drawn by the miniature ponies, and an Indian village. Its newest feature is the Medieval Heritage Center, complete with jousting tournaments, medieval fare, and performances of Shakespeare. In addition, you can explore what the farm is here for; they grow herbs for essential oils that are used in holistic medicines. Call or write to 3700 North Highway 91, Mona 84645 to get their calendar of events.

Utah's Heart

The drive along Highway 89 from Fairview to Junction is a journey through Utah's heritage. Highway 89, the first road to span the state of Utah from north to south, travels through some of Utah's oldest communities, where preservation is thankfully a high priority with its residents.

Mormon pioneers settled the **Sanpete Valley** not long after they settled the Salt Lake Valley. Their legacy is felt all over the place, especially during all the summer festivals for which Sanpete County has become noted. In what was probably the first and only instance of Indians ever offering land to the white man, Ute Chief Wakara invited the Mormons to settle in Sanpete Valley. Before the Mormons moved in, Sanpete Valley was inhabited by the San Pitch Indians, relatives of the Northern Utes and possible descendants of the Fremonts. (Sanpete is a corruption of San Pitch.) For years the Northern Utes raided the San Pitch encampments, often kidnapping their children and selling them to Mexican slave traders. By 1870 only fourteen San Pitch Indians remained; the rest were killed off by diseases brought by settlers. Not much is known about the San Pitch today, thanks to scavengers who have cleaned out most of the archaeological sites in the valley.

Today, **Sanpete County** boasts a healthy concentration of historic homes and buildings, many of which are now bed-and-breakfasts. Although it's in the heart of Utah, Sanpete County is strangely isolated, drawing few out-of-state tourists, making it an ideal destination for the off-the-beaten-path traveler.

First stop on Highway 89 in Sanpete County is the ***Fairview Museum of History and Art*** (435-427-9216) at 85 North 100 East in **Fairview**. Bought for $20 in the 1960s, the 1900 schoolhouse-turned-museum houses an eclectic, almost eccentric collection of stuff, much of which has been culled from the attics of local townsfolk. Nineteenth-century Mormon furniture, spinning wheels, household items, and agricultural equipment make up the historical collection of the museum. Noted Utah artist ***Avard Fairbanks*** donated a number of his sculptures to the museum, including one titled *The National Shrine to Love and Devotion*. This sculpture depicts Fairview natives Peter and Celeste Peterson, married for eighty-two years. Both lived more than one hundred years, making them the oldest married couple in the country. The newest addition to the museum is a life-size replica of a Colombian mammoth skeleton, unearthed from a peat bog in 1988 during the construction of nearby Huntington Reservoir. The 11,000-year-old mammoth was so well preserved that scientists were able to determine his age when he died (sixty-five) and what his last meal included (pine tree). The mammoth apparently required a new building, added to the museum in 1995. The wing also showcases an abundance of work by local artists. Hours are 11 a.m. to 5 p.m. from May to Oct.

Heading east of Fairview, Highway 31 ascends through Fairview Canyon to the top of the **Wasatch Plateau**, providing a bird's-eye view of the Sanpete Valley from the plateau summit. Huntington, Cleveland, and Electric Lake Reservoirs sit in the plateau's basins, amid lush alpine meadows and pine and aspen forests. Picnic areas and campgrounds line the highway, most heavily in Huntington Canyon, through which Highway 31 drops down the eastern slope of the plateau on its way to Huntington (see Northeastern Utah). The highway is kept open in the winter, giving cross-country skiers, snowmobilers, and ice fishermen a chance to pursue their pleasures. For advice on mountain biking, cross-country skiing, or hiking on the western side of the Wasatch Plateau, contact the Sanpete Ranger District office (435) 283-4151 at 540 North Main Street, Ephraim.

utah'srocky mountains

The **Uinta Mountains**—a primitive, relatively untouched range that runs east and west—are considered part of the Rocky Mountains because they were formed at the same time.

The magnificent Wasatch Mountains, like other Utah ranges, are younger mountains and technically are not part of the Rockies. The "Basin Range" comprises a number of long, narrow, north-south ranges in Utah.

It's not often that an entire town gets listed on the National Register of Historic Places, but **Spring City** has achieved just that. Known locally as the "Williamsburg of the West," Spring City got its start in 1852. Drawn by the locale's springs, the settlers of Spring City abandoned the town twice for fear of Indian attack. You can attribute the town's remarkable preservation to the steady decline of residents since 1895, when the town's population peaked at 1,250. With no incentive to tear down and redevelop, the town has retained a great deal of its architectural heritage. You can also attribute the town's preservation to its location—a few miles off Highway 89, away from the hubbub that usually spawns convenience stores, gas stations, and fast-food joints.

The best time to visit Spring City is the Saturday of Memorial Day weekend. **Spring City Heritage Day** is the occasion for residents to open their historic homes to the public. Another good time to visit is during **Spring City Pioneer Days**, usually from July 21 to 24. Everything from the parade to the music to the prices reverts to the old days for this event. Pioneer Days' big attraction is the food, usually something like barbecue mutton or turkey.

The **Lazy Inn Bed and Breakfast** (11650 Canal Canyon Rd.; 435-255-2350) sits on twenty acres in Spring City at the base of Horseshoe Mountain. The three rooms are available and the price is reduced if you stay for more than one night. They provide soaps, lotions, and bath salts—made in the community specifically for the inn—for each room's private bath. Hot chocolate, apple cider, and popcorn are always on hand to be enjoyed in the parlor or while watching the wildlife out the window. (Deer and elk are plentiful here, as are the hawks and eagles soaring above.) Find more information about the inn at thelazyinn.org.

Horseshoe Mountain Pottery (278 South Main St.; 435-262-0582) is the studio, gallery, and home of Joseph and Lee Bennion, two artists who settled in Spring City in 1977 to do the work that has made Joe a nationally acclaimed

Utah Trivia

In December and January, Snowbird averages more than 200 inches of snow.

The **Fish Lake National Forest** provides 1.2 million recreation visitor days, 4 million board feet of timber, and 9,000 Christmas trees.

Utah's birth rate is the second highest in the nation; its death rate is the second lowest.

The state's population is younger than the national average—25.7 years compared with 32.7.

Hikers along Utah's Wasatch Front can still find fossilized shoreline evidence of the Great Lake Bonneville that once covered most of Utah and portions of Idaho and Nevada.

Spanish Fork, at the base of the Wasatch Mountain Range, has become the livestock center of Utah.

Utah County has the most apple and peach trees in Utah.

The City of Omni was renamed Richfield because the soil was so fertile and the crops so lush.

The largest US Swiss cheese factory is located in Utah.

One-third of Utah is considered desert.

Utah is a leading producer of prosthetic human body parts.

A Festival for Everyone

Every month in Utah, cities find something to celebrate. This is especially true during the summer months in Utah Valley. In June, Lehi hosts the **Lehi Roundup**, Springville celebrates **Art City Days**, and strawberries are in abundance at Pleasant Grove's **Strawberry Days**. The last week in June and first part of July, Provo hosts one of the nation's largest Fourth of July celebrations, **America's Freedom Festival**, which includes an art festival, a carillon concert, hot-air balloon races, and a fireworks extravaganza (freedomfestival.org). Also in July, you can help Payson honor **Scottish Days**, complete with kilts and bagpipes, or head to Spanish Fork's **Llama Fest**. If you like folk dancing, Springville's **World Folkfest** features more than 400 dancers from around the world (worldfolkfest.com). During August many cities celebrate their heritage and the county fair. In addition, Orem has the **Timpanogos Storytelling Festival**, which brings in celebrated performers from around the nation (timpfest.org). By September things are starting to wind down, but be sure not to miss the **Festival of India** in Spanish Fork.

potter and Lee an equally acclaimed painter. As a potter, Joe has become so praiseworthy that he was the subject of **The Potter's Meal**, a documentary film by Steve Olpin, featured at the Sundance Film Festival in 1993. Lee's paintings have made their way into galleries and museums across the country. By the look of them, you can tell she has a love affair with the kind of life her family has nurtured in this sleepy, pastoral town. Horseshoe Mountain Pottery has no regular hours, so it's best to call ahead before you stop by.

Farther south along Highway 89, *Ephraim* takes its name from a tribe mentioned in the ***Book of Mormon***. Swedes, Norwegians, and mostly Danes settled the town in the early 1850s, building a fort that became the valley's refuge during the Black Hawk War with the Indians. Today Ephraim is widely known around Utah as the home of Snow College, a two-year college noted for its agricultural program. In celebration of the town's heritage, the town throws an annual *Scandinavian Festival*, held Memorial Day weekend.

Next destination along Highway 89 is *Manti*, the first Mormon settlement south of Provo and the state's fourth-oldest town. As the first settlement in the Sanpete Valley, Manti has the distinction of being founded by an Anglo and an Indian, Brigham Young and Ute Chief Wakara.

The town's landmark is, of course, the ***Manti Temple***, completed in 1888 after eleven years of volunteer labor and at a cost of more than $1 million. Brigham Young dedicated the site in 1877, just three months before his death. Constructed of oolitic limestone quarried from nearby mountains, the temple perches on a hill above town, drawing attention from points throughout the

Sanpete Valley. Only Mormons in good standing can enter the temple, but anyone is welcome at the visitor center.

For such a small town, Manti has an incredible concentration of bed-and-breakfasts. The reason for so many of them is the number of weddings occurring in Manti year-round. Mormons from around the state gravitate to this quaint little town to be married in its temple. Wedding guests follow, filling the bed-and-breakfasts that receive nary a regular tourist.

As the first home built in Manti, the **Manti House Inn** (401 North Main St.; 435-835-0161 or 800-835-7512) certainly has a right to its name. Built of the same stone used to construct the Manti Temple, this bed-and-breakfast has had a long and illustrious history connected to the building of the town's most famous structure. Andrew Van Buren built the original section of the house in the late 1860s and soon after added another section and converted his home into a hotel, hosting Mormon dignitaries such as Brigham Young and Joseph F. Smith.

The Manti House Inn was totally renovated in 1987. Named after the Mormon prophets who lodged at the hotel, each of the seven rooms at the Manti House is finely decorated with period antiques and Mormon knickknacks. The **Carriage Restaurant** is open by reservation.

Visitors to Manti should explore the town's side streets, where you'll find a host of Old West structures not commonly seen in many places around the West. One such structure is the **Yardley Inn and Spa** (190 South 200 West; 435-835-1895). This late nineteenth-century Victorian bed-and-breakfast renders all the charm and comfort of an old English inn.

The three rooms in the main house (all with private baths) are tastefully decorated with poster or brass beds. No expense has been spared in the two suites, which come with a whirlpool, fireplace, and private decks that look out across town. The inn also has its own health spa. The innkeepers have a passion for the business and enjoy pampering their guests, many of whom return year after year. To see the rooms, visit theyardleyinnandspa.com.

Traveling farther south along Highway 89, you'll move out of the Sanpete Valley and into Sevier Valley, where the landscape colors segue from alpine green to desert browns and vermilion. At the northern reaches of the valley is **Salina**, a dusty cowboy town named for its ready supply of salt—*salina* in Spanish. Sitting at the crossroads of Interstate 70 and Highways 89 and 50, Salina makes a good stop-off for people heading in all directions. Salina is certainly a rowdier place than its neighboring towns, which all but shut down after nightfall.

About a forty-five-minute drive from Salina, **Fish Lake** sits in a serene volcanic basin of the **Fish Lake Mountains**. Extending 5 miles in length and up to a mile in width, Fish Lake is surrounded by thick stands of aspens and spruces. At 8,800 feet, Fish Lake offers a cool respite from the heat down below. Anglers pull splake and rainbow trout from the waters, as well as Mackinaws, lake trout, which can weigh up to thirty pounds. Hiking or mountain biking along the shoreline and into the mountains is also an option for having fun.

Fish Lake Lodge, a venerable log structure dating from the 1930s, is the centerpiece for several outlying lakefront cabins. Most of the cabins are brand new, offering great views of the lake from large decks. Prices vary depending on the accommodations. Many of them have well-equipped kitchens and wood-burning stoves. Call Fish Lake Resort Associates at (435) 638-1000 to make reservations. The lodge is open year-round, but on a limited basis in the winter. Snowmobilers and, more recently, cross-country skiers have found Fish Lake an excellent place to engage in their winter pastimes. To get specific details about each cabin and see photos of the lake, visit fishlakeresorts.com.

To access Fish Lake from Salina, continue along Highway 89/I-70 and take the exit at Sigurd, a mile or so southwest of Salina. Head south on Highway 24 for about 35 miles until you reach the turnoff for Fish Lake (Highway 25)—another 8 or so miles to the east.

Traveling along Highway 89, 24 miles south of Richfield and 9 miles south of I-70, you'll see what **Burl Ives** referred to when he sang "Big Rock Candy Mountain." Though "Haywire Mac" **Harry McClintock** never actually saw Big Rock Candy Mountain, he wrote a song about it, picturing it as some luscious mound of caramel.

Time has seemed to slip past the town of **Marysvale**, located on Highway 89 about 15 miles south of I-70. If there ever were a village in the state of Utah,

The Fish Lake Ghost

Folks say that Fish Lake is haunted, but don't you believe it! In fact, some have gone so far as to suggest that she (the ghost is female) even lives in Fish Lake Lodge. In the late afternoon when the wind dies, you can hear her over the water, sounding mournful. Rumor has it she's lonely and looking for anglers to drown. You're supposed to get off the water fast before she tips your boat and makes you a ghost, too.

The truth is, there's no ghost in the afternoon. It's a rumor started by some jealous fishermen who wanted the lake to themselves when the fishing was good. Seems they wanted to scare the competition away, and ghost stories were the best way to do it.

Everyone around here knows the Fish Lake Ghost doesn't come out until midnight . . .

it would have to be this quaintest of towns that has yet to pave most of its streets. Sitting at the eastern foot of the ***Tushar Mountains*** in the canyon of Pine Creek, Marysvale has held on to pieces of the town's history and heritage. Nowhere in town is this more evident than at ***Lizzie & Charlie's Rag Rug Factory*** (210 East Bullion Ave.; 435-326-2078).

Ron and Glenda Bushman have kept alive the family's weaving tradition that began with Ron's grandfather, Charlie Christensen, who emigrated from Denmark to Utah in 1894. Forty years later he and his wife, Lizzie, set up shop in an old J. C. Penney store, where they both worked until Charlie's death. Ron recently renovated the building that he and Glenda continue to operate as a loom factory. The factory is filled with eight or nine restored antique looms, on which you can see Ron, Glenda, and their apprentices weave rag rugs by hand—a folk art that's scarcely practiced these days. If you're itching to try your hand at weaving, Ron will help you. Of course, Ron and Glenda are also in the business of selling their rugs, and there are hundreds to choose from. Stop in Mon through Sat, 9 a.m. to 5 p.m.

Another great example of Marysvale's heritage is found at the restored ***Moore's Old Pine Inn*** (60 South St.; 435-326-4565). The illustrious history of the Pine Inn goes back more than 110 years. During its heyday, when the train ran through town, it lodged the likes of locally born Butch Cassidy and Western icon ***Zane Grey***.

Randy and Katie Moore relocated to Randy's hometown and bought the venerable structure that seems to loom large in Marysvale's history. Preserving the authenticity of the old hotel, Katie and Randy have thankfully kept and restored the old wood floors and the iron beds. Each of the four rooms and three suites is individually and tastefully decorated. In addition to the rooms in the main house, the inn offers lodging in two cabins located on its spacious

Competitive Twinkle Fingers

If you're in the Salt Lake area in June and you like classical piano, you're in for a treat. June is Piano Month in the Beehive State. There are recitals and competitions galore for those so inclined, perhaps the most prestigious being the world-renowned *Gina Bauchauer International*. This affair has become one of the top piano competitions in the world.

During the Gina Bauchauer International, fifty-six musicians from more than twenty countries compete in Salt Lake's Abravanel Hall. Each of the six finalists performs a concerto with the Utah Symphony on the final two evenings. Competition and concert tickets range in price. Visit the website for pricing information at bauchauer.com.

grounds. The cabins are nicely furnished, with kitchens and living rooms. The Moores wanted to add more rooms and decided to build a replica of an Old West Main Street. To see their Western-themed rooms and the Old West town, visit oldpineinn.com.

In the late 1800s, previously untapped gold and silver veins spurred a mad rush to the 12,000-foot Tushar Range. In 1868 the Ohio Mining District was born, its port located in **Bullion Canyon** above Marysvale. By the 1870s **Bullion City** had turned into a reasonably sized town, boasting a population of more than 200 and claiming Piute County's seat. The Old Sylvester-Soderberg Stamp Mill was erected, as were fifty buildings, including a saloon, a gambling hall, and boardinghouses. But gold found in other canyons of the Tushars sent miners and prospectors scrambling to other camps, such as Kimberly. In a few short years after its reported peak population of 1,651 in 1880, Bullion was deserted.

climatefastfacts

Central Utah's climate:

winter, 12 to 40 degrees

summer, 60 to 95 degrees

about 16 inches of precipitation

But its relics remain and are on exhibit at the **Miner's Park Historical Trail**, located at the Bullion townsite above Marysvale. As the little outdoor museum tells you, Americans weren't the first to prospect for gold at Bullion. In the mid-1800s, prospectors found piles of ore and an arrastra (a device for processing the ore). Historians suspect that Spanish conquistadors, scouting for gold in the late 1700s, left these things behind, as well as several veins of untapped gold.

The ¼-mile historical trail circles around an old miner's cabin relocated from the mountains. Along the trail you'll see samples of tools and equipment found in the area, including an original mucker (work car). On your way to the historical trail, you'll pass the old mill as well as an old mine shaft. From Marysvale head east on Center Street (Bullion Avenue). Take a left on Bullion Canyon Road and follow it up a rough dirt road for 7 miles. Take the right fork at the sign for Bullion City and continue a ½ mile to reach the Miner's Park Historical Trail. Low-clearance, two-wheel-drive vehicles can usually make the ascent if the road is completely dry. Ask in Marysvale for road conditions, or call the Beaver Ranger District office in Beaver at (435) 438-2436.

Those enchanted with the legends of the Wild West will want to check out the hometown of one Robert LeRoy Parker, better known as **Butch Cassidy**, whose story has been mythologized in countless books and articles and in the movie *Butch Cassidy and the Sundance Kid*. The tiny town of **Circleville**, 10 or so miles south of Junction, is where Cassidy spent most of his boyhood years, before he joined the Wild Bunch and robbed banks, trains, and payrolls throughout the West. Though some believe Cassidy died in South America, his relatives who remained in Circleville claimed that he returned to his boyhood digs before settling down somewhere in the Northwest, where he lived the rest of his days a lawful man. The old Parker log cabin, Butch Cassidy's boyhood home, is 2½ miles south of Circleville beside Highway 89. The cabin is open to the public.

Places to Stay in Central Utah

EPHRAIM

Iron Horse Motel
670 North Main St.
(435) 283-4223
Standard

MANTI

Legacy Inn Bed & Breakfast
337 North 100 East
(435) 835-8352
legacyinn.com
Moderate

Manti Country Village Motel
145 North Main St.
(435) 835-9300 or
(800) 452-0787
Standard

Manti House Inn
401 North Main St.
(435) 835-0161 or
(800) 835-7512
mantihouseinn.com
Moderate

TOP ANNUAL EVENTS IN CENTRAL UTAH

AUGUST

Harvest Days
Midvale
(801) 567-7204

Salem Days
Salem City
(801) 423-2770

SEPTEMBER

Juab County Fair
Nephi
(435) 623-3400

Sanpete County Fair
Manti
(435) 835-1351

Sevier County Fair
Richfield
(435) 893-0457

Utah County Fair
Orem
(801) 768-7411

Wayne County Fair
Loa
(435) 836-2650

FOR MORE INFORMATION ABOUT CENTRAL UTAH

TRAVEL COUNCILS

Mountainland Travel Region
586 East 800 North
Orem 84097
(801) 229-3800
Fax (801) 229-3801

Bus Schedules
Provo
(801) 743-3882

Road Conditions
(800) 492-2400

The Yardley Inn and Spa
190 South 200 West
(435) 835-1861 or
(800) 858-6634
yardleyinnandspa.com
Moderate

MARYSVALE

Moore's Old Pine Inn
110 S. Main St.
(435) 326-4565 or
(800) 887-4565
marysvale.org/pine/oldpine
.htm
Moderate

MIDWAY

The Homestead
700 North Homestead Dr.
(435) 654-1102 or
(888) 327-7220
homesteadresort.com
Deluxe

NEPHI

Super 8
1901 South Main St.
(435) 623-0888
Standard

PROVO

Chuck-a-Rama
1081 South University Ave.
(801) 375-0600
Inexpensive

Days Inn
1675 North 200 West
(801) 375-8600
Standard

**The Hines Mansion
Luxury Bed and
Breakfast**
383 West 100 South
(801) 374-8400 or
(800) 428-5636
hinesmansion.com
Deluxe

LaQuinta Inn
1555 North Canyon Rd.
(801) 374-6020
Standard

Ruby River
1454 South University Ave.
(801) 371-0648
Expensive

RICHFIELD

Days Inn
333 North Main St.
(435) 896-6476
Standard

Fish Lake Lodge
fishlake.com
Moderate

SPRINGVILLE

Days Inn
520 South 2000 West
(801) 491-0300
Standard

Places to Eat in Central Utah

OREM

Mi Ranchito
1109 South State St.
(801) 225-9195
Inexpensive

SPRINGVILLE

**Art City Trolley
Restaurant**
256 North Main Street
(801) 489-8585
Moderate

Northeastern Utah

The northeastern region is startlingly diverse. Its landscape is spotted with soaring mountains, sinuous canyons, lofty plateaus, and high-desert flatness. The **Uinta Mountains** sit like a crown on top of the northeast region of the state. Named after the Ute Indians, or Uintats, who claim this region as their homeland, this chain of mountains is the largest in the lower forty-eight states to run along an east-west axis. Its peaks are the highest in the state; **Kings Peak** is 13,528 feet. Thousands of lakes sit like specks of crystal among old-growth spruces, lodgepole pines, aspens, Douglas and white firs, and the occasional ponderosa. Above the timberline, at about 11,000 feet, rocky alpine tundra scours the peaks, making their superior heights clear among the rest of the wooded mountains. Mule deer, moose, elk, raccoons, porcupines, and Rocky Mountain goats commonly make an appearance on the mountain slopes. Black bears, mountain lions, bobcats, and other animals keep to themselves but are spotted now and again. The lakes and streams are a fisherman's paradise.

Flat desert floors stretch south of the Uintas across the **Uinta Basin**, segueing into the **Colorado Plateau**. The Green River flows calmly and assuredly through the Basin,

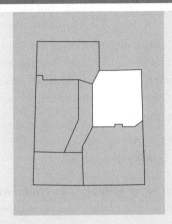

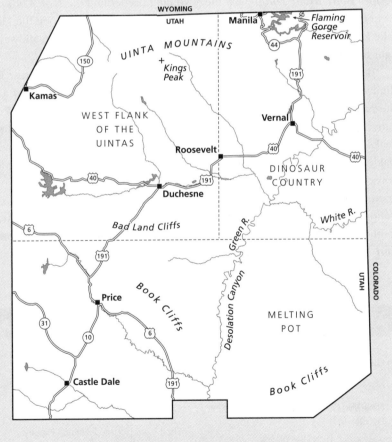

on course to the Colorado River. This is the home of the ***Uintah and Ouray Indian Reservation***.

Farther southward in Northeastern Utah, Castle Valley is sided by the Tavaputs and the Wasatch plateaus. Towns such as Price and Helper became the permanent destination for thousands of immigrants seeking employment and a new life in America. Places such as Nine-Mile Canyon and the northern section of the San Rafael Swell promise wide-eyed fascination.

West Flank of the Uinta Mountains

"Gateway to the Uintas," ***Kamas*** sits at the bottom of ***Mirror Lake Highway*** (Highway 150)—your access road into the western half of the Uinta Mountains. Besides ***Bear River Lodge*** near the Wyoming border and the scores of campgrounds lining the road, you won't find any accommodations along the Mirror Lake Highway. So you many want to consider staying in Park City, Midway, or right here in Kamas.

Before committing yourself to the heavily trodden spots off Mirror Lake Highway, first consider the ***Smith and Morehouse Recreation Area*** as an alternative destination. The recreation area is set in a serene fork of Weber Canyon, offering pretty views of aspen- and pine-covered slopes and distant peaks. From Kamas head 7 or 8 miles north on Highway 32 to the town of Oakley, then go 16 miles east on Weber Canyon Road. The Smith and Morehouse Recreation Area is centered around a small, picturesque reservoir, open to anglers and wakeless boats only. At each end of the reservoir are campgrounds, laid out underneath the canopies of lodgepole pines. At the southern end of the reservoir, past the ***Ledgefork Campground***, the ***Smith and Morehouse Trailhead*** marks the beginning of an alpine excursion to

AUTHOR'S FAVORITES IN NORTHEASTERN UTAH

Green River	Western Mining and Railroad Museum
Mirror Lake Highway	Christmas Meadows
Nine-Mile Canyon National Back Country Byway	Ouray National Wildlife Refuge
Cleveland-Lloyd Dinosaur Quarry	Utah Field House of Natural History
Green River	Uintah County Heritage Museum

Erickson Basin or the "Lakes" country to the south. Although it is heavily used, Mirror Lake Highway (Highway 150) is still Utah's most astounding high-country byway, taking you to the crest of the western half of the Uintas. The drive starts out at an elevation of 6,500 feet in Kamas and peaks at 10,678 feet on top of Bald Mountain Pass. You will have to pop your ears at least once or twice. The road soars among the Uintas' lakes and back country accessing campgrounds, rivers, and hiking and cross-country ski trails. Because of the extreme amount of snow that gets dumped in the Uintas every winter, most of the highway closes October through May. But thanks to the snowplows, you can go as far as *Soapstone Basin* (15 miles from Kamas) on the southern end or the *Bear River Campground* (about 30 miles from Evanston, Wyoming) on the northern end. This means you can still go cross-country skiing or snowshoeing in the tranquil fir and aspen forests. For hiking, skiing, campground, or any other information on areas in the southwestern section of the Uintas, contact the Heber/Kamas Ranger District office (435) 783-4338 at 50 East Center Street, Kamas. For the same information on the northwestern section of the Uintas, contact the Evanston Ranger District office (307) 789-3194 at 1565 Highway 150, P.O. Box 1880, Suite A, Evanston, WY 82930.

Six miles east of Kamas, the *Beaver Creek Cross-Country Trail* parallels the highway but keeps you at a comfortable distance from the road. Snowmobiles are not allowed on the trail, so you can enjoy the innate peace and quiet of the snow-blanketed forests. The 5½-mile trail is fairly easy and

Strawberry Reservoir Means Big Fish and Fast Fishing

A trip to **Strawberry Reservoir** is a must for anglers. The 'Berry, as it's fondly called by locals, is one of the best fishing waters in the West. If you like big fish and fast fishing, this is a wonderful place to wet a line. It's premier cutthroat water, hosting the aggressive Bonneville strain.

There are more than 17,000 acres of fin-infested waters to fish. The lake is 23 miles southeast of **Heber City** on Highway 40. There are campgrounds, day-use, and picnic sites. There are several paved boat ramps and two marinas at **Strawberry Bay** and **Soldier Creek Recreation Sites**, as well as a pier for handicapped anglers.

In the winter the area is popular with snowmobilers. Winter fishing for "cold footed" anglers is hot. Whether you're a blue-blooded dry fly snob, a spin caster, or a worm dunker, there's a fish in the 'Berry with your name on it . . . and there's a chance it could be a real lunker. Fish from the bank, a float tube, or a boat, or cut a hole in the ice.

accesses other, more strenuous trails, one of which goes to the ***Lower Provo River Campground***, 10 miles east of Kamas. Set on the banks of the rushing Provo River and in the shade of pines and spruces, the campground is an excellent place to pitch your tent in the summer. Water is available here in the summer.

Spring Canyon Road veers off to the left (east) 24 miles from Kamas and shortly arrives at Trial Lake, where you'll find a campground and an opportune spot to fish. Just past the lake's dam is the Crystal Lake Trailhead, the beginning of two possible hikes. One takes you 6½ miles past a series of lakes and through The Notch to the upper reaches of the Weber River. An additional 3½ miles will bring you up to Bald Mountain Pass. The other possible trail heads 3 miles past several lakes before connecting with the Smith–Morehouse Trail.

Beginning at ***Bald Mountain Pass*** (29 miles from Kamas), the 2-mile Bald Mountain National Recreation Trail is a steep, strenuous ascent to the summit of this appropriately named peak. The top-of-the-world view at the summit is well worth the hard work. From here you can look out across the High Uintas and see the Wasatch Range out on the horizon.

Coming down from Hayden Pass, Mirror Lake Highway passes several more campgrounds, eventually reaching the turnoff for ***Christmas Meadows*** (46 miles from Kamas and about 40 miles from Evanston, Wyoming). The 4-mile dirt road (negotiable for two-wheel-drive, low-clearance vehicles) veers past a stretch of meadows, finally arriving at ***Christmas Meadows Campground*** and the ***Stillwater Trailhead***—a gorgeous, off-the-beaten-path setting to hike, camp, or fish. The trail runs parallel to the Stillwater Fork River on the edge of lush meadows before ascending into the ***High Uintas Wilderness Area***—about 3 miles from the trailhead.

Adjacent to Christmas Meadows is the ***Bear River Campground*** (48 miles from Kamas), located right on the banks of the river in a grove of lodgepole pines. The campground also marks the spot where the northern section of Mirror Lake Highway dead-ends in the winter and where the ***Lily Lake Ski Trail*** begins. At 8,400 feet, the skiing is always good and can last into April or May. And because of its distance from populated areas, the ski trails here attract only a handful of skiers. But you'll have to go the extra mile to get here in the winter, which means taking Interstate 80 across the border to Evanston, Wyoming, then going about 35 miles south on Highway 150 back into Utah and the Uinta Mountains.

Just below Bear River Campground, at ***Bear River Lodge*** (801-798-1008), you'll find a general store, cafe, fishing ponds, and thirteen surprisingly comfortable log cabins. The cabins, outfitted with private baths and electric heat, sit within hearing distance of Bear River's rushing waters. From the main lodge and cabins, it is a short stroll down to the river and the two fishing ponds stocked with trout. One is catch-and-release, the other is catch-and-keep. The cafe, open daily 8:30 a.m. to 6 p.m. or 8 p.m. depending on the season, serves homemade Western basics. Cabins are open year round. Visit bearriverlodge .com for specials.

Dinosaur Country

In the northeastern shoulder of the state, the Uinta Mountains stoop down to meet the high desert. The diversity in geology, from the glacial-sculpted peaks of the Uintas to the river-carved canyons below, makes for a thrilling ride. Also thrilling are the dinosaur remains, dating from 140 million years ago. The dinosaur legacy comes to life at *Dinosaur National Monument*, where geological and climatic forces have tilted, warped, and eroded the earth's crust to reveal a treasure trove of fossils.

Our journey through the northeastern corner of Utah begins on the west side of Flaming Gorge Lake. Branching off Highway 44 about 10 miles south of the town of *Manila*, the scenic loop through *Sheep Creek Canyon Geological Area* is a tour past towering canyon walls, representing a billion years' worth of variegated rock strata. The paved road through the canyon points out the different formations that were exposed when the earth's crust broke along the *Uinta Crest Fault*. The drive eventually takes you out of the canyon and into the high country of the Uinta Mountains, where an excellent perspective of Sheep Creek Canyon comes into view. The gothic spires and towers in the canyon promise to keep you enthralled, as does the alpine scenery high above the canyon. The 13-mile scenic loop (closed in the winter) meets up again with Highway 44 about 10 miles south of where you left off.

But before you get back on Highway 44, you might want to consider venturing farther into the interior of the Uinta Mountains, where Utah's highest peaks crown the range. A good place to take in the mountains is from the top of the *Ute Tower*. Constructed by the Civilian Conservation Corps in 1934, the Ute Tower was the first fire lookout built in Utah. The restored tower, now listed as a historic site, is a testament to early fire prevention, before aircraft replaced towers in fire detection. Several newlywed couples spent their first summers together spotting fires. Ute Tower is open Memorial Day through Labor Day. Check with the Flaming Gorge Ranger District in Manila (435) 784-3445, P.O. Box 279, Manila 84046, for days and hours of operation, which change from year to year. From Sheep Creek Geologic Loop, take Forest Route 221 (posted as Browne and Spirit Lakes) a mile west along a dirt road manageable for low-clearance cars. Take a left on Forest Route 5 and go another

"Dino" Power

Younger kids love dinosaurs. Head to **Vernal** and show your kids the real stuff—or at least the remains of the real stuff. While there are a lot of bones and complete skeletons—and digs in progress—there are a number of "interpretive" displays the kids will love, too.

The Vernal area may indeed be the "dino" capital of the world. You can spend several days looking about and never see it all.

1½ miles to the tower. If you don't have a high-clearance vehicle, you should probably walk or bike the last 1½ miles.

About 17 miles east of Ute Tower, **Spirit Lake** sits in a wonderfully remote location at an elevation of 10,000 feet on the outside edge of the **High Uintas Wilderness Area**. Situated in the shadows of the High Uinta peaks, the lake is a great place to fish, camp, or just lounge. Trails from the lake access seventeen other lakes that are within a distance of 3 miles.

Mountain bikers, hikers, and cross-country skiers will enjoy the ascents and descents along **Dowd Mountain Trail**, a 10-mile loop beginning at the base of Dowd Mountain Road (at the junction of Highway 44 and the north end of Sheep Creek Geologic Loop). The moderately strenuous trail leads to **Dowd Mountain Overlook**, where you can catch your breath while comprehending the drop-dead-gorgeous views of Red Canyon, Flaming Gorge, and the High

Matt Warner Reservoir— The Mormon Kid

Between Vernal and Dutch John, there is a reservoir named **Matt Warner**. Matt Warner was a famous outlaw who was a close friend of Butch Cassidy. He was also a member of the Wild Bunch. His real name was William Erastus Christiansen—a young Mormon boy from Nephi, Utah. One evening he thought he had killed a rival fighting over a girl after a dance. Grabbing his rifle, he said goodbye and escaped across the mountains because he thought he might be hanged. He was afraid of Indians camped in the Strawberry Valley, but he managed to slip by. He made his way to the Diamond Mountains in Northeastern Utah. He changed his name to Matt Warner to protect his family and escape the law. Known as the Mormon Kid, he started rustling cows and took up the outlaw trail. Outlaw Matt became good friends with Butch Cassidy. Matt was not as careful, however, and he got caught. He did time for his crimes and reformed. He became a famous lawman.

The Green River

If you like to fly-fish, the Green River below Flaming Gorge Dam is one of the finest fishing waters in the country . . . bar none. Fly casters will be in heaven. This water draws world-wide attention. And yes, the river is very green. Think lots of large trout. It is not unusual to have a twenty- to thirty-fish day, some fish easily breaking the 20-inch mark.

You can walk the banks or book a guide and float—the fish are there. Equipped with a standard selection of flies or spinners, a pair of waders, a hat, and lunch, you're ready for a blue-ribbon day with trout. There are miles of exciting fishing below the dam. Please catch and release! I'll be watching—I'm there a lot!

Uintas. To save yourself from a really steep climb, take the loop in a counterclockwise direction.

Red Canyon Lodge (435-889-3759), located on Red Canyon Road just off Highway 44 and a few miles east of the Highway 191 junction, offers accommodations in several cabins that encircle East Green Lake, a tranquil natural lake stocked with rainbow trout. You can choose from the lodge's luxury or alpine cabins. The dinner menu features a wide variety of pasta, seafood, and steak. Hours vary seasonally. Red Canyon Lodge is open full-time April through October and on weekends during the winter. For more information, write them at 790 Red Canyon Road, Dutch John 84023, or visit redcanyonlodge.com.

Cross-country skiers, hikers, mountain bikers, and campers should consider **Red Canyon Rim** a place to pursue their endeavors. There are several groomed trails in the vicinity, including **Canyon Rim Trail**—a 6½-mile route skirting Red Canyon. Two trailheads provide access to the trail: One is at Red Canyon Lodge; the other is at Greendale Rest Area, located on Highway 44 just east of the Highway 191 junction. If you're traveling through, then be sure to at least check out the overlook at the Red Canyon Visitor Center, located at the end of the paved, 4½-mile Red Canyon Road. The overlook sits on a precipice high above the dammed waters of **Flaming Gorge Lake**, snaking through the 1,400-foot-deep Red Canyon. Open daily, 10 a.m. to 5 p.m. Memorial Day weekend to mid-September, the visitor center has exhibits dealing with the ecology of the area and the Indian and Anglo cultures that once lived here.

Another historic site on the east flank of the Uintas, **Swett Ranch** (435-789-1181) is a testament to Oscar Swett's self-sufficiency and ingenuity, representing the bygone homestead era. In 1909, Oscar was only sixteen years old, which meant he was too young to file for a homestead at the location he had picked out in the Uinta Mountains. So his widowed mother did it for him. In 1913 Oscar and his wife, Emma, moved to the isolated, high-country ranch and lived in a one-room cabin that Oscar relocated from another ranch. At the time of his death in 1968, Oscar and Emma were the last remaining homesteaders in the area, having accrued 397 acres and constructed eighteen buildings, three of which were homes for his wife and constantly expanding family of nine kids. In 1972 the Forest Service bought the ranch and has subsequently turned it into a working historical site, where you can get a taste of the homesteading years and what it took to make a living so far away from civilization.

The three Swett Ranch homes have been restored and decorated with items donated by Oscar's daughters. Swett Ranch is open Memorial Day through Labor Day, Thurs through Mon 10 a.m. to 5 p.m. Look for the sign on Highway 191, a half mile north of the Highway 44 junction. A 1½-mile dirt road, manageable for regular cars if it isn't muddy, leads to the ranch.

An option for having fun in the *Flaming Gorge National Recreation Area* is rafting the Green River below the Flaming Gorge Dam. The waters here are friendly and don't require any special navigation skills. *Dutch John Resort* (435-885-3191) rents rafts, provides a shuttle service, and offers guided

Utah Trivia

Duchesne is located near the largest cedar forest in the world.

The bridge across Starvation Reservoir is the longest in Utah.

When you look at the Book Cliffs from a distance, they look like the leaves of a partly opened book.

There are 1,253,142 acres of aspen trees in Utah.

The Uinta Mountains run east and west (one of the few ranges in the world to do so) and are part of the Rocky Mountains.

Kings Peak, at 13,528 feet, is the highest point in Utah.

The Uinta National Forest provides 3.5 million recreation visitor days; 70,000 sheep and 12,000 cattle graze on the forest each year.

Notable in Utah's ancient history is the abundance of dinosaurs that once roamed the region.

Today the state is home to two of the largest dinosaur graveyards in North America: Dinosaur National Monument in the northernmost part of the state and the Cleveland–Lloyd Quarry in East-Central Utah.

The blue spruce was chosen by the Utah State Legislature in 1933 as the state tree.

Brown's Hole and Its Outlaw Past

Brown's Hole, sometimes called Brown's Park, is a beautiful valley with wonderful fly fishing. In the 1830s it was trapped by the mountain men. At the turn of the 19th century, however, it was a bloody no man's land. Homesteaders and small ranchers fought a brutal range war against land-hungry cattle barons who ran their kingdoms like feudal fiefdoms. The small ranchers sheltered the outlaws such as Butch Cassidy, the Sundance Kid, Matt Warner, and Kid Curry. The large ranchers hired professional gunmen like the killer Tom Horn to do their dirty work. It was a savage land work. They said if a lawman rode into the hole, he'd ride out draped over his saddle. Tom Horn killed at least two local ranchers. He stalked his victims in barefoot and shot them in cold blood. He put a few stones by their dead bodies as his calling card. He called it "the system that never fails." As you visit this part of Utah, you are capturing a part of the Wild West.

scenic trips along the river. They'll even transport your equipment and your car if need be. In addition to specializing in rafting, they offer guided fishing trips. They also have a fly shop and an RV park for your convenience. You'll find Dutch John Resort at the turnoff for ***Dutch John.***

The John Jarvie Historic Property, located along the banks of the Green River in Brown's Park, is almost as remote as it was in the days when Jarvie hosted Butch Cassidy and the Sundance Kid. Settling here in 1880, this industrious Scottish immigrant ran a post office, a store, and a ferry across the Green—all in addition to maintaining his ranch. Guided tours through the original corral, blacksmith shop, and stone house give you an idea of what it was like being a rancher in the late nineteenth century. This was Jarvie's first home before the house was built and supposedly a secret meeting place for outlaws from all over the West. What makes this place all the more ripe for legend is the way Jarvie met his death in 1909: He was murdered by a couple of transient workers from Rock Springs, Wyoming, who sent his body down the Green River on a raft. The murderers were never caught.

You can visit the ranch at any time. Tours are conducted Wed through Sat, May through Oct, 10 a.m. to 4:30 p.m. There are three ways of getting to the Jarvie Ranch. From Highway 191, head east on 22 miles of maintained gravel road that begins a mile north of the Utah-Wyoming border. Another approach (the easiest of the three) begins in Maybell, Colorado. Head west on paved Highway 318 to the Utah border. Continue 8 miles on a maintained gravel road. The final approach is from Vernal. Go north on Vernal Avenue to 500 North, then east 25 miles on a paved road to Diamond Mountain and Brown's Park turnoff. Then head 16 miles north on an infrequently maintained dirt road to

Brown's Park and the Jarvie Ranch. It's best to have a high-clearance vehicle if you take this route from Vernal. For information on road conditions or anything else regarding the historic site, contact the park ranger at (435) 885-3307.

Your backdoor approach to **Dinosaur National Monument** begins at **Jones Hole National Fish Hatchery** (435-789-4481), set at the bottom of some spectacular 2,000-foot-high canyon walls. Natural springs at Jones Hole provide the water in which thousands of trout are raised. After maturing, the trout are transported to Flaming Gorge and other lakes in the area. Behind the hatchery is Jones Hole Trailhead, the beginning of an easy, 4-mile hike into Dinosaur National Monument, ending at the Green River in Whirlpool Canyon. The trail follows Jones Creek through enchanting canyon scenery and past Fremont pictographs. (Please do not touch the rock art; oils from your hands damage it.) Remember to bring plenty of water, and be prepared for extreme, high-desert conditions. From Vernal go north on Vernal Avenue and then east on 500 North. Follow the paved road 38 miles to the hatchery. For more information, write to 1380 South 2350 West, Vernal 84078.

Vernal is a great hub. In the heart of Dinosaur Country, it hosts the **Utah Field House of Natural History State Park** (496 East Main St.; 435-789-3799). This is one of my favorite places—a must see. The *allosaurus* skeleton welcoming visitors at the entrance sets the tone for this museum, where you'll get the lowdown on 600 million years' worth of fossil history recorded in the Uinta Basin and see artifacts from the Fremont and Ancestral Puebloans, as well as artifacts from the Ute culture. But the real reason to visit the Utah Field House is the prehistoric animals poised in the dinosaur garden outside the museum. Elbert Porter sculpted the fourteen life-size models based on skeletons he had studied across the country. The effect is somewhat campy, but fun. In the garden you'll find a *diplodocus* and a *meganeura*—a prehistoric dragonfly with a wingspan of 2½ feet and a body length of 15 inches. But Porter's crowning achievement has to be the woolly mammoth, whose fur looks like an overgrown shag carpet. The museum is open daily, 9 a.m. to 5 p.m. (March through Memorial Day); 9 a.m. to 7 p.m. (Memorial Day through Labor Day); and 9 a.m. to 5 p.m. (Labor Day through Oct). October through March it is open Mon through Sat, 9 a.m. to 5 p.m. and closed on Sunday.

While you're in Vernal, see the **Uintah County Heritage Museum** (155 East Main St., 435-789-7399, uintahmuseum.org). It preserves the heritage of Uinta County and has some treasures for those interested in West. There are displays of the pioneers, Native American Indians, miners, soldiers, lawmen and outlaws who helped shape the history of this region. If you like history, visit the **Daughters of Utah Pioneers Museum** (2670 S. 500 W; 435-790-3907).

Josie Bassett Morris: A Woman for All Seasons

Josie was a farmer and rancher who lived a full life and ended her days in this cabin. Legends tell of her adventures as a cowgirl, including that she married and divorced five times, shot one husband, poisoned another, and ran yet another off with a frying pan. Some rumors even say that Butch Cassidy courted her. Josie built the cabin in 1935 and lived here by herself for about fifty years, raising animals and crops in the area. For more information about this trail, inquire at the Dinosaur Quarry visitor center.

While you're at Dinosaur National Monument, you might want to try the Cub Creek Trail. Take a left turn out of the parking lot and follow the signs to the trail. Along the trail you'll see Split Mountain, which looks as though it's been cleft in two by the Green River, and Turtle Rock. After you cross Cub Creek, you'll see rock art; a little farther on you'll find a cabin that belonged to Josie Bassett Morris.

Vernal's ***Dinah "Soar" Days & Hot Air Balloon Festival*** is in May. It is a three-day event, Thursday, Friday and Saturday, each day starting with an early morning hot air balloon launch. There is a night launch where the balloons look like giant lightbulbs in the sky. In July the ***Dinosaur Roundup Rodeo*** attracts competitors from all over the country for the four-night competition. For more information on Dinah "Soar" Days and the rodeo, call (800) 477-5558.

There is definitely no better way of seeing Dinosaur National Monument than taking a river trip through it. Based in Vernal, ***Don Hatch River Expeditions*** offers rafting excursions down the Green and Yampa Rivers through the stunningly beautiful canyons of Dinosaur National Monument. You can choose from a three-, four-, or five-day adventure. Hatch also offers one-day trips and, on a more limited basis, two-day trips through Split Mountain Canyon. Contact Don Hatch River Expeditions (435-789-4316) at P.O. Box 1150, Vernal 84078, or see their website at hatchriver.com.

For world-class pictographs, visit ***McConkie Ranch***, about ten miles outside of Vernal. Go north (Hwy 121) to Maeser. Turn north on 3500 West. Follow the road to Dry Fork Canyon. The first rock art to see is about 4 miles past the ranch. It is fantastic. Some can be viewed from the road; other areas require some hiking. Some impressive things are just over the hill. The fertility panel, a favorite, is quite a hike.

Take the trail—about a mile round trip. It can be steep in a few areas, but it is an easy hike if you take it slow. It can be hot in the summer, take a hat, a water bottle, and sunscreen. There are many petroglyphs—some are large and close—others are further away. Look at the figures with fascinating head gear or very large feet. This is up-close and personal—a unique opportunity. The admission is free and this collection is on private land. Consider donating a few dollars at the booth. Of course, don't touch or deface the rocks, or leave any litter—remember these images are over a thousand years old.

Spread out along the Green River south of Vernal, **Ouray National Wild-life Refuge** (435-545-2522) hosts an unexpected wealth of migratory birds out in the middle of the desert. A must see. More than 200 species feed and find shelter here; April through November, bird populations are high. Bald and golden eagles, Canada geese, whooping cranes, and ospreys are just a hand-ful of the species you might see along the 9-mile auto tour of the 11,480-acre refuge. At the information center, pick up an interpretive brochure that explains twelve sites along the road and tells you what species you're liable to see. To get to the refuge, drive 15 miles west of Vernal on Highway 40, then turn left (south) on Highway 88 and go 13 miles until you see a sign marking the entrance to the refuge. The refuge is open daily during daylight hours. Visit ouray.fws.gov or contact the refuge at HC69 Box 232, Randlett 84063 for more details.

Taking you back a number of years before fast food meant a drive-up window, **Marion's Variety** (435-722-2143) at 29 North Main Street in **Roo-sevelt** features an old-fashioned soda fountain, one of the last in the state. The shakes and malts served at Marion's are thick and luscious. And the ham-burgers, marinated in homemade barbecue sauce before grilling, are superb. Marion's goes back to 1933, when Danish immigrant Marion Mortenson opened a novelty, gift, and ice cream store. Today, Marion's grandnephew runs the place, keeping alive the old-time feel. Stop in Mon through Sat 10 a.m. to 9 p.m.

Uinta Canyon Trail makes for an excellent high-country excursion. The trail ascends into the High Uintas along the Uinta River, accessing a number of other trails that crisscross the range, giving you the option of a day hike or backpack trip. If you want to do some car camping, you can choose from several campgrounds lining the road into Uinta Canyon.

If you plan on traveling south from Duchesne to the Price area via High-way 191, you may consider taking the **Nine-Mile Canyon National Back Country Byway**, spanning from Myton (between Roosevelt and Duchesne on Highway 40) to Wellington (a few miles south of Price on Highway 6/191). The well-maintained dirt road (okay for passenger cars) cuts through Wells Draw, Gate Canyon, and the Nine-Mile Canyon (it's actually 40 miles long). Make sure you have plenty of gas; there are no services along the byway. From Myton travel west 1%₁₀ miles on Highway 40. Take a left (south) on the first paved road out of town and go a half mile to the beginning of the byway, where you'll see an information kiosk.

The 80-mile byway is a testament to the closing of the frontier in this region of Utah. In 1886 the all-black Ninth US Cavalry constructed it, linking their base at Fort Duchesne with the nearest railhead and telegraph line at Price. It later served as a major stagecoach and mail route, as well as the main thoroughfare between Carbon County to the south and the Uinta Basin to the north. Hundreds of settlers flocked northward along the road beginning in 1905, when President Roosevelt issued a proclamation that allowed whites to homestead pieces of the Uintah and Ouray Indian Reservation. Some settlers didn't go all the way to the basin but rather dug in at various points along the way. Today, you can see remnants of these old settlements and ranches, including the ghost town of **Harper**. The road travels past a number of Fremont ruins; consequently, you'll also see a wonderful concentration of rock art. Please do not touch the rock art.

Melting Pot

Starting out in the northern reaches of Castle Valley, the town of **Helper** looks as if it came off the canvas of an Edward Hopper painting. Its dusty Main Street, stretched out at the bottom of high terraced cliffs, is lined with Victorian architecture, most of which is vacant and in a state of dilapidation. Despite its down-on-its-luck appearance, Helper's Main Street looks poignantly authentic, as if it has been left untouched since its days as a raucous mining and railroad town in the early twentieth century.

Helper got its start when the Denver & Rio Grande Western Railroad built a depot here in 1883 to service its new line over Soldier Summit. In 1892 a standard gauge railroad replaced the narrow gauge over the summit, which meant additional engines, or "helpers," were needed to haul cars up the steep grade. But the railroad did more than give the town its name. It also brought in thousands of immigrants from around the world to work in the scores of mines that emerged in the area. It makes sense then that an informal census conducted in the 1930s found people from thirty-two different countries congregated in a Helper pool hall.

With the downslide of the mining and railroad industries, so slipped Helper. But the past has not been forgotten. Case in point is them must-see **Western Mining and Railroad Museum** (296 South Main St.; 435-472-3009), documenting the heyday of Helper and the industries that made it thrive. The defunct Helper Hotel houses the four-story museum, filled with memorabilia representing just about every aspect of Carbon County's past, down to the shoes its residents wore. Equipment and tools used by miners and railroad workers aren't the only things on exhibit here. You'll see several photographs of immigrants, including one of an Italian miner handing his first pay to his wife, who then sent the picture back to Italy to prove to her parents that her husband was taking care of her. One of the more fascinating features of the museum is its collection of art commissioned by the Work Projects Administration (WPA) during the Depression. Be sure to check out this wonderful museum, open Mon through Sat 10 a.m. to 6 p.m., May through Sept; Tues through Sat 11 a.m. to 4 p.m. the rest of the year. The website (wmrrm.org) contains detailed information about the museum's exhibits.

Many of the paintings that the museum has added to its collection are now on exhibit at the "phantom galleries" lining the upper section of Main Street. Instead of letting their storefronts sit empty, Helper has created galleries out of them. The exhibits rotate, and most are extremely good.

To get a better look at the area's faded mining industry and the towns it left behind, take a drive up **Spring Canyon**, where you'll see the densest concentration of ghost towns that Utah has to offer. On the east side of Highway 6/191 in Helper, take Canyon Street to see the ruins that litter the sides of this 6½-mile road. You'll see several foundations and a few buildings that are still intact.

The first ghost town you'll come to in Spring Canyon is **Peerless**, 3 miles from Helper. Not much remains of this coal-mining town that had a peak population of 300. Founded in 1912, Peerless thrived until the 1930s, when fuel oil and natural gas crushed the coal market. A mile farther, Spring Canyon City was the brainchild of Jesse Knight, the Mormon best known for building Knightsville. Population topped at 1,000 but couldn't be sustained. The town finally died in the 1950s after most of the miners were laid off.

Five miles up Spring Canyon, **Standardville** set the "standard" for other mining towns. The Standard Coal Company made the town a showpiece of its benevolence, planning and building a community with modern homes and a snazzy business district. The town's attractive appearance couldn't prevent the coming of trouble, however. In 1922 a riot erupted in Standardville after a deputy sheriff killed a Ku Klux Klan leader. Martial law went into effect, and the governor of Utah sent the state police to quell the tension. As if riots weren't enough, Standardville was also the site of a mining explosion that left twenty men dead.

A mile from Standardville, the old Liberty Fuel Company office building signals the rise and decline of **Latuda**, which got its start in 1917 as a company town but met its demise not long after an avalanche swept through town in 1927, taking a number of homes with it. At the end of the road is *Mutual*, known in its time as the prettiest town in Spring Canyon. Here you'll see several stone ruins, including the old Mutual Store.

Although *Price* (a few miles south of Helper on Highway 6/191) started out as a typical Mormon agrarian community in 1879, the railroad put an end to that bringing thousands of immigrants to work in the coal camps. As in Helper, a WPA census in the 1930s revealed folks from thirty-two different nations living in Price. Price unfortunately didn't escape the racism and exploitation that were rampant in other coal-mining towns across the country.

Unlike Helper and the other towns in the area, Price has continued to prosper. Despite repeated setbacks in the coal market over the last seventy years, coal mining is still Price's biggest industry, making it the "black gold" capital of Utah. A great depiction of Price and Carbon County's history is painted on the foyer walls at the Price Municipal Building, located on the corner of Main Street and 200 East. A native of the area, *Lynn Fausett*, worked on the Price Mural from 1938 to 1941, drawing on his own experiences and on numerous historical photographs. Check out the mural Mon through Fri, 8 a.m. to 5 p.m.

Price's biggest attraction has to be the *USU Eastern Prehistoric Museum* (435-613-5060 or 800-817-9949), set in a handsome, modern structure at 155 East Main Street, Price. The museum has culled its collection from excavations around Eastern Utah, including the Cleveland–Lloyd Dinosaur Quarry south of Price discussed later in this chapter. An exciting feature at the museum is the two *Utahraptors*. Discovery of the Utahraptor, the largest slashing dinosaur species, coincided with the making of Jurassic Park, adding to the dinosaur-mania surrounding this film. Also poised at the museum are the *stegosaurus, camarasaurus, camptosaurus, allosaurus*, and the oldest dinosaur egg yet found, in addition to a number of artifacts from the Fremont, Ute, and Navajo cultures, as well as another Lynn Fausett mural depicting the rock art found in Barrier Canyon. Hours at the museum are 9 a.m. to 5 p.m. Mon through Sat; closed Sun. Check out the website at usueastern.edu/museum.

It should come as no surprise that with its rich, multicultural heritage Price would host the *Price City International Days*, a three-day event held in late July. Performers from around the world, garbed in traditional clothing, demonstrate songs and dances reflecting their native countries. Call (435) 636-3180 for specific dates and locations.

Your best bet for food in Price might be at the *El Salto Mexican Cafe* (801 E. Main St.; 435-637-6545). Noemi Taberna cooks delicious enchiladas, smothered burritos, chimichangas, and other Mexican recipes that have been passed down to her from previous generations. Don't miss eating here Mon through Sat, 11 a.m. to 9 p.m.

A few miles southeast of Price in the town of **Wellington** is where **Nine-Mile Canyon National Back Country Byway** begins (or ends). The byway spans 80 miles from US Highways 6/191 in Wellington to Highway 40 in Myton (see page 64 for the northern approach). The highway's namesake, **Nine-Mile Canyon**, is actually 40 miles long, comprising about half the byway journey. But it is the most interesting section of the road, because it was here that Fremont Indian ruins going back more than 900 years were discovered. Although only a trained eye can spot the Fremonts' pit dwellings, those who keep their eyes peeled will see hundreds of figures etched (petroglyphs) or painted (pictographs) on the canyon walls. Most of the rock art is Fremont, but not all of it. You'll also see figures done by the Archaics, who left their mark around 2000 BC (Archaic rock art is identifiable by its ghostlike, anthropomorphic forms and its frequent absence of arms and legs).

You'll also catch sight of historic Ute rock art, identified by horse-and-rider figures. White settlers couldn't help themselves either, adding their names and dates to some of the panels. Start looking for the rock art about 7 miles beyond where the pavement ends. As has been said several times, please do not touch or damage the rock art in any way. Skin oils hasten its deterioration and lessen the possibility that future generations will have the same opportunity to view the art.

The maintained gravel road is fine for regular passenger cars if it's dry. Contact the BLM office in Price (435) 636-3600 at 125 South 600 West, for road conditions. You may want to stop by anyway and pick up the Nine-Mile Canyon/San Rafael Swell brochure, which gives a step-by-step account of the panels found in the canyon, mileage included.

The Wonder of Nine-Mile Canyon

In 1869 the great explorer John Wesley Powell was guiding a federal expedition to explore some of the more unknown parts of the territory. His friend and topographer did a triangulation from a place he called Nine-Mile Creek (which happened to be about 9 miles from the mouth of Desolation Canyon). This splendid 40-mile-long canyon picked up the name Nine-Mile Canyon—named after the creek.

Nine-Mile Canyon is home to some of the finest Native American rock art in the country. It's also a perfect place to study geology, go rock hounding, see old ruins, or simply get lost in wild country. This is the middle of nowhere. If you want to explore off-the-beaten path, put this canyon at the top of your list. It has a rich history. Dinosaurs and fierce ice age creatures wandered these lands. So did Native Americans. You can wander it, too. Nine-Mile has some of the best, accessible, rock art in the West. Don't miss it.

Don't forget some extra water, a shovel, and a few candy bars. Take US Highway 6 out of Spanish Fork and go past Price. Follow the signs. It's another 24 miles to Nine-Mile Ranch (435-637-2572), where you can stop and ask directions (or stay at the bed-and-breakfast).

Dinosaur enthusiasts shouldn't miss the *Cleveland–Lloyd Dinosaur Quarry*, located 30 miles south of Price. About 150 million years ago, the site was a shallow lake with a muddy bottom. Dinosaurs that wandered into the lake often got trapped, their remains preserved beneath layers of sand, mud, and volcanic ash after the lake dried up. Since the University of Utah began excavation here in 1929, the quarry has yielded thirty complete skeletons, 12,000 individual bones, and several dinosaur eggs. Recognized worldwide as the greatest source of *allosaur* skeletons, the quarry has a reconstruction of this flesh-eater's skeleton at its visitor center. In the enclosed quarry you'll also see paleontologists in action. The quarry is open weekends (weather permitting) May 1 through June 30, 10 a.m. to 5 p.m. During the summer and fall, the quarry is open to groups by appointment only. From Price, head 13 miles south on Highway 10, then 17 miles on Highway 155 and graded dirt roads. From Huntington, drive 2 miles north on Highway 10, then 20 miles east on Highway 155 and dirt roads that, when dry, are fine for passenger cars. Signs point the way. For road conditions or other information call the BLM office in Price at (435) 636-3600.

A great excursion into the high country of the *Wasatch Plateau* begins in *Huntington* at the mouth of Huntington Canyon. A scenic byway, Highway 31 lifts you from the desert floor of Castle Valley, taking you through Huntington Canyon alongside its raging river. Several great campgrounds line the road on its way to the top of the plateau, where Electric Lake, Huntington Reservoir, and other bodies of water sit amid verdant alpine meadows and stands of pine trees. Highway 31 drops down the eastern side of the Wasatch Plateau into Fairview (see Central Utah), 50 miles from Huntington.

If you can't seem to get dinosaurs off the brain, then check out the *Museum of the San Rafael* (435-381-5252) at 70 North 100 East in *Castle Dale*. This handsome museum houses several dinosaur skeletons and remains, including the massive skull of a *Tyrannosaurus rex* and the first dinosaur egg

thesegolily

The **sego lily** (*Calochortus nuttallii*) grows 6 to 8 inches tall in open grassy areas and sage flats. It is found throughout the Great Basin area during the summer months.

The early Mormon pioneers ate the bulbs of the sego lily during their first winter in the valley, when food was in short supply. It was made the official state flower in 1911.

Sagebrush Barbecue, Utah Style

You haven't lived until you've had a sagebrush barbecue somewhere in the lonely stretches of Utah. It's a favorite tradition. Few things are better than a good steak, slow-cooked over sagebrush coals. The good news is there's an abundance of sagebrush and miles of lonely country, so you can dine in peace.

To start, find a safe place for the fire. Dig a pit, put a couple of rocks on the edges, and set up a grill. Start collecting dead sage branches, which can be found everywhere. (They burn quickly, so you'll need quite a bit.) Put a few cans of beans on the edges of the coals to simmer, and grill the steaks—don't rush them! Put the steak on a plate, smother it with beans. Serve with fresh bread and Coke, then sit back and enjoy the scenery while you listen to your arteries harden.

Let your fire burn out—then pour a couple of gallons of water over the coals to make sure they are dead. Don't leave until the coals are cool to the touch.

discovered in North America. It is open Mon through Fri, 10 a.m. to 4 p.m., and 10 a.m. to 2 p.m. on Sat.

Off to the east of Castle Dale sits some of Utah's most treasured wilderness—**San Rafael Swell**, a mammoth dome of rock pushed up by geological forces in the earth's interior. The rock later eroded into a mosaic of buttes, canyons, pinnacles, and mesas, stretching 80 miles long and 30 miles wide. This is perhaps the last "undiscovered" region in Utah due to lack of accessibility. Interstate 70 cuts through the middle of it but is the only paved road that does so. You can still get around the terrain via well-maintained dirt and gravel roads, many of which are fine for regular passenger cars if the weather cooperates. Remember to bring plenty of water and a full tank of gas. This is wilderness, so no services exist out here. If you hike or mountain bike, be sure to stay on established trails, slickrock, or washes—don't destroy any fragile desert vegetation. For road conditions or other information, contact the BLM office in Price (435) 636-3600 at 126 South 600 West, Price.

To experience some of the mind-boggling terrain of the San Rafael Swell near Castle Dale, head east on a gravel road that branches 1⁶⁄₁₀ miles north of town off Highway 10. (Look for the turnoff just north of an old log corral standing next to the highway.) The first stretch of road takes you across a flat desert floor, giving you little preparation for the geological wonders ahead. Mesas dot the landscape, and Cedar Mountain looms in the background.

At 12¹⁄₁₀ miles you'll come to Buckhorn Flat Junction. From there go 6 miles south, staying left at the fork. Brace yourself for what lies at the end of the road—a phenomenal view of "Little Grand Canyon" from Wedge Overlook.

Here, a 1,000-foot drop separates you from the San Rafael River meandering below.

If the scenery has you hooked, go back to Buckhorn Flat Junction and continue traveling east on the same road that brought you in. Two miles east of Buckhorn Flat Junction, the road forks. The left (north) fork takes you 29 miles across dramatic terrain littered with buttes, mesas, and pinnacles, finally connecting with Highway 6/191, 16 miles north of Green River.

The right fork heads southward, headlong into **Buckhorn Draw**. This road passes through imposing cliff walls and affords views of several pinnacles rising out of the desert floor. You'll pass a 100-foot-long panel filled with rock art 6⁸⁄₁₀ miles from the fork. After passing the petroglyphs, the road meanders past several beautiful canyons that make for excellent hikes.

As you come out of Buckhorn Draw, look to your left for two pinnacles, Hall Peak and Window Blind Peak, lined up one in front of the other. At 12¹⁄₁₀ miles from the fork you'll come to the San Rafael River, where the Civilian Conservation Corps built the Swinging Bridge in 1938, now used as a footbridge. Across the river you can camp or picnic at the **San Rafael Campground**, where you'll find tables and outhouses but no water. From the campground it's a 24-mile drive to Ranch exit 129 and I–70. From Ranch exit 129 you can continue through more drop-dead scenery of the southern sections of the San Rafael Swell (see Southeastern Utah).

climatefastfacts

Northeastern Utah's climate

winter, 8 to 29 degrees

summer, 50 to 89 degrees

about 10 inches of precipitation

TOP ANNUAL EVENTS IN NORTHEASTERN UTAH

AUGUST

Carbon County Old-Fashioned Fair
Price
(435) 636-3233

Summit County Fair and Rodeo
Coalville
(435) 336-3221

Uintah County Fair
Vernal
(435) 789-1660

Places to Stay in Northeastern Utah

ALTAMONT

Falcon's Ledge
Stillwater Canyon, Hwy 87
(435) 454-3737 or
(877) 879-3737
Deluxe

LC Ranch
14535 4000 N
(435) 454-3750 or
(435) 724-1504
lcranch.com
Deluxe

CHRISTMAS MEADOWS

The Cabins at Bear River Lodge
(801) 798-1008
bearriverlodge.com
Deluxe

DUTCH JOHN

Flaming Gorge Resort
155 Greendale, US 191
(435) 889-3773
fglodge.com
Moderate

Red Canyon Lodge
790 Red Canyon Rd.
(435) 889-3759
redcanyonlodge.com
Moderate

PRICE

Greenwell Inn
655 East Main St.
(435) 637-3520
Standard

Holiday Inn Hotel and Suites
925 Westwood Blvd.
(435) 637-8880
Deluxe

VERNAL

Dinosaur Inn and Suites
251 East Main St.
(435) 789-2660
Standard

Places to Eat in Northeastern Utah

KAMAS

Dick's Drive Inn
235 Center St.
(435) 783-4312
Inexpensive

Gateway Grille
215 S. Main St.
(435) 783-2867
Moderate

Summit Inn
80 S. Main St.
(435) 783-4453
Moderate

VERNAL

Betty's Cafe
416 West Main St.
(435) 781-2728
Inexpensive

FOR MORE INFORMATION ABOUT NORTHEASTERN UTAH

TRAVEL COUNCILS

Dinosaurland Travel Region
55 E. Main St.
Vernal 84078
(435) 789-6932 or
(800) 477-5558
Fax (435) 789-7465
dinomaster@dinoland.com

Carbon County Travel Bureau
155 E. Main St.
P.O. Box 1037
Price 84501
(435) 637-3009 or
(800) 842-0789
Fax (435) 637-7010
cctr@priceutah.net

Road Conditions
(800) 492-2400

Country Grub
2419 S. 1500 East
(435) 789-7000
Inexpensive

Stella's Kitchen
3340 N. Vernal Ave.
(435) 789-5657
Moderate

ROOSEVELT

Marion's Variety
29 N. 200 East
(435) 722-2143
Inexpensive

PRICE

China City
350 E. Main St.
(435) 637-8211
Expensive

El Salto Mexican Cafe
19 South Carbon Ave.
(435) 637-6545
Inexpensive

Ricardo's
655 E. Main St.
(435) 637-2020
Moderate

HELPER

Pinnacle Brewing Company
1653 N. Carbonville Rd.
(435) 637-2924
Moderate

West-Central Utah

A succession of mountain ranges and valleys characterizes the topography of the Great Basin, where West-Central Utah sits. Around 15,000 years ago, the area was mostly submerged beneath the waters of Lake Bonneville, an inland sea that spread across a third of Utah and into neighboring Idaho and Nevada. What remains of Lake Bonneville are the Great Salt Lake (the Lake Bonneville puddle, if you will) and the Bonneville Salt Flats. Perhaps Utah's most unusual sight, this floor of salt spanning a part of the Great Salt Lake Desert is so starkly flat that you purportedly can see the curvature of the earth.

Pioneers and explorers usually chose to skirt the Great Basin on their way to California. And wisely so. Finding a way across this seemingly vast wasteland was a brave endeavor. John C. Fremont, an explorer and surveyor for the government, conducted studies of the Great Basin in 1845, during which he named a number of its features. Today much of West-Central Utah remains uninhabitable and off-limits to visitors because the military uses the region for bombing and gunnery exercises.

What most people see of West-Central Utah are the sights they pass going 80 miles per hour along Interstate 80 or 15.

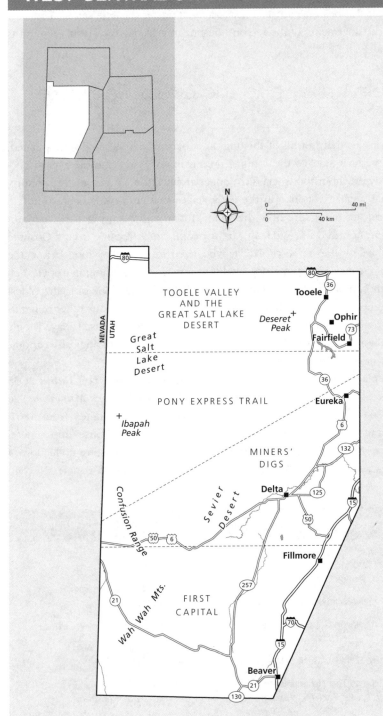

Getting off the beaten path is as easy as getting off the interstates. You may want to consider many of the region's destinations as day trips from other parts of the state.

Tooele Valley and the Great Salt Lake Desert

Tooele proves that not all of this region is barren, remote, and unpopulated. On the western side of the Oquirrh Mountains, Tooele surprises its visitors with shady neighborhoods, classic pioneer architecture, and several opportunities to see what it was like in the early stages of Utah's settlement. Although no one can be quite sure how the valley, town, and county got the name of Tooele (pronounced too-WILL-ah), most people agree it came from a Goshute Indian chief by the name of Tuilla, who lived in the valley long before the Mormons arrived. Seeing the potential for farming and ranching in Tooele Valley, Mormon pioneers founded the town in 1849, making it one of Utah's oldest communities. Miners moved in when gold, copper, and various other minerals were discovered in the Oquirrh (pronounced O-ker) Mountains. Today, Tooele has the dubious honor of being the recipient of America's biological weapons, stored at nearby Tooele Army depot.

The place to start is at the *Tooele Pioneer Hall and Log Cabin* at 35 East Vine Street, home of the *Daughters of Utah Pioneers Museum*. The small stone edifice, typical of early Mormon structures, dates from 1867. Throughout the ages it has been used as a jailhouse, courthouse, and general city office. Now a museum, the pioneer hall has an interesting collection of artifacts, clothing, and photographs from the early days of Tooele. Next to

AUTHOR'S FAVORITES IN WEST-CENTRAL UTAH

National Wildlife Refuge, west of Simpson Springs

Deep Creek Mountains, north of Callao

Bingham Canyon Copper Mine, east of Tooele

Bonneville Salt Flats, east of Wendover

Pony Express Trail National Back Country Byway, Fairfield to Ibapah

Frisco, west of Beaver

Elk Meadows Ski and Summer Resort, east of Beaver

Oquirrh Mountains, east of Tooele

Deseret Peak Wilderness Area, southwest of Grantsville

Bonneville Salt Flats International Speedway, east of Wendover

The Great Basin

The Great Basin lies across a large portion of western Utah and is nearly 5,000 feet above sea level. This basin is made up of rugged mountains, deserts, and valleys. Utah's main population center and all the major cities are on the eastern fringe of this basin next to the Wasatch Mountains.

The early explorer John C. Fremont noticed that the rivers and watersheds in this expansive area seemed to have no outlet to the Pacific Ocean. So he called this land a "Great Basin."

He wasn't that far off, either. In days of yore (like a couple million years ago), Fremont's "basin" was the floor of a giant lake known as Bonneville. When Lake Bonneville receded, it not only helped to carve the current landscape, it also became the present-day Great Salt Lake.

the Pioneer Hall is one of the first log cabins built in Utah, constructed by Zachariah Edwards in 1855. The museum and log cabin are open on Fri and Sat beginning the first Fri in May through the last Sat in Sept, from 10 a.m. to 4 p.m. It is closed in the winter except by appointment. For further information, visit duptooeleco.org.

Tooele County Railroad Museum (435-882-2836), located at the 1909 Tooele Train Station at 35 North Broadway, Tooele, offers a look at a later age. A steam engine, a dining car, and a number of cabooses sit outside the restored station now serving as a museum, documenting the rise of industrialism in the county. Photographs of gritty railroad workers and smudged-faced miners provide telling images of an era come and gone, as do the tools and other artifacts from nearby mines and boomtowns that have since gone bust. Here you'll learn about the Tooele Smelter, built and controlled by the International Smelter and Refining Company, which employed as many as 3,000 people during World War II. Open Tues through Sat 10 a.m. to 4 p.m. from Memorial Day to Labor Day.

For a jaunt into the *Oquirrh Mountains*, try the road going up Middle Canyon and arriving at the Oquirrh Overlook, looking into the Kennecott Canyon Copper Mine, the largest open-pit mine in the world. This is a good place to marvel at or get concerned about the technology capable of taking down mountains. From the overlook, perched at an elevation of 9,400 feet, you also have a stunning view of the Salt Lake and Tooele Valleys. From downtown Tooele, head east on Vine Street. The road is paved until it reaches a picnic site 7 miles from Tooele. It then turns to gravel and continues up another 3 steep and winding miles before reaching the overlook. If you have a 4WD vehicle you can descend into the Salt Lake Valley by way of a dirt road that continues down the eastern slope of the Oquirrhs.

Another vision of Tooele County's past is the ***Benson Grist Mill***, located 10 miles north of Tooele and a half mile west of the Highways 36 and 38 junction. E. T. Benson, grandfather of the late Mormon president Ezra Taft Benson, developed the mill in 1854 under the instructions of Brigham Young. The structure, one of the oldest standing in Utah, was built using mortised timbers from the Oquirrh Mountains and held together using strips of rawhide. In 1986 volunteers renovated it and much of the original machinery, which you can now see Thurs through Sat, 10 a.m. to 6 p.m. from May to Oct. Call (435) 882-7678 for an off-season tour or write to 325 SR 138, Stansbury Park 84074.

Located 20 miles south of Tooele, ***Ophir*** is a town that refuses to become a ghost town. This silver-mining boomtown peaked at a population of 1,200 and displayed all the signs of mining success: saloons, dance halls, houses of ill repute, hotels, and so on. The mining camp was born in the late 1860s, when soldiers under Colonel Patrick Connor tracked down Indian silver mines. Within a few weeks the prospectors had extracted more than $1 million. By the end of the century nearly 3,000 claims had been staked, and the town had reaped a total of more than $13 million. A US senator from Montana who owned mining property at Ophir built a short-line railway linking the town with the major railway lines. The ore veins, however, proved to be shallow and were soon depleted. Although the population has at times dwindled to fewer than a dozen, Ophir refuses to die. From Tooele head 12 miles south on Highway 36. Take a left onto Highway 73, and then follow the signs to Ophir. Paved roads take you all the way there.

Marine life in the desert? Believe it or not, yes. Utilizing geothermal pools near the Great Salt Lake, Bonneville Seabase has done the unthinkable, filling the pool with groupers, trigger fish, damsels, angels, clownfish, and even lobsters. Because of the natural-salt composition of the water, the marine life has adapted well to its high-altitude, desert habitat. This microcosmic "ocean" now provides landlocked Utahans with a place to test their scuba diving and snorkeling skills in a simulated marine environment. An air-filled habitat underneath the surface enables divers to talk and observe.

Hiking in the alpine heights of the ***Stansbury Mountains*** provides a good opportunity to see the ecological diversity in the desert of Western Utah. Lush meadows, Douglas firs, and aspens cover ***Deseret Peak Wilderness Area***, where the views contain scores of mountain ranges to the east and the barren floors of the Great Salt Lake Desert to the west. A moderately strenuous 7½-mile round-trip trail begins at the Loop Campground, located 10 miles southwest of Grantsville. Take South Willow Road out of Grantsville and follow the signs to South Willow Canyon Recreation Area. Loop Campground is at the end of the paved road.

One of the stranger chapters in Mormon history took place on the western slope of the Stansburys. Iosepa was founded by a group of Polynesian Mormon converts, who came to Utah in 1889 because there was no temple in their homeland that could serve their religious needs. The Polynesians settled for 1,280 acres in Skull Valley, an appropriate name, considering the harsh desert climate and barren landscape. The settlers named the town Iosepa (Hawaiian for Joseph) out of reverence for the missionary who brought Mormonism to Polynesia—Joseph F. Smith, the sixth president of the LDS church. Although the community was well planned and had even won the state prize for best-kept and most progressive town, Iosepa could not tame the unforgiving environment on which it was dependent. Crops failed miserably, and, to make matters worse, leprosy reared its ugly head. By 1916 the settlers had given up. Some went back to Hawaii to help build the Laie Temple. Others moved to Salt Lake City, where descendants of the original Iosepa settlers live to this day.

climatefastfacts

West-Central Utah's climate:

winter, 19 to 40 degrees

summer, 60 to 94 degrees

about 11 inches of precipitation

What remains of the town are a few houses, inhabited today by those who run the large ranch on which Iosepa's townsite is located. Behind the houses (about ½ mile east) is the lonely cemetery, where crumbling, Hawaiian-inscribed tombstones create a poignant memory of the doomed town and its faithful residents. A large marble memorial crowned with the bust of a Polynesian warrior stands at the cemetery, which is surrounded by a fence and flagpoles.

Descendants of Iosepa's settlers hold an annual luau here on the Friday and Saturday preceding Memorial Day. Poi is served, Hawaiian arts and crafts are shown, and famous Hawaiian singer and Mormon convert Al Harrington performs. The public is invited. Iosepa is located along Skull Valley Highway, 15 miles south of I–80 and Rowley Junction (exit 77). Although the ranchers don't mind if people visit the cemetery, it's a good idea to ask first at one of the houses.

About midway between Salt Lake City and Wendover on I–80 is something of an oddity that never fails to elicit a comment from those driving past it: a giant sculpture of a tree with planetary-shaped fruit dangling on steel limbs or else resting on the ground below. Titled *Tree of Utah*, the sculpture is about the only thing standing for miles around, which makes it all the more peculiar.

When **Karl Momen**, an Iranian artist living in Stockholm, drove through the salt flats in the early 1980s, he apparently saw the white landscape as a natural canvas, a backdrop for a steel sculpture that would cost him $1 million to construct. He immediately went to work, employing Don Reimann, a local contractor. Together they built what Momen thought of as a "symbol of life," planted in the most life-negating place on earth—the Bonneville Salt Flats. *Tree of Utah* seems to be more appreciated overseas than it is in Utah. Reportedly, Europeans who are familiar with Momen's work go out of their way to see the tree when they come to the West. In Utah, hardly anyone knows what to make of it, let alone what to call it.

Silver Island Mountains, on the border of Utah and Nevada, add to the strangeness of the salt flats. From one of the flattest and driest places on earth, Silver Island's jagged peaks rise, creating a wondrous contrast. Silver Island Mountains' sediment, composed of mud and marine animals, indicates that the mountains were once the floor of an ancient sea and later an island in Lake Bonneville, which formed with the melting of Ice Age glaciers. The salt flats are, in turn, the salt and mineral remains of the evaporated Lake Bonneville. Existing roughly 15,000 years ago, the lake covered more than one-third of the state of Utah and was comparable in size to Lake Michigan.

Traveling along the **Silver Island Mountains National Back Country Byway** gives you a pretty good idea of why people consider this the most unusual, if not most bizarre, natural place in America. The byway loops around the range, allowing you to get an eyeful of the horizontal salt flats and the vertical mountains. The road, good enough for high-clearance passenger vehicles, is 54 miles long and takes about two hours to complete. At the north end of the

Twinkle, Twinkle, Utah's Little Star

Utahans love their symbols. In addition to the old standards like birds and flowers and plants, there is a state cooking pot, a state dance, and a state fossil, but it doesn't stop there. Utah now has a state star.

House Bill 140 designates Dubhe as Utah's own personal star, giving the state an astronomical symbol, too: the Beehive Cluster. Both Dubhe and the Beehive Cluster were featured in the Hansen Planetarium's centennial show, Space, Time, Utah.

Dubhe, which means "bear" in Arabic, is one hundred light-years away. It's one of the "pointer stars" on the Big Dipper (Big Bear), located on the corner of the cup.

loop, you'll cross over the mountains at the same place as the Donner–Reed party did in 1846. To access the byway, get off I–80 at exit 4 (120 miles west of Salt Lake City and a few miles east of Wendover). Go north about a mile, take a left onto a gravel road, and then a right at the sign for Silver Island Mountains. Take this road only in dry weather. For information on road conditions, call the BLM office in Salt Lake City at (801) 977-4300.

If you want a good look at the terrain without having to take a dirt road, drive to the ***Bonneville Salt Flats International Speedway***, accessed by exit 4 on I–80. The paved causeway heads 5 miles out into this blank space on the landscape, where speed freaks in their outlandish machines have been setting land-speed records for more than eighty years.

W. D. Rishel first saw the potential for racing here in 1896, when he plotted a bicycle route across the salt flats for Randolph Hearst. It wasn't until 1911 and the advent of the automobile that Rishel had his need for speed sated, convincing the makers of the first Packard to test their machine on the 44,000-acre salt flats. But it was Teddy Tetzlaff who first made the record books, when in 1914 he reached 114 miles per hour in his Blitzen Benz. In 1926, Ab Jenkins, driving his Mormon Meteor III, drove for twenty-four hours straight, traveling 2,710 miles at an average speed of 112 miles per hour. By 1940 Utah native Jenkins had set eighty-one land-speed records. By the 1960s, jet and rocket engines were stuffed into car bodies designed like bullets, and speeds of more than 600 miles per hour were regularly obtained. The peaks of Silver Island Mountains are named in honor of the daredevils who set land-speed records on the salt flats.

Today, the fascination with speed in all its variations continues in the ***World of Speed***, held every year in late September. Entrants try for records in scores of different categories and machines during this three-day event. Call Utah Salt Flats Racing Association at (801) 485-2662 or visit saltflats.com for more information on World of Speed. Other events, such as ***Speed Week***, occur during summer and early fall. Call the BLM office in Salt Lake City at (801) 977-4300 for information on any of the events.

Because the area is so remote, ***Wendover*** was also a perfect place for a military base. During World War II, Wendover Air Base provided a training ground for the bomb crews who later dropped the atomic bombs on Hiroshima and Nagasaki. This base was the largest military reserve in 1943, home base to more than 17,000 troops. ***The Historic Wendover Airfield Museum***, located in the operations building of Icarus Aviation on the base, honors the people who worked here. The museum is open Mon through Fri 11 a.m. to 4 p.m., and Sat 9 a.m. to 5 p.m. For more information call (435) 665-7724. Across from the Peppermill Resort on Main Street stands the ***Enola Gay Monument***, named after the plane that dropped the first atomic bomb. To get to the base, take exit 2 off I–80, then turn left at the airport sign onto Main Street.

On the Pony Express Trail

Very few enterprises have stirred the American imagination quite like the Pony Express. It encapsulates the spirit and romance associated with the settlement of the frontier and stands as one of the finer examples of the raw, independent grit that helped distinguish American identity. The enterprise ended after a short nineteen months, when it was rendered obsolete by the telegraph. Despite being short-lived, the Pony Express and its riders acquired near-mythological stature in American history.

From 1860 to 1861 the Pony Express did more than offer a quick mail service between St. Joseph, Missouri, and Sacramento, California. The Express enabled California to become more involved in the affairs of the nation and consequently helped maintain the state's alignment with the Union at the outbreak of the Civil War. The Pony Express also served as a great experiment for crossing the West in the worst kinds of weather, proving to naysaying members of Congress that a transcontinental railway was indeed feasible.

In West-Central Utah, you can follow in the hoofprints of the Pony Express riders by taking the **Pony Express Trail National Back Country Byway**, stretching 133 miles across West-Central Utah from Fairfield to Ibapah. This BLM-administered byway can be negotiated by regular passenger vehicles if the weather is dry, something that is certainly not unheard of here in the desert. Plan on a day's worth of travel if you decide to take the entire route, which ends up 58 miles from Wendover and I–80. (The road from Ibapah to Wendover is paved.) Have a full tank of gas, a spare tire, plenty of water, and whatever else you need to get you through the next 130 miles of desert travel. There is sometimes gas available at the end of the byway in Ibapah, but don't count on it. The next service is in Wendover, 58 miles from Ibapah. It's a good idea to have a detailed map of the area, because roads branching from the byway can sometimes be misleading. For road conditions, maps, or any other information, stop in at the BLM office in Salt Lake City at 2370 South 2300 West, Salt Lake City, or call (801) 977-4300.

The first stop along the Pony Express Trail National Back Country Byway is **Camp Floyd** and the **Stagecoach Inn State Park**, located in **Fairfield** (36 miles northwest of Provo on Highway 73). Attracted by the fertile ground and abundance of water, John Carson and his family founded the town of Fairfield in 1855. Fearful of Indian attack, they built and lived inside a tiny stone fort, which didn't prevent Carson's two brothers from getting killed by Indians.

Then in 1858, some 3,500 US soldiers nervously marched through Salt Lake City on their way to this remote spot. Citing the barbarism of Mormon polygamy and the potential for an uprising in Salt Lake City, Secretary of War John B. Floyd (for whom the camp is named) ordered federal troops stationed outside the Mormon capital in case a rebellion had to be quelled. But there was more to Floyd's reasoning for sending so many soldiers to Utah, where 5,500 enlisted men (more than one-third of the Union Army) were stationed just before the beginning of the Civil War. As a supporter of the Confederacy, Floyd saw the opportunity to divert manpower and resources away from the East and create a weakness in the Union defense. (Floyd was later forced to resign when he was charged with fraud and malfeasance—later he became a brigadier general in the Confederate Army.)

With the soldiers' occupation of Fairfield, the town boomed, overnight becoming the third-largest city in Utah and the country's largest military post. Between 300 and 400 buildings were erected, and several businesses moved in to cater to the soldiers' needs, the largest of which was seemingly whiskey, as some seventeen saloons opened that summer. A motley assortment of gamblers, prostitutes, actors, and thieves also gravitated to Fairfield, raising its population to more than 7,000 by 1860. They were drawn to Fairfield because of the Army payroll at Camp Floyd, the only place west of the Rocky Mountains where legal tender appeared at that time.

A Mormon elder, John Carson, took advantage of the situation as well. Seeing that his tiny fort was no longer necessary, he tore it down and built a two-story adobe hotel, calling it the Stagecoach Inn. Luckily for Carson, the South-Central Overland Route, plotted by Captain J. H. Simpson of Camp

Utah Trivia

There are 864,279,750 hectares—2,134,770.9 acres—of open water in arid Utah.

Most of Utah is on a plateau higher than 4,000 feet above sea level.

It took almost fifty years for lawmakers to admit Utah as an official member of the Union.

The word Utah came from the Ute Indian tribe and means "the tops of the mountains."

The California gull (Larus californious Lawrence) has been the state bird since 1849, when seagulls saved the early Mormons' crops from crickets.

There were 140,300 marriages and 13,100 divorces in Utah in 1994.

Floyd, ran directly in front of the hotel's front door, making the Stagecoach Inn a popular waystation for those traveling between Salt Lake City and California. Forbidding the consumption of liquor and round dancing, the Stagecoach Inn served as a dignified oasis amid all the hell-raising for which Fairfield was notorious. After Camp Floyd was disbanded, the Stagecoach Inn kept its doors open to stagecoach passengers, Pony Express riders, and everyone else who passed along this main Utah thoroughfare. After Carson died, his family took over, running the business until 1947, when it finally was boarded up. During its time, the Stagecoach Inn hosted such notables as Mark Twain, Porter Rockwell, Bill Hickman, and Sir Richard Burton.

Today you can tour the Stagecoach Inn, designated a state park in 1964. Completely restored in 1995, the inn is replete with period furniture, looking as it did back in the mid-1800s. Across the street is the only building remaining of Camp Floyd—the Army commissary. From Salt Lake City, go south on I–15. Exit at Lehi and head 21 miles west on Highway 73. From Tooele take Highway 36 south to Highway 73. The state park is open daily Apr through Oct 15, 9 a.m. to 5 p.m. It is closed on Sundays the rest of the year. To contact the park, call (801) 768-8932 or write to 18035 West 1540 North, P.O. Box 288, Fairfield 84013.

From Camp Floyd the Pony Express Trail continues on Highway 73 until it forks off onto a gravel road about 5 miles west of Fairfield. Or you can pick up the trail farther west at Faust Junction on Highway 36. Either of these starting points is where backcountry travel begins, and preparedness is essential.

About 25 miles west of Faust Junction, Simpson Springs Station was for years a dependable Indian watering hole. Captain J. H. Simpson stopped here in 1858 while plotting an overland mail route between Salt Lake City and California. That same year George Chorpenning built a mail station here, which was later used by the Pony Express and Overland Express. Several other buildings were later built and destroyed. A stone building, reconstructed on a site that dates from the period, gives you an idea of the original mail station. A BLM campground, located nearby on a hillside to the east, has drinking water, toilets, and fourteen campsites.

Forty-one miles west of Simpson Springs is *Fish Springs National Wildlife Refuge* (435-693-3122). With more than 10,000 acres of marshes and lakes, the refuge supports a wealth of bird and animal life. An 11 mile road, built on top of dikes, makes a loop through the refuge, allowing bird-watchers several good opportunities to break out the binoculars. Mostly waterfowl—ducks, geese, herons, and so on—flock to the refuge. But you're also liable to see raptors preying above. Stop at the kiosk for more information on the different species of birds found here.

Attention, Bird-Watchers

Bird-watching is very popular in Utah. A variety of species can be found in the diverse environments. If bird-watching is your interest, the rivers and lakes in the Vernal area may prove to be particularly enjoyable. The **Ouray National Wildlife Refuge** south of Vernal is bird-watching heaven. Waterfowl and shorebirds can be found in abundance. Look for the rare eastern kingbird and the Lewis' woodpecker.

There are many places in Utah to see waterfowl and shorebirds. A few places to try are the **Bear River Migratory Bird Refuge**, **Matheson Wetlands Preserve**, the Logan River bottoms, Desert Lake in Price, and Clear Lake in Delta.

For a bird-watching trip that's really off the beaten track, the **Fish Springs National Wildlife Refuge** in the west desert of Utah is a prime choice. It's rather out of the way (a few hours off the freeway), but for the enthusiastic ornithologist, it's well worth the extra traveling time. The refuge offers stunning desert beauty and is home to many birds of prey. Spring and fall are the best times to visit. Summer can be very hot. It's a good dirt road, but it can be messy in the winter even with a 4WD. You'll want to dodge snowstorms—the wind and snow can really blow.

Take binoculars and a bird book. Keep an eye out for rattlesnakes. Call (435) 693-3122 to check on road conditions.

An abundance of water, cottonwood trees, and desert grassland made **Callao** an oasis for travelers along the Overland Trail. Originally called Willow Springs, the town changed its name because so many towns in Utah already had the same name, which frustrated the postal service. An old miner recommended "Callao," the name of a mining camp in the Peruvian Andes that apparently had similar surrounding scenery. Located 54 miles west of Boyd Station, Callao is today a tiny ranching community, where the children still attend a one-room schoolhouse.

Towering above Callao to the west are the **Deep Creek Mountains**, one of the few mountain ranges in the Great Basin with an abundance of water. You can access several canyons of the Deep Creek Range or just get a good look at them by getting off the Pony Express Trail and heading south at Callao on the Snake Valley Road. Healthy flora and fauna thriving at unexpectedly high elevations make this range of mountains an exception to the sun-baked Great Salt Lake Desert. Six perennial streams flow down from this 12,000-foot range of mountains and support a population of Bonneville cutthroat trout, a species of fish that originated in prehistoric Lake Bonneville. Wildlife include mule deer, bighorn sheep, mountain lions, antelope, grouse, and chukars. Aspens, Engelmann spruces, white firs, Douglas firs, and bristlecone pines grow in the mountains, along with more than 600 kinds of plants. What's even more incredible is that few people know about these mountains, which are every bit as impressive as the Wasatch but certainly not as accessible. Trails are generally primitive and unmarked, making topographic maps and a compass essential if you plan any serious hiking or backpacking. A first-aid kit and experience in backcountry survival are certainly beneficial, considering you are far away from civilization. For road conditions, topographic maps, or any other information on the Deep Creek Mountains, contact the BLM House Range Resource Area office (435) 743-3100 at 35 East 500 North, Fillmore.

From Callao the Pony Express Trail winds northward around the Deep Creek Mountains and past the last of the featured sites along the byway.

About 7 miles north of Canyon Station and accessed from either Callao or Ibapah is *Gold Hill*, a town that was twice reborn before it finally fizzled out. Gold was first discovered here in 1858 by people traveling on the Overland Route. But problems with Indians stalled settlement until the 1870s. For nearly a decade, Gold Hill reaped millions in gold and copper deposits. A sizable business district grew, despite the fact that most people lived in tents. One of those who came to Gold Hill to make their fortune was Jack Dempsey. Later crowned heavyweight champion of the world, Dempsey apparently had better luck in the ring than at the mines.

By the end of the century, most of the gold had been extracted. The town was all but forgotten until World War I, which opened up a whole new market for deadly minerals—something Gold Hill had plenty of. With its rich concentrations of arsenic and tungsten, the town boomed again. When the war ended, so did the military's need for the minerals. Gold Hill again died. What the town needed was another war, and it got one. But World War II sustained Gold Hill only as long as the war lasted, after which the town died a permanent death. Several dilapidated structures and the old cemetery today render the memory of a town that had three lives. The town hasn't been abandoned completely, however. Several people still call it home.

Although there is little that draws tourists to the *Tintic Mining District*, it is worth your while to at least get a look at the district base camp of *Eureka* if you happen to be in the area. Set in the narrow Ruby Gulch, Eureka is somewhat of an oddity for the state of Utah. Mormons had little to do with the growth of this community, which is probably why it lacks the uniformity of other Utah towns. Mines dug out from the sides of the canyon sit above Main Street, winding its way across the canyon floor. Decrepit Victorian houses in dire need of paint huddle around the center of town or creep up the hills toward the mines. With its rough-and-tumble appearance, Eureka looks as though it could be located in an Appalachian state, such as Kentucky or West Virginia.

A Mormon shepherd first discovered silver in Ruby Hollow—Eureka's original name. In the 1860s, the time of the discovery, Mormons were discouraged from gold or silver mining, so the discovery remained under wraps. But in 1869 a Gentile (non-Mormon) cowboy by the name of George Rust, who couldn't have cared less about Brigham Young's advice about prospecting, found the silver that the Mormon shepherd had kept a secret. He and seven other cowboys staked their claims, and they were soon digging up ore, averaging 10,000 ounces of silver ($1,500) to the ton. By 1871, 500 claims had been made in the area. New discoveries of gold, copper, lead, and zinc fueled the frenzy. By 1910 the Tintic Mining District, as the area was called, had twelve towns and a population of 8,000. Eureka, the center of all the activity, itself acquired a peak population of 3,400.

Now down to 700 inhabitants, Eureka's glory years are far behind, although the miners are still in business. Eureka fared better than the rest of the district's towns, which are today no more than havens for ghosts. *The Tintic Mining Museum*, housed in the Old City Hall on Eureka's Main Street, 241 W. Main St., tells the story of the Tintic Mining District. The museum is open Wed, Fri and Sat, 12 p.m. to 4 p.m. Call (435) 433-6842 for more information.

Located about 40 miles south of Eureka, *Delta* is a town that lived up to Brigham Young's prophecy that the desert would bloom. The area was long considered hopeless for farming, until a businessman from Fillmore took a risk in 1905. He bought 10,000 acres of land, along with water rights to the Sevier River Reservoir. With an extensive irrigation system, the land bore impressive crops of wheat, corn, barley, hay, and especially alfalfa seed. (At one time nearly one-fourth of all alfalfa seed sold in the United States came from the Delta region.) Lots were sold to homesteaders, and the town developed into an important agricultural center for Utah.

Rock Hounding Heaven

Some folks think the western part of Utah is mighty desolate—and they're right. It's a lot of lovely nothing—well, almost nothing. There are a few dozen human sorts, antelope, desert mule deer, rocks, sage, mountains, and rattlesnakes, as well as a few cattle and sheep.

It's a great place to lose yourself, to get away from microchips, cell phones, and twenty-first-century madness. It's also a great place to wander if you're a rock hound. There are hundreds of square miles of rocky hills, rocky plains, and, well, rocky mountains. You can wander until you drift into a rock-hound nirvana.

Topaz: An Historical Gem

After the bombing of Pearl Harbor, paranoia and fear of a threat to national security led to many Japanese–Americans being placed in internment camps for the duration of World War II. One of these camps, Topaz, operated from 1942 to 1945 outside Delta, Utah. In 1943 it reached a peak population of 8,130, with most of the internees coming from California. Now it is a ghost town. Many foundations remain, and those who visit may find an artifact or two lying in the dust. A memorial museum in a barrack building contains many artifacts and pictures that show what life was like in the *Topaz Camp*. To get there, follow State Road 6 west out of Delta on the way to Topaz Mountain. Signs will point out the camp.

About 45 miles west of Delta looms *Notch Peak*, part of the greater House Range. Towering above Highway 50/6 at Skull Rock Pass, Notch Peak and its sheer 3,000-foot limestone cliffs rise to an altitude of 9,700 feet, making it the largest limestone monolith in the state and the second-highest mountain in the House Range. Bizarre rumblings are said to come from deep inside this mountain.

To the north of Notch Peak, *Swasey Peak* is a famed source of fossil trilobites, dating from 500 million years ago. More than 3,000 specimens found here have gone to the Smithsonian Institution.

Surprisingly good dirt roads wind through the House Range, making travel by two-wheel-drive passenger cars feasible. Two roads, one crossing Dome Canyon Pass and another crossing Marjum Pass, connect at both their ends to make a 43-mile loop through some of the Houses' best scenery. You can access the loop via several dirt roads that branch off Highway 50/6. One option is to turn off the highway 10 miles west of Delta onto old Highway 50/6 (unpaved) and travel 25 miles to connect with the loop. Another is to take the dirt road signed Antelope Spring (32 miles from Delta) and go 10 miles. An option from the west side of Notch Peak is to exit Highway 50/6 at the road signed painter spring, 63 miles from Delta (30 miles east of the Utah–Nevada border), and go 14 miles. This road, however, isn't as regularly maintained as the others. The map to North-Central Utah clarifies these routes, which shouldn't be attempted in wet weather.

There are no marked trails in the House Range, making topographic maps and a compass essential if you decide to do any serious hiking or backpacking. Popular day hikes include ascents to the summit of either Notch or Swasey Peak. You can buy maps, check road conditions, or gather any other information on the House Range at the BLM House Range Resource Area office (435)

743-3100 at 35 East 500 North in **Fillmore**. Due to the remoteness of the House Range, you'll have no problem finding solitude here. But be prepared for the heat (or cold), the scarcity of water, and the extreme distance from civilization in general.

First Capital

In 1851 Brigham Young and the Utah Territorial Legislature decided that the Pavant Valley was an appropriate site for the capital of the anticipated state of Utah, because it lay in the approximate center of the Utah territory, which at that time included all of present-day Utah, Nevada, and parts of Colorado and Wyoming as well. A town, mind you, had not yet been erected. But plans for the building of a statehouse were implemented anyway. Truman Angell, architect of the Mormon temple and tabernacle in Salt Lake City, designed the building that would consist of four wings in the shape of a cross. Although only the south wing was ever completed, the Utah Territorial Statehouse in Fillmore began housing legislative sessions in 1851. Expected federal appropriations for the statehouse got tied up in disputes between the Mormons and the US Congress, and the funds for completion never came through. Because of the lack of housing and the difficulty of traveling between Salt Lake and Fillmore in midwinter, the statehouse served its purpose for only four short years before the legislature adjourned in the middle of one of its sessions to Salt Lake City.

The Territorial Statehouse, Utah's oldest existing governmental building and the first statehouse west of the Mississippi, now operates as a state park and museum, telling the story of Fillmore's pioneer heritage and its attempt

Watch for Flash Floods

Flash floods are always a possibility in desert country, and it pays to be cautious. In the desert, rainfall is rather infrequent, and these areas simply can't handle a heavy rainfall or even a moderate one.

The dry desert soil and the thin-rooted vegetation have a difficult time absorbing more than a small amount of moisture. A saturation level occurs quickly and water drains rapidly into creeks and rivers. Canyons and gullies run with torrents of water. Radical, violent flash floods occur as a result.

During a flash flood, boulders the size of a compact car are easily uprooted—as is any unwary hiker caught in the torrent. A dry canyon can have a 20-foot wall of dirty, swirling water rushing down it in minutes. Avoid narrow canyons or gullies and keep a weather eye for storms, even those in the surrounding hills.

to become Utah's first capital. The statehouse, at 50 W. Capitol Ave., Fillmore, is open 9 a.m. to 5 p.m., Mon through Sat. Call (435) 743-5316 for more information.

When Lake Bonneville covered the region 12,000 to 24,000 years ago, a series of volcanic eruptions spewed ash and cinder, creating a ring of tuff that rose above the surface of the water at a diameter of 3,000 feet and a height of 250 feet. A second series of eruptions spilled molten lava into the ring and filled it, turning the ring into an island. ***Tabernacle Hill*** is what remains of the tuff ring, one-third of which has been lost over time.

Named for its supposed resemblance to the Salt Lake City Tabernacle, Tabernacle Hill is a treasure trove for geology buffs, who come here to check out the collapsed caldera (measured at 1,000 feet across and 60 feet deep), pit craters, cinder cones, and other volcanic features. A lava tube extends from the caldera for about a mile. Collapses along the roof of the tube have opened up caves, in which bats, rattlesnakes, and other undesirable creatures live.

Although Tabernacle Hill is accessible by roads leading out of Fillmore, the simplest way there is via Meadow. Take the Meadow exit on Interstate 15 (about 8 miles south of Fillmore). Drive into town and take a right (west) at the road signed White Mountain. Follow the road under I–15 and past White Mountain. Five miles from Meadow and about a half mile past White Mountain, take a left (west) and head toward Tabernacle Hill. After about 1½ miles take another left and drive 2 miles to the center of the caldera.

Near the junction of Interstates 15 and 70 is Cove Fort (435-438-5547), a historical stone fort built in 1867, originally intended as a way station for those traveling between Fillmore and Beaver. The name "Cove" comes from natural rock and a steady water supply near the fort. The fort was built from rock quarried nearby, but it was never needed for defense.

Now, a frontier kitchen, bedrooms, parlors, and eating rooms are all restored to look as they did a hundred years ago. On the surrounding grounds stand a number of buildings, including a blacksmith shop and a barn built to

Utah is a Hunting State

Hunting and guns are politically incorrect in some circles, but they're part of the culture here. In fact, many schools let the kids off the Friday before the annual deer hunt. Hunting has been a way of life since pioneer days. Outside the Wasatch Front, you'll be hard-pressed to see many pickups without a gun rack in the back window. Utah has a wonderful safety record, and lots of blaze-orange clothing (400 square inches) is required on big-game hunts.

Watch the Birdies: Migrating Raptors

Utah is a major fly zone, not only for migratory waterfowl but also for big raptors. Lots of them.

Enjoy big birds of prey, feathered friends with hooked beaks and big, sharp talons. Want a bird's-eye view? If you're in Utah around the end of September, you might be interested in the *Official Raptor Watch Day*, sponsored by the Utah Division of Wildlife Resources and Hawk Watch International.

There will be folks at Wellsville Mountains, southwest of Wendover; Squaw Peak, east of Orem; Big Mountain between Mountain Dell and East Canyon; and Fish Creek near Microwave Tower. Even if you can't be part of the Official Raptor Watch, you can still hang around and watch or photograph. Officials are on hand to help you identify birds and field any questions you might have. For information, call Robert Walters, Division of Wildlife Resources (801) 538-4771, or email him at bobwalters@utah.gov.

And if you're not there for the official day, you can still see lots of these creatures a few weeks before or after. To be a prepared bird-watcher, a good pair of field glasses are a must. Take a water bottle and a few sandwiches, and don't forget your favorite bird book.

the original specifications. Look at the buildings from 9 a.m. 'til dusk. Be sure to take a break under one of the shady trees on the grounds.

Beaver is a small town with no pretenses about its size. Its downtown, a wide avenue that could comfortably accommodate four diesel trucks side by side, is only a few short blocks, filled mainly with mom-and-pop stores, one of which advertises "Free Advice on the Area." Although the town started out as a sleepy Mormon agrarian community in 1856, it didn't take long after gold and silver were discovered for it to wake up. Miners swept in from Frisco to raise Cain while Mormon farmers stood by wondering if their town had become the modern-day Gomorrah. Suspicion mounted on both sides, and both called in federal troops to keep the peace.

The *Beaver County Courthouse* (just off Main on Center Street) is a testament to better days, when gold and silver still came out of the San Francisco Mountains to the west. Although the 1889 structure stands in dilapidation, renovation is under way. The onion-domed clock tower, topped by a weather vane, is the building's most interesting feature, even though the time is a little off. Inside is the *Daughters of Utah Pioneers Museum* that tells the story of the town through pictures, historical documents, and an 1882 wedding cake. It's open June through Aug, Tues through Sat, 11 a.m. to 5 p.m. Call (435) 438-2975 or write to 90 E. Center Street, Beaver 84713.

A Man from Out of the Past

Western Utah is mining country, and some are still doing it the old-fashioned way.

You never know who you'll meet in the desert backcountry. Several years ago, in some very rugged high-desert country, fifteen rolls of film and five days from the truck, we made camp by a seep in a canyon. Out of the desert, coming toward us in the fading light, was a curious sight.

A grizzly miner leading a donkey (right out of a Grade B Western movie) made his way to our camp. The old man said his name was Roy. He had a long, dark beard, a cowboy hat, logging boots, and a .45 on his belt. (Soon it was obvious he'd not been near a bar of soap for several years.) Roy said he'd been wandering the Utah–Nevada desert for more than a decade trying to make it big. He filled up his canvas water bags, let his donkey drink, and started making coffee.

Roy was starved for conversation and talked nonstop for two hours. Seemingly out of place in a world of digital cameras and cell phones, Roy was from a different age. He left a small gold nugget and took what was left of the hot chocolate mix. He also left the backstrap off a mule deer (poached, no doubt) and pointed us to where the largest bucks stayed on some distant plateaus.

Could this have been the twilight zone?

If you have interest in the development of television, you might want to check out the **statue of Philo T. Farnsworth** ("the Father of Television") in the little park next to the courthouse. A Beaver native, Farnsworth accrued 160 patents, starting with vacuum tubes and going on to the electric microscope, the baby incubator, and the medical gastroscope.

But the real reason that you are in Beaver is to be on your way to the **Tushar Mountains**. Follow the scenic byway of Highway 153 east out of Beaver and into Beaver Canyon, and then make sure you don't get too distracted by the scenery, or you're liable to topple off one of the high switchbacks. Big ponderosa pines, aspens, and innumerable opportunities for hiking, biking, and downhill and cross-country skiing await in one of the more secluded alpine areas in the state.

Stop in at the Fishlake National Forest office in Beaver (435-438-2436), 575 S. Main St., Beaver, to learn about other options for exploring the Tushars. When the snow begins to fall, Highway 153 closes where the pavement ends—just above Elk Meadows. In the summer and early fall, you can manage to get down the steep 21-mile dirt road in most vehicles. At the bottom is the town of Junction and Highway 89. (See Central Utah.)

West of Beaver, in the remote San Francisco Range, is what remains of **Frisco**, the richest and wildest silver-mining town ever to be erected. The

Horn Silver Mine extracted an astounding $50 million in silver, the largest single body of silver found anywhere at any time. Add an extra $10 million from other mines in the area, and you can imagine what sort of heyday this town had. Twenty-one saloons appeared in a matter of weeks after silver was discovered in 1875. Scores of stores, hotels, houses of ill repute, and opium dens arose in one big boom that attracted a population of more than 6,000. But as famous as its mines were for tapping into the silver bounty, so were the gunslingers of Frisco for piling the bodies high. It got so bad that city officials had to hire a meat wagon to pick up the bodies. But all this euphoria came, literally, to a crashing end. On February 13, 1885, the Horn Silver Mine caved in, sending boulders and rubble down to the streets of Frisco. Luckily for the miners, they were between shifts, which meant no one was killed or even injured. But the rumble was so loud and so hard it broke windows 15 miles away in Milford. A few days later the town was deserted.

What remains of Frisco are several foundations, a few buildings, and a lot of rubble. High above the townsite stand four or five picturesque charcoal kilns, made out of stones and shaped like beehives. As with most ghost towns, the most poignant part of Frisco is the cemetery, where the tombstones tell sad stories about the children who perished in Frisco.

To get to Frisco head 47 miles west of Beaver (15 miles west of Milford) on Highway 21. Look for a dirt road between Mileposts 62 and 63, just before the Frisco monument. You can see the townsite and kilns from the highway. The cemetery is located away below the mine. At the monument, take the dirt road off to the left and follow it about a half mile until you see the cemetery on your right. Be sure to stay on the dirt roads, as walking near the old mines and collapsible buildings can be quite dangerous. While you're there, you'll probably see some treasure hunters scavenging the land with metal detectors. In the last few decades, people have apparently found lost gold and silver buried beneath the dirt and rubble at Frisco.

TOP ANNUAL EVENTS IN WEST-CENTRAL UTAH

SEPTEMBER

Millard County Fair and
Rodeo
Delta
(435) 864-3660

Places to Stay in West-Central Utah

BEAVER

Best Western Butch Cassidy Inn
161 S. Main St.
(435) 438-2438
Standard

Country Inn Motel
1450 N. 300 West
(435) 438-2484
Inexpensive

Days Inn
646 W 1400 N Main St.
(855) 516-1093
Inexpensive

DELTA

Budget Motel
75 S. 350 East
(435) 864-4533
Inexpensive

Days Inn
527 Topaz Blvd.
(800) 760-7718
Inexpensive

Deltan Inn Motel
347 E. Main St.
(435) 864-5318
Inexpensive

TOOELE

Best Western Inn
365 N. Main St.
(435) 882-5010
Moderate

Hampton Inn
461 S. Main St.
(435) 843-7700
Moderate

Hotel American
491 S. Main St.
(435) 882-6100
Standard

Places to Eat in West-Central Utah

TOOELE

Perkins Family Restaurant
281 N. Main St.
(435) 833-0111
Inexpensive

Sun Lok Yuen
615 N. Main St.
(435) 882-3003
Inexpensive

DELTA

Lotsa Motsa Pizza
340 E. Main St.
(435) 864-3131
Inexpensive

Top's City Cafe
313 W. Main St.
(435) 864-2148
Moderate

BEAVER

Mel's Diner
155 N. Main St.
(435) 438-5600
Inexpensive

Maria's Cocina
1419 E. Canyon Rd.
(435) 438-5654
Inexpensive

Southwestern Utah

Southwestern Utah is where the Mojave Desert, the Great Basin, and the Colorado Plateau all come together in an assembly of extremes. From the scorched desert earth of the Joshua Tree Forest to the lush alpine meadows of the Markagunt Plateau, the variations of terrain, climate, and color are startling. Depending on the time of year, a two-hour drive can mean the difference between sweating in the heat of the low-lying desert or freezing in a mountain blizzard. But there's one thing that's consistent: It never fails to inspire awe.

Vegetation comes in as many forms as the vast variety of rock formations and depends on the elevation. Joshua trees dot the parched lower elevations in the far southwest corner of the state. Farther up, pinyon pines and junipers scrape out an existence in the dusty soil. Forests of ponderosa pines, Gambel oaks, and Rocky Mountain junipers grow strong and tall, starting at about 7,000 feet. Douglas firs, Engelmann spruces, and aspens thrive in the lush elevations above 8,000 feet, where the snow piles high and takes until June or July to finally disappear. Mule deer, coyotes, and herds of elk migrate with the seasons, making their way down from the higher elevations in search of food not covered by the snow. Mountain lions make

SOUTHWESTERN UTAH

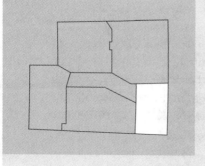

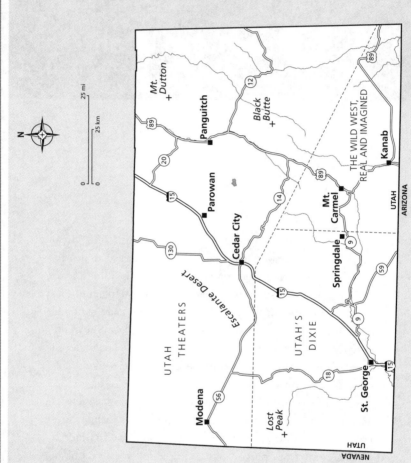

rare appearances, and hopefully you'll be at a comfortable distance if you run into one.

The Southern Paiutes, possible descendants of the Paleo-Indians, inhabited this region when the Mormons came to colonize and convert the Indians in the early 1850s, not long after the first party of pioneers landed in Salt Lake City. With hardly time enough to unload their wagons up north, Mormon families answered the call to move south and establish missions for the sake of producing needed materials, such as iron and cotton.

Utah's Dixie

You can imagine the state of the first Mormon pioneers' clothing when they finally settled in Utah after the long and arduous journey from the Midwest. The Mormons were in dire need of cotton, a commodity that the South (the actual Dixie) was selling mostly to Europe. The Mormon response, as it had been to most everything they needed, was to produce their own. Brigham Young, hearing reports on Southern Utah's temperate climate, sent a delegation of 300 to establish a "Cotton Mission" on the banks of the Santa Clara Creek, which in turn led to settlements along the Virgin River. The first year yielded 100,000 pounds of cotton. After the Civil War cheaper cotton soon arrived on the transcontinental railroad, erasing the need for cotton to be grown in Utah.

The capital of Utah's so-called Dixie is *St. George*, in the far southwestern corner of the state. St. George has, since its incarnation, been Utah's Riviera, even though it has no coastline. Its year-round warm weather draws folks from the colder climates up north. The largest of the early Mormon settlements in

AUTHOR'S FAVORITES IN SOUTHWESTERN UTAH

Zion National Park, south of Cedar City	Cedar Breaks National Monument, east of Cedar City
St. George Temple, St. George	
Utah Shakespearean Festival, Cedar City	Kodachrome Basin State Park, southeast of Cannonville
Snow Canyon State Park, north of St. George	Cedar City
Coral Pink Sand Dunes, north of Kanab	Joshua Tree Forest, west of St. George

Southern Utah, St. George got its name from one of the pioneers that Brigham Young sent south from Salt Lake City—George A. Smith. Smith, an enormous man who had special chairs built to support his weight, served as the head of the Iron Mission in Cedar City. Smith lost his wife and two kids to scurvy during the first Mormon pioneer trek to Utah. He earned his title of "saint" by delivering potatoes, then considered a scurvy preventive if eaten raw, to parties of pioneers traveling across Utah. Young named the city in honor of Smith—a "Latter-day Saint."

The first stop in St. George is the **Brigham Young Winter Home** (67 W. 200 North; 435-673-2517). It is named after the city's first and most famous winterer, who came to soak up Dixie's sunshine and find some relief for his rheumatism. He also came to supervise the cotton mission and the building of the **St. George Temple** (on the corner of 400 East and 200 South). A Mormon missionary takes you on a free tour of the house and each of its rooms, which have much of the original furniture, including a chandelier that was thought to be lost until one of Young's descendants happened to come across it in a pawn shop in San Francisco. Tours are conducted 9 a.m. to dusk daily.

Kitty-corner to the Brigham Young Winter Home is the **Seven Wives Inn** (217 N. 100 West; 435-628-3737). After polygamy was banned in Utah, the attic of this bed-and-breakfast served as a hideout for several local polygamists running from the law. One of them was Benjamin F. Johnson, the great-grandfather of Donna Curtis, one of the present innkeepers.

Winter in Southern Utah

Some people think the only thing Utah's good for in the winter is snow sports. There's another Utah, a wonderful Utah that few take advantage of in the winter.

Few tourists think of going south when the weather turns chilly in the northern mountains. A southern winter is unforgettable, especially for visitors who want the place to themselves. Motel room rates drop drastically and there are lots of available camping spots for those willing to brave a little chill.

The most popular hiking places become secluded and silent. This is the time to visit Delicate Arch, Grandstaff Canyon, and the boardwalked Matheson Wetlands Preserve. The awe-inspiring experience of the Delicate Arch amphitheater is made much more personal without the hundreds of other noisy tourists. This is a wonderful time to see the sun rise over red bluff and walk the canyons of Zion.

Donna, along with her husband, Jay, her daughter, Alison, and her son-in-law, Jon Bowcutt, runs a tight ship. Jon's artwork, mostly drawings of Alison, add a personalized touch to the rustic old home that was recently put on a "Best of the West" list for bed-and-breakfasts in Sunset magazine, the only one in Utah to get such a mention. The inn is actually composed of two buildings, the other named the "Presidents' House," because many early Mormon presidents stayed here, supposedly so they could get a meal from the owner's wife. Ask for the "Jane" room and sleep where the polygamists once hid from the law. See the rooms at sevenwivesinn.com.

The **Rosenbruch Wildlife Museum** (435-656-0033) allows you to travel the world without ever leaving St. George. Replicated habitats from every continent contain nearly every type of large mammal in the world. Visitors will see over 200 species, many of which are posed as if in motion. Hand-held wands provide visitors with information about the animals that they are seeing. This 25,000-square-foot building also contains a theater, an art gallery, and an extensive insect collection. Children will be pleased to explore the petting room. The museum is located at 1835 Convention Center Drive, St. George. The museum is open Mon through Sat, 10 a.m. to 5 p.m. A preview of some of the exhibits can been seen at rosenbruch.org.

In **Santa Clara**, 4 miles northwest of St. George, is the **Jacob Hamblin Home** (435-673-2161), which is easy to find along the main road at 3325 Hamblin Dr. In 1854 Brigham Young sent Hamblin to Santa Clara on a mission to establish peace with the Paiutes. Already known as a pacifist when it came to dealing with the Indians, Hamblin was later sent to other parts of Southern Utah and Northern Arizona to negotiate with the Indians, as well as preach the gospel. Hamblin built the house in 1863 to accommodate himself, his two wives, and twelve children. (He had four wives and twenty-four children in all, but not all lived together.) The house, including all the wood, is original. After the free tour is over, be sure to pick up and read a free copy of Hamblin's rules on dealing with the Indians. Open Mon through Sat, 9 a.m. to 4:30 p.m., and Sun 1 p.m. to 4:30 p.m.

By going northwest 5 or 6 miles beyond the Hamblin Home on Santa Clara Drive (which becomes Highway 91), or by going about 9 miles north of St. George on Highway 18, you'll come to **Snow Canyon State Park**, a name that refers not to the snowfall that's unlikely to happen here but to two of the area's early pioneers, Lorenzo and Erastus Snow. Shaped like giant fingers and knuckles, the towering Navajo sandstone cliffs enclosing the canyon range in color from red to white to black. Beginning across the street from the Shivwits Campground, **Hidden Pinyon Trail** takes you over slickrock and lava flows, allowing you to get up close and personal with the rock. At 1½ miles, it's a fairly easy hike. You can venture out farther by connecting with other trails along Hidden Pinyon, such as the **West Canyon Trail**, the longest in the park (7 miles round-trip). It takes you through the bottom of Snow Canyon up to West Canyon, where the rock turns white. If you want more information on the trails or would like to reserve a campsite, call (435) 628-2255.

Still going along Highway 18, about 27 miles north of St. George, is the turnoff for **Pine Valley**, the name of the mountains and the town nestled among aspens and Douglas firs. Coming into town, you'll see a little white church that looks as though it would be more appropriately placed in New England. Ebenezer Bryce, who also homesteaded in Bryce Canyon and for whom the park is named, said he built the **Pine Valley Ward Chapel** like a ship, the one thing Bryce had experience in building before he went to work on the church in 1868. The church is said to be the oldest continuously used house of Mormon worship. It keeps no regular visitation hours except, of course, on Sunday.

About 35 miles north of St. George, still on Highway 18, is the **Mountain Meadows Massacre Historic Site**. The name refers to a bizarre and horrifying event that occurred here in September 1857. A Mormon mob, disguised as Indians and led by John D. Lee, attacked the Fancher party, a California-bound group of Arkansas pioneers. One hundred twenty men, women, and children were killed. The reason for the massacre is shrouded in mystery, but the event points to widespread paranoia among early settlers, who feared that the federal government, leery of Mormon customs, would order an attack on Mormon settlements.

After the massacre, Lee fled to the Grand Canyon, and the federal authorities went on a manhunt. During his flight from the law, he ran a ferry service crossing the Paria River at a slot in the cliffs now known as Lee's Ferry. Lee, a polygamist, was captured years later in Parowan while visiting one of his wives. A firing squad executed him on March 23, 1876, at the site of the massacre. He was the only one tried and punished for the murders.

Overlooking the valley where the emigrants were besieged, the memorial is a poignant homage to the Fancher party. Embedded in the hillside, the granite memorial lists most of the names of those who were killed and the infants who were spared. Most striking are the ages of some of the victims (as young as seven) and the size of some of the families who were all killed (the Fancher family lost eleven).

In the very southwest corner of the state, traveling along Highway 91, you'll find yourself surrounded by trees you know you've seen in pictures but never in reality (unless you've been to a certain park in California). **Joshua Tree Forest** can make you wonder if you've completely left the civilized world, which is exactly what makes it so special. The trees, which are mistakenly attributed only to California, dot the unforgiving landscape, where there is no sign of water or shade. (Don't be fooled into thinking that because it's called a forest there is respite from the heat. There's not. So bring plenty of water and a hat.) From the forest is an amazing view of the **Mojave Desert** and the desert-tarnished cliffs and rugged canyons of the **Beaver Dam Mountains**. There are no marked trails in the forest, but a number of dirt roads give you access through the fences. (It's a designated BLM recreation area; don't worry about trespassing.) Instead of driving your car through this godforsaken land, it's best to park at one of the entrances and then walk or bike around on the designated roads, but not on the vegetation. You might even see one of the elusive desert tortoises that can live for thirty-five years. Apparently they are most active in the spring and summer. Around early April is an excellent time to see the desert wildflowers and cactus blossoms.

Outside Leeds (17 miles northeast of St. George off Interstate 15) are two interesting sites, one historical and one natural. **Silver Reef**, at its peak in 1880, had more than 1,500 residents and had extracted more than $8 million

Symbolic Nature of Native Rock Art

Utah has a number of interesting people. Few are more intriguing than a lady in Payson named Kristine Peele, an expert on Utah deserts. She's especially knowledgeable on Native American rock art—specifically, what it means.

"It's all symbolic," she says, "and the symbols have basic meanings." Snakes, for example, are a common image in Indian work. The serpent was held in high esteem by early cultures. A snake is symbolic of rebirth and renewal because it sheds its skin. It knows how to adapt to the harsh land and survive.The owl, silent and deadly, was a symbol of death or ill omen. To show that it was wet or raining, an artist would draw a cloud or a river. The sun meant a spirit or father; the earth, mother.

On one rock panel, there are four figures with arms raised in prayer. Next to these is a lady climbing with a papoose on her back. Peele suggests that this could mean the lady and child were grateful for escaping some type of danger.

Once you start to make sense of what is there, it becomes more meaningful.

If you'd like to read more, consider the following books: Kenneth Castleton's *Petroglyphs and Pictographs*; Garrick Mallery's *Picture-Writing of the American Indians, Volumes 1 & 2*; LaVan Martineau's *The Rocks Begin to Speak*; and Elizabeth C. Welsh's *Easy Field Guide to Southwestern Petroglyphs*.

worth of silver from its mines, the only mines in the world to extract silver from sandstone. Silver Reef could also boast of having six saloons, two newspapers, two dance halls, a Chinatown, and three cemeteries, as well as a reputation for being one of Utah's most rip-roaring, good-time towns. Although Silver Reef today defies its classification as a ghost town by also being a newly developed subdivision, it still feels like a late-nineteenth-century mining town. Stop in the restored Wells Fargo Bank to view old mining tools, guns, bottles, and other artifacts left over from the old days. Silver Reef is easy to find by following the signs once you get into Leeds. The cemeteries are a little tricky to locate, however. Heading toward Silver Reef from exit 23, take a left at the first dirt road you come to. A hundred feet and you'll be faced with three roads to choose from. Take the middle road and keep an eye out for one of the gravesites, which looks like a miniature version of the Washington Monument and is surrounded by an ornamental metal fence. This is the gravesite of one Henry Clark, Silver Reef's most notorious gambler, shot down by a saloon owner who happened to be quicker on the draw than Clark.

Red Cliffs Recreation Site could be considered a misnomer. Depending on the direction of the sun, orange, blood red, or black might be more like it. Whatever color it really is, it's spectacular. The bulbous sandstone cliffs, aged and wrinkled by the wind, look like they've been handblown in a furnace. Several caves and crags can skew your sense of dimension inside the canyon, which can be also be reached by following the signs once you land in Leeds. At the RV park, you need to take a right on the road that runs under the interstate and follow it until you reach the Red Cliff campground and picnic area. Desert Trail, starting at the beginning of the loop in the campground, takes you past small pools and precariously situated boulders and runs into Quail Creek a half-mile up. If the creek is running, you'll be forced to wade. Be careful you don't step on any lizards; they like to dart across the trail at breakneck speeds.

Getting away from the mobs in Zion National Park isn't always easy, especially during the summer months, when the crowds reach traffic-jam proportions. Fortunately, there are shuttle buses in the more congested areas where cars are not allowed.

However, you must see **Zion National Park**. It is a world-class park that can't be overlooked. It has stupendous scenery. In fact, there is nothing like it on earth. Take a few short hikes, and see the scenic finales at trail's end. There are hundreds of flowers, animals, and rock formations to identify and make up names for, and even in the hottest summer weather, there is always a shady picnic spot.

Zion is Utah's first national park. A section of the current park was set aside as a monument in 1909 by President Taft. In 1918 the monument was enlarged

Zion National Park: In More Detail

Watching nature is a favorite pastime at Zion, and the park is very obliging with its diversity and depth of "watchables." In spring, summer, and fall showy flowers can be seen. Look for the purple Zion daisy and the bright red cardinal monkey flower—there are 899 plant species. For the wildlife enthusiast, there are sixty species of birds and sixty-eight species of mammals. There are thirty-six different reptiles and seven amphibians. The campgrounds are open on a first-come basis. They have fire grates, picnic tables, water, and modern rest rooms.

and given the name Zion. In 1919 it was made a national park by an act of Congress. Many of Zion's trails and viewpoints were marked and interpreted decades ago. Most of the trails are hard-packed—a few are paved.

While the actual boundaries are immense—147,000 acres—Zion Canyon, where most tourists congregate, is relatively small. About 6 miles long, the canyon is as deep as it is wide and it terminates at The Narrows. Take a hike, if you don't mind heights. Anyone who has wandered in Zion's sandstone glow or ventured into its cool grotto canyons knows that words are not enough to explain its appeal. Visitors young and old are awestruck by its magnificent splendor. Famous natural stone landmarks such as The Watchman, The Sentinel, Court of the Patriarchs, and Mountain of the Sun must be viewed at least once in a lifetime—never mind Paris. It is said that nonreligious explorers named many of the stone monuments, but only religious terms seemed appropriate. You'll notice that the terms *temple, cathedral, patriarch, throne,* and *angel* are common nomenclature.

The Virgin River runs a green lazy course through the red rock. The river carries an equivalent of 180 carloads of ground rock out of the park each day.

Easier hikes include **Weeping Rock**, a half-mile, self-guided trail, ending at a rock alcove that features dripping springs and hanging gardens of wildflowers; **Emerald Pools**, a 1.2-mile roundtrip that leads past three waterfalls and the small pools they have created; and **Riverside Walk**, a paved 2-mile walk that follows the Virgin River upstream, past hanging gardens and marshy wetlands, to The Narrows. The trail to **Angels Landing** and the **West Rim** is a more challenging hike but has sections along the way, such as Walter's Wiggles and Refrigerator Canyon (where early inhabitants once stored their perishables).

The **Canyon Overlook** hike requires a drive out of Zion Canyon along Mt. Carmel Highway east of the tunnel. This 1-mile trail passes under low-hanging rocks and by (but not too close to) steep drop-offs. It ends with a spectacular viewpoint of Zion and Pine Creek canyons. A guidebook that interprets the plant and animal life along this trail is available at the Visitor Center. And speaking of Zion's long tunnel, you'll want to take a drive through this engineering marvel constructed in 1930. It carves through rough terrain to connect lower Zion Canyon with the high plateaus to the east. Look around when you enter because when you exit the landscape will look very different. On one side are the massive cliff walls of Zion Canyon—on the other are fantastically eroded colorful sandstone formations. ***Checkerboard Mesa*** is crisscrossed with cracks that are geometrically patterned.

It can be busy, but a trip to Zion is always worth it. Spring and fall are comfortable, but many visitors come in summer. If you use the two backdoor entrances at the northwest corner of the park, venture out farther than most people are willing to go. Then you have the chance of finding yourself in solitary awe of the park's monolithic peaks and vast canyons. One of these back doors is Kolob Canyons Road, along I–15, about 15 miles south of Cedar City. The other is Kolob Terrace Road, branching off Highway 9 in Virgin. The road ascends through juniper and piñon pine woodlands, winds past the Guardian Angel Peaks, and ends up at Lava Point (by then a dirt road), where the panoramic view takes in the Cedar Breaks area to the north, the Pink Cliffs to the northeast, Zion Canyon Narrows to the east, and the Sentinel to the southeast. Needless to say, the view is no less than mind-bending. From about November 1 to May 1 the snow buildup may prevent you from reaching Lava Point, but it's worth checking several of the trails along the way. One reaches Lava Point from below. During late fall, winter, and early spring, you're unlikely to see

Utah Sandstone

There are marvelous examples of sandstone all over the state, but this sedimentary rock is especially noticeable in the southwestern corner.

Sandstone is composed primarily of quartz, cemented together with small amounts of other minerals. The colors you'll see (the luscious reds, browns, and yellows) in exposed sandstone walls are influenced by the "cement" holding the pieces of quartz together. For instance, those haunting red walls you enjoy at Red Cliffs and Capitol Reef have a high iron content.

There are different types of sandstone, each named according to when it was formed. Navajo sandstone, which is very prevalent in Southwestern Utah, is older than Entrada, Dakota, and Wahweap sandstones, and younger than Wingate formations. It was formed in the Triassic and Jurassic periods, 144 to 245 million years ago.

more than a handful of people. Undoubtedly, these are the best times of year to visit the park.

Left Fork Trail, beginning from the first parking lot just inside the park boundaries, drops 420 feet into the canyon of Left Fork North Creek and follows the creek 4½ miles to "The Subway," a narrow slot carved deep in the rock, resembling an empty subway tunnel. At 9 miles round-trip, the hike is fairly strenuous, especially during the hot summer months, so bring plenty of water.

But the best trail for amazing views along Kolob Terrace Road is the *Wildcat Canyon Trail*, starting 16 miles from Virgin and leading to Lava Point, 6 miles from the Wildcat trailhead. The trail goes through plenty of lush vegetation, including aspens, white firs, maples, and a variety of wildflowers. North Guardian Angel and several other imposing domes appear around each corner, the view climaxing at the trail's end—Lava Point. If you do this hike, you might want to consider taking a shuttle from Zion Lodge in Zion Canyon. The shuttle drops you off at the trailhead and then picks you up at the trail's end, so you don't have to double the mileage by retracing your steps. What would otherwise be an overnight backpacking trip can become a day-hike. For scheduling and fee information, contact the transportation desk at the lodge at (435) 772-3213. There's also a backcountry shuttle board at the Zion Canyon Visitor Center for hikers who want to coordinate rides with other hikers.

Along the short stretch of Highway 9 from Virgin to Springdale are a number of bed-and-breakfasts. And no wonder. The scenery is some of Utah's most awe-inspiring. The problem is choosing among them.

As you are heading east out of Rockville on Highway 9, look for Bridge Road (200 East), the access road to Grafton. *Grafton* might strike you as someplace you've seen before, that is, if you've ever seen *Butch Cassidy and the Sundance Kid*, which used this ghost town for one of its scenes. All that remains of this onetime county seat started in 1859 is a charming little schoolhouse, a church, and a dusty graveyard at the foot of some sandstone cliffs.

Grafton lies 2½ miles from Rockville. Follow the signs once you get on Bridge Road. The last 2⁹⁄₁₀ miles are not paved, but any car should make it during dry weather.

As far as Utah towns go, *Springdale* is a gem. Springdale is located at the mouth of Zion Canyon, which puts it in the back row of one the greatest natural cathedrals on earth. With the town's location at the south gate of Zion National Park, Springdale exhibits some of the signs of theme-park mentality. The town has maintained, for the most part, an air of authenticity not found on the outskirts of most national parks. Ranchers and park officials—now joined by a host of artists, writers, and bed-and-breakfast owners—make up this tightly knit community of 350.

As anyone who lives in the area will tell you, the place to eat in Springdale is the ***Bit & Spur Saloon*** (435-772-3498) at 1212 Zion Park Boulevard, Springdale. "The Bit," designed and built by Springdale native Mark Austin, has an old-saloon-crossed-with-a-mountain-lodge atmosphere. Beyond that it makes no nostalgic attempts at evoking the Old West. You're more likely to hear Ella Fitzgerald on the stereo than you would any Western crooner. The food here is straight-ahead contemporary and some of the best you'll find in Southwestern Utah. Most of it is Mexican/Southwestern based, but with a signature style. The Bit also has a bar, which means you can order a bottle of wine or a mixed drink. It is open from 5 p.m. to 12 p.m.

The price for Springdale's commitment to staying small is a lack of accommodations for its visitors. The large number of bed-and-breakfasts doesn't mean you don't have to worry about finding a room. You do, especially in the summer, when the streets are jam-packed with tourists. Wherever you decide to stay, make sure you call well in advance.

Under the Eaves (435-772-3457), 980 Zion Park Boulevard, Springdale, is a rustic inn in two houses, one reminiscent of an old English cottage and the other a restored cabin relocated from Zion National Park. Besides providing a great view of the Virgin River Valley and the canyon, the porch is simply a perfect place to spend the evening chatting. Visit undertheeaves.com for more details.

Good local and regional pottery abounds at ***Worthington Gallery*** (789 Zion Park Blvd.; 435-772-3446). Owner Greg Worthington creates his pottery on-site, but he also receives work from potters all over the West. Greg borrows techniques from the ancient Ancestral Puebloan cliff dwellers, using original designs and making each piece only once. The store also carries a good amount of raku, a Japanese style of pottery. The gallery is open daily 10 a.m. to 7 p.m. in the spring and fall. In the winter you can never tell when it will be open. You can see some of the pottery at worthingtongallery.com.

Harvest House Bed and Breakfast (29 Canyon View Dr.; 435-772-3880) stands in a perfect spot for guests to absorb all the majesty of Zion Canyon with a relaxing garden, a Koi pond, and a year round outdoor hot tub. Two of the four rooms, all with their own bathrooms, have private decks that face the park, which in itself is worth the price of the room. The Harvest House is convenient for access to local shops, restaurants and the Zion National Park Shuttle. Your stay includes breakfast vouchers to two local restaurants. See the rooms at harvesthouse.net.

The Wild West, Real and Imagined

Flanked by the imposing Vermilion Cliffs, the dusty town of **Kanab** must have been an easy sell to the filmmakers and television producers seeking out locations for their projects. Named by the Paiute Indians, Kanab means "place of the willows," but the people of Kanab would also like you to remember it as the setting for more than 90 feature films and 200 television shows. Kanab's Hollywood exposure began in 1924, when the Parry brothers (Gron, Whit, and Chaunce) were hired as drivers for the first film ever shot in the Kanab area, *Deadwood Coach*. The brothers, anticipating the possibility of more film production coming to Kanab, became acting solicitors for the town, going to Hollywood and peddling the area to producers. Not only did they sell the area to Hollywood, but they also provided the props, extras, transportation, and accommodations (at Parry's Lodge, of course). But with the decline of the Western genre, so went much of Kanab's Hollywood exposure.

If **Kanab**'s Hollywood bug has bitten you or you'd like to imagine yourself back in the days of the Wild West (as portrayed in the movies), then you might be interested in visiting the ***Johnson Canyon Movie Set***, located 15 miles east of Kanab off Highway 89. The set, still available for filming, has been used in more than twenty movies, including *The Rainmaker*, *The Dalton Girls*, and *The Outlaw Josie Wales*. It was also used in the television series *Gunsmoke*. Miss Kitty's Longbranch Saloon and Doc's office are just a few of the twelve buildings that make up the three streets of the movie set. Follow the signs to Johnson Canyon, 10 miles east of Kanab. The movie set, accessible by a paved road, is another 5 miles north of the highway. Because of its location in the middle of nowhere, the set appears like a ghost town, which, to some extent, it is.

Strange-Sounding Names

Did you ever wonder where all these strange-sounding Southern Utah names come from?

Kanab, the town and the creek off Highway 89, was settled in the 1860s by the Hamblins. Indian attacks were always on the settlers' minds. In fact, the town had to be vacated in 1871. The name Kanab is Paiute for "willows". In olden times, Kanab Creek was lined with jungles of willows.

Kaiparowits is a 50-some-mile plateau in the Escalante area—one point overlooks Lake Powell. The Native American name means "a mountain's little brother."

Farther east on Highway 89 is another opportunity to visit the Wild West, real and imagined. ***Pahreah Townsite and Movie Set***, like Johnson Canyon, was first the locale of a farming settlement back in the 1800s and then that of movie production in the mid-1900s. ***Pahreah***, named for a Paiute Indian word meaning "muddy water," was first settled in 1870 by a group of pioneers fleeing the attacks Paiute Indians waged on the previous settlement at Rockhouse, 5 miles downstream. The settlers' new location at Pahreah was easier to defend and better suited for farming. Visited by such notables as John Wesley Powell and Jacob Hamblin, Pahreah flourished, attracting more than forty-five families, not to mention a host of polygamists hiding out from the law, who found the town's isolated location comfortable during the polygamy trials of the 1880s. By 1890 floods had washed away most of the farmland, and the farmers deserted the town in search of a more habitable location. The town was all but forgotten when gold was discovered there in the early twentieth century. A small gold mining operation went up in 1911 but soon proved to be fruitless. One miner, an old bachelor, hung on until the 1930s.

But in 1963 the town rose again, so to speak. A mile south of the original location of Pahreah, a movie set was erected for the making of *Sergeants Three*, starring Frank Sinatra, Dean Martin, and Sammy Davis Jr. (not exactly the sorts you would immediately identify with the Wild West). Take Highway 89, 30 miles east of Kanab. Turn north at the historic marker and head up the dirt road, which isn't passable when wet. You'll first come to the movie set, about 4 miles from the highway. The old townsite is another mile farther on. Look for the old cemetery just beyond the movie set.

Paria Canyon is a backpacker's backcountry dream. The trail follows the Paria River and its tributaries through the bottom of this 2,000-foot-deep gorge, where the sculpted sandstone walls allow as little as 4 feet of passage. This is no leisurely jaunt into the wilderness. Flash floods are a threat, especially in July, August, and September. To hike the entire 37-mile length of the canyon, from White House Ruins in Southern Utah downstream to Lee's Ferry in Northern Arizona, takes four to six days and requires a high degree of backpacking experience and self-sufficiency, as help can be days away. If you're up to the task, then you must obtain a permit twenty-four hours in advance of the hike from the Paria Canyon Ranger Station (at the White House Trailhead) or from the BLM Area Office (435-644-2672) in Kanab at 318 North 100 East. If you would rather go into the canyon and come out on the same day, then you only need to register at the White House Trailhead. It's a good idea to wear canvas shoes (better than heavy leather hiking boots in the water) and carry a walking stick (for support in the swift currents). To get to the White House Trailhead, go 43 miles east of Kanab on Highway 89. The trailhead begins 2 miles south

If the Movie Scenery Looks Familiar, It's Utah

From John Ford Westerns and *Indiana Jones* to television shows like *Touched by an Angel* and *Promised Land*, Utah is Hollywood's favorite back lot. Southern Utah is one of the cowboy capitals of the film industry, but it hasn't stopped there. While Westerns may have dimmed, Utah's movie future as a whole looks very bright indeed. In fact, it's the third most popular state for filming movies.

And why not? The state has everything you'd need for a movie or television show—mountains, forests, valleys, plains, farms, deserts, rivers, cities, towns, wildlife . . . cheap extras. Utah has about every setting imaginable, except ocean beaches (guess you can't have everything).

This is advantageous to budget-minded executives conscious of the meter ticking. A production company doesn't have to send the crew and actors all over the world to film. Everything can be done in one state, a state that embraces this sort of involvement.

of the highway at the end of a dirt road, at the site of an old homestead called **Whitehouse Ruins**. If it happens to rain while you are in Paria Canyon and you then hear something akin to a locomotive crashing down the canyon, climb to higher ground and wait for the flood to pass.

To the north of Kanab is something that is a bit hard to fathom—an animal sanctuary, home to more than 1,500 dogs, cats, birds, horses, rabbits, pigs, burros, and other companion animals. **Best Friends Animal Sanctuary** (435-644-2001) is the largest of its kind in the United States, taking in animals that have been neglected, abused, injured, and are otherwise unadoptable by common animal shelters. The sanctuary formed when a group of friends in Arizona, who had sheltered a lot of animals on their own behalf, decided to put their efforts together and create a haven for animals that would otherwise be killed, something Best Friends does not do. They chose a ranch outside Kanab. It has turned into a cause for Hollywood celebrities, receiving support from such notables as Ellen DeGeneres, Kelsey Grammer, Rene Russo, and director Wolfgang Petersen. Besides the stars who support and promote the organization, Best Friends is supported by donations from its members, 50,000 strong, who become "Guardian Angels" when they adopt a pet.

Best Friends offers one-hour tours two or four times a day, depending on demand. There is no charge for the tour, but they do ask for a donation. You must reserve ahead by calling (435) 644-2001. To get there, go 7 miles northwest of Kanab on Highway 89. Follow the signs to Kanab Canyon between

A Rare Snail Discovered in Kanab Canyon

When people think of Utah, pioneers and national parks come to mind. Few think of snails—let alone a new species of snails. This is a desert, after all. Nevertheless, Utah is apparently a good home for snail populations, and there are still some left to be discovered.

Vicky Mertsky teaches at Indiana University; her specialty is conservation biology and ecosystem ecology. She was on a bushwoman's holiday in Kanab Canyon, enjoying the sights and wonders of Southern Utah. She was also observing, collecting, and looking for "stuff," specifically snails. Looking for stuff, after all, is what professors do.

In the wetlands of Kanab Creek, quite by accident, Vicky discovered ambersnails while looking at other snail groups. Utah now has a new snail—or an old snail we simply weren't aware of.

Mileposts 69 and 70, and then follow the signs to the Best Friends Welcome Center. For more information visit the website at bestfriends.org or write them at 5001 Angel Canyon Rd., Kanab 84741.

High winds, funneled through a notch between the Moquith and Moccasin Mountains, carry eroded sandstone from the mountains and deposit it on what is today known as the ***Coral Pink Sand Dunes***, named for the color of this surprisingly soft, light sand. The wind sketches its course on the dunes, disrupted in places by the tracks of elusive mule deer, coyotes, kit foxes, or jackrabbits. Here you'll find an unsuspected variety of plant and animal life. Scores of wetlands, the result of snow melt, sit in the pockets of many of the dunes, supporting amphibian life, such as salamanders and toads.

Go west on Hancock Road (which branches off Highway 89, 8 miles north of Kanab). The dunes will be off to your left, 4 or 5 miles from the junction. You'll find fewer people in this BLM-controlled section of the dunes than you will in the designated state park. It is a good idea to park your car on Hancock Road and just wander around this wonderland to the south. The state park, 12 miles from Highway 89, has some of the bigger, more impressive dunes and maintains a campground and picnic sites. Call (800) 322-3770 if you want to reserve a campsite. The Coral Pink Sand Dunes area is a mecca for off-road vehicles, and hikers have to put up with the noise and danger of these vehicles, which seem more prevalent in the state park than on the BLM land. If you're coming from the north on Highway 89, take a right (south) 3½ miles south of the Mt. Carmel Junction, then go another 11 miles until you reach the state park.

If it weren't for the ***Historic Smith Hotel Bed and Breakfast*** (435-648-2156), you would most likely drive through the town of ***Glendale*** without blinking an eye. Located 30 miles north of Kanab on Highway 89, Glendale has about 200 residents. Built in the style of a country manor, the Smith has been run as a hotel on and off since 1927. More than any other bed-and-breakfast in Utah, the Smith has a pastoral feeling about it. The seven rooms, all renovated with private baths, are simply and sparingly decorated but still retain an old-time feel, just like the rest of the house. An interesting feature of the old hotel is its sign, designed out of stained glass and nicely illuminated at night. Contact the hotel at 295 North Main St., Glendale or visit historicsmithhotel.com.

Utah's Theaters

As did St. George, ***Cedar City*** began with a need, this time for iron. A group of pioneers, under the orders of Brigham Young, left Provo in 1850 and headed south on a mission to mine iron ore and coal deposits and to build a furnace and iron foundry that would supply northern settlements. Soon after the factory began producing the commodity, cheaper iron arrived from the East, putting the Iron Mission out of business by 1858.

Frontier Homestead State Park (635 N. Main St.; 435-586-9290) tells the story of the Desert Iron Manufacturing Company. The most interesting aspect of the museum, however, is its collection of horse-drawn vehicles, one of the biggest in the West. In addition to the several varieties of buggies, sleighs, and surreys, you'll see "the Rolls Royce of carriages"—the Clarence, featuring beveled glass, broadcloth upholstery, and a horizontal fender over the back wheel to prevent mud from splashing on the glass. Almost as nice as the Clarence is the hearse, decked out with fancy lamps, railings, urns, and glass. Also be sure to check out the Overland Stagecoach, which has a bullet lodged in it, suggesting the sort of rides it must have been on. And don't miss the stagecoach's displayed rules of etiquette. (Rule 5: "Don't snore loudly while sleeping or use your fellow passenger's shoulder for a pillow; he or she may not understand and friction may result." Sound advice, indeed.) Behind the museum is the oldest log cabin in Southern Utah, built in 1851 and the birthplace of twenty-four children. The park is open 9 a.m. to 5 p.m. Admission is $4 per person, $2 if an Iron County resident; kids under 7 are free.

The Pizza Factory (131 S. Main St.; 435-586-3900) is a Cedar City original. The founder, Bill Kringlen, moved to Cedar City twenty years ago and missed the Italian food he grew up with in California, so he decided to start his own restaurant. Now it is always full of locals there to enjoy the light crust pizza, breadsticks with chunky marinara sauce, large plates of pasta, and fresh-squeezed raspberry lemonade. The restaurant is open from 11 a.m. to 10 p.m., Mon through Thurs, and until 10:30 p.m. Fri and Sat.

What puts this small community of Cedar City on the present-day map is the *Utah Shakespearean Festival,* held each summer at Southern Utah State University.

Founded by Fred C. Adams in 1962, the festival started out with a budget of $1,000 and an attendance of 3,276. Now, with a multi-million-dollar budget and an annual attendance of more than 125,000, the festival has reinvigorated the town of Cedar City. Hailed by critics from around the globe as one of the best Shakespearean festivals in the world, the one here in Utah has something going for it that most don't: a theater patterned after drawings and research of sixteenth-century Tudor stages. Experts say it comes respectfully close to the Globe Theatre, where Shakespeare presented his plays. "We searched world-wide to find a replica of Shakespeare's theater," BBC producer Peter Wineman said, "and found it in Utah."

The Adams Shakespearean Theater is quite an oddity on the tiny pine-strewn campus of Southern Utah University. It's a roaming theater—ranging from Elizabethan music and dance, to impromptu sword fights, to *Punch and Judy* shows—all in addition to what's presented in the Adams and in the university's newest theater, the *Randall L. Jones Theater.*

Besides the three or four Shakespearean plays produced all summer long, the festival presents two others at the Randall Theater, usually contemporary works by playwrights considered "the best of the rest." Featured in *Architecture* magazine in 1990, the Randall Theater is perhaps one of Utah's most attractive modern structures, presenting plays and musicals throughout the year. And just to make sure you've caught the significance of all that you're seeing and hearing, the festival offers literary and production seminars that address the plays presented on the previous day. Actors, costumers, and musicians sit in at the production seminars, contributing their insight to the discussions. If all this has you inspired, you can participate in one of the workshops the festival sponsors. Renaissance dance, actor training, and medieval falconry are just a few of the skills you can take home with you.

The Utah Shakespearean Festival generally runs from mid-June to the middle of October. Call (435) 586-7878 or (800) 752-9849 in advance for tickets. Call (435) 586-7880 for workshop information. If you don't happen to be in Cedar City during the summer, you can still wander into the Adams Shakespearean Theater for a look.

Some of the best food in town can be found a couple of blocks east of the Shakespearean Festival. *The Pastry Pub* (86 W. Center St.; 435-867-1400) serves fresh baked breads and pastries and gourmet salads and sandwiches

Shakespearean Festival

With a 2000 Tony award for America's Outstanding Regional Theater, given to theaters that have "displayed a continuous level of artistic achievement contributing to the growth of theater nationally," the Utah Shakespearean Festival has earned bragging rights. USF has ranked among the four best Shakespearean festivals in the United States for several years and is in the process of becoming a year-round theater.

You might be interested to know that the USF also has the world's most accurate replica of the Globe Theatre. Indeed, it is so true-to-life that the BBC used it to film their Shakespeare series after a worldwide search.

Be sure to see the Green Shows, part of the festival experience that shouldn't be missed. Actors dressed in Elizabethan garb present a noteworthy half-rehearsed/half-improvised presentation while they mingle with the audience.

Despite the increased popularity of the festival caused by the Tony win, tickets are accessible and affordable. For ticket information log on to bard.org, or call (800) PLAYTIX.

brimming over with fixings. There is also an espresso bar. The Pub is open from 7:30 a.m. to midnight, Mon through Sat (it closes at 10 p.m. the rest of the year), so you can enjoy an iced latte or a slice of cheesecake after the plays.

The eight rooms at *Bard's Inn Bed and Breakfast* (150 S. 100 West; 435-586-6612; thebardsinn.com) are named after characters in Shakespeare's plays. The Inn is tastefully decorated with a liberal amount of antiques and accomplishing an English cottage feel. The rooms are replete with rich wood furnishings and an ample number of windows. Behind the house is a cottage that serves as a two-bedroom suite in the summer. It is common for most of the summer rooms to be reserved a year in advance. If you want to stay at the Bard, keep this in mind.

Bulloch Drug (91 N. Main St.; 435-586-9651) has an old-fashioned soda fountain and candy counter right in the front window. Try a frosty root beer float or an ironport, a Southern Utah soda. While you enjoy your ice cream, mill around the other rooms full of nostalgic gifts and toys. The store is open 9 a.m. to 9 p.m., Mon through Fri, and until 7 p.m. on Sat.

The best approach to Zion National Park is 19 miles south of Cedar City along Interstate 15. Even though the paved Kolob Canyons Road is only 5 miles long, the view at the top extends across much of Southern Utah. The road skirts Kolob's "Finger Canyons," its red-rock monoliths resembling enormous fingers reaching up to the sky. The scenery from the road is some of the most dramatic in the park, but some of the least beheld for car travelers. A couple of excellent hikes are possible from the road. Taylor Creek Trail, beginning 2 miles from the Kolob Canyons Visitors Center, forges upstream into the Middle Fork of Taylor Creek. You'll see a couple of homestead cabins dating from 1929, which don't compare to the thrusting, monumental cliffs and the small pools and waterfalls also encountered along the way. The trail ends at Double Arch Alcove, a cool, florid recess in the canyon, where cliff columbines drape the dripping rock walls. The trail is 5⁵⁄₁₀ miles round-trip.

La Verkin Creek Trail, a longer, more strenuous hike, begins 4 miles beyond the visitor center. Dropping 1,000 feet to La Verkin Creek, the trail is an excellent opportunity to embrace the sight of Kolob's red cliffs and canyons. The destination is **Kolob Arch**, the largest freestanding arch in the world. At 14 miles round-trip, the hike is tough to do in a day, especially in the summer, when you'll need to carry at least a gallon of water for the day. You may want to backpack it so that you have more time to explore the area. (In that case, don't forget to obtain a permit from the Kolob Canyons Visitors Center.)

North of Cedar City, the **Parowan Gap Petroglyphs** represent an accumulation of work dating from a thousand years ago, beginning with the Sevier–Fremont, an agricultural-based tribe that lived in the region. The seminomadic ancestors of the present-day Southern Paiutes are also suspected of contributing to the assorted renderings of geometrical designs, snakes, lizards, mountain sheep, bear claws, and human figures. What these prehistoric designs mean is still largely a mystery to archaeologists. Whatever they mean, they enchant. The location, a gap through the Red Hills, appears in the distance like a great portal, augmenting the strangeness of this place, which can be reached two

Utah Trivia

Utahans rank number four in the United States in the "longest lifetime category" at 75.76 years.

About 2,000 years ago, the Ancestral Puebloans began raising corn in the valleys of Southern Utah; these farmers were the first stationary residents in Utah.

The beehive symbol and the word "Industry" became Utah's official emblem and motto on March 4, 1959.

Utah consumes more ice cream, Jell-O, and marshmallows per capita than any other state in the Union.

The state of Utah contains every setting imaginable, except an ocean beach.

ways. From Cedar City go north on Main Street (or take exit 62 on I–15) to Highway 130. Continue north 13½ miles, then turn right (east) and go 2½ miles on a good gravel road to Parowan Gap. From the town of **Parowan**, go north on Main Street and turn left (west) on 400 North. Go 10½ miles on good gravel road until you reach the gap. Please do not touch the petroglyphs. Oil from your hands hastens erosion of the rock and its art.

If you do come from Parowan or decide to go there after visiting the petroglyphs, you'll drive by Little Salt Lake. Paiute Indian legend suggests that a windstorm swept across the lake one day, prompting a large monster to emerge. Water rushed onto the shore, allowing the monster to swim over and grab one of the Indian maidens camped there. The maiden, so the story goes, was never heard from again. The name Parowan, a Paiute Indian word meaning "evil waters," comes from this legend.

The Indians call **Cedar Breaks National Monument** the "Circle of Painted Cliffs," perhaps a better name than the one now popularly used. The natural amphitheater spans 3 miles in diameter and drops 2,500 feet. The formations are the result of different erosional forces at work—water, frost, snow, wind, and so on. If you have a hard time picking a predominant color in the rocks, don't feel bad; color analysts claim to see more than fifty different hues. Cedar Breaks National Monument is, for the most part, inaccessible by car in the winter and unpleasantly crowded in the summer. Highway 148, the road cutting across the east section of the monument, closes once the snow begins to fall, around the latter part of October or early November.

In the winter this leaves a couple of alternatives for seeing the massive natural amphitheater. One is by snowshoe, and the other is by cross-country skis. Georg's (435-677-2013), just below the Brian Head Hotel, rents a complete cross-country ski package and can also provide you with maps of the trails in the area, including the North Rim Trail, a short tour that skirts the rim of Cedar Breaks and overlooks the amphitheater and its strange pinnacles. The North Rim Trail begins about 5 miles north of Brian Head at the North View parking area. You can also ski on the snow-packed Highway 143, but you'll have to put up with snowmobiles. Winter is a particularly nice time to see Cedar Breaks because of the variation in color the snow adds to the red rock of the amphitheater.

If you want to stay in the Cedar Breaks area, consider B&Bs in Cedar City or Parowan. Or accommodations in **Duck Creek Village**, 30 miles east of Cedar City on Highway 14. The village sits on the perimeter of a large meadow at an elevation of 8,400 feet. In the winter this location becomes a snowy haven for snowmobilers. More and more cross-country skiers are, however, waking up to the Nordic possibilities. In the summer there are scores of great hiking

Bryce Canyon National Park: In More Detail

Bryce Canyon is the "fairy princess" of Utah's National Parks—you'll love the densely placed, delicate pink spires and turrets. For more information, contact the Bryce Canyon National Park Service at (435) 834-5322 or nps.gov/brca/planyourvisit/index.htm.

The early Anglo settler's names for the rocks remain—Queen's Garden, Grand Staircase, and Fairy Castle, to name a few. Earlier Paiute Indian residents saw the rocks in a more surreal light. They named it Land of the Legend People. They believed the chimney shaped rocks were evil folks who had been turned to stone, in the midst of saying bad things. If you're inside the canyon at dusk, look up at the monolith "faces." You'll know what those Paiutes had in mind. The park takes its name from one of the first Mormon Pioneers who tried to run cattle in the area. Ebenezer Bryce will forever be remembered by his statement of exasperation over the myriad of hiding places in the canyon. He said, "It's a hell of a place to lose a cow!"

The top of the plateau remains intact, and is a delight to folks who come looking for the rock expanses and sunset colors—for which Bryce is famous. The flat top supports a vast evergreen forest and many kinds of wildlife. Wildflowers bloom throughout summer, spring, and fall. Autumn is a season to visit. The aspens turn bright yellow against the green pines. One note of warning: The ground squirrels in the area have become so tame that they harbor no fear of humans. Don't feed them since they may carry diseases.

Fairlyland Point is located just inside the park boundary, and you'll see its turn-off sign before you reach the pay station. You're overlooking Fairyland Canyon here, a petite, self-contained bowl well worth the mile drive off the main road. Immediately after passing the pay station, you'll find the Visitor Center on your left. This is a good place for all sorts of information, including weather, hikes, wildflowers, ranger talks, and orientation. If you would like to take a guided walk with a ranger, ask for the schedule. You will also find restrooms here.

Next up are *Sunrise* and *Sunset Points*, with their exponentially expanded views. You're overlooking the *Bryce Amphitheater* from both of these pullouts, and it seems as if you

and mountain biking trails from which to choose. Check duckcreekvillage.com for further information.

On the northeast side of the *Markagunt Plateau* on Highway 89, the town of *Panguitch* (Indian word for "big fish") has a main street that's retained a lot of its early-twentieth-century charm.

If you're going to eat anywhere in Panguitch, make it *Cowboy's Smokehouse Cafe* (95 N. Main St.; 435-676-8030). When you're walking on Main Street, your nose will probably lead you here. The Cowboy's Smokehouse uses the old cowboy methods, smoking meats over pecan, oak, hickory, and can see most of the world in the distance. Closer up, just below the concrete, find the famous exposed-root pine trees, which continue in a most steadfast way to survive, even though their underpinnings are continually being washed downward. Notice the birds that enjoy showing off their skills here, swooping through the canyon and making sudden, picture-perfect stops on top of the pinnacles.

Inspiration Point is a favorite viewpoint because of its vista of Silent City. If you've seen a science fiction movie that portrays an abandoned metropolis, think about the Silent City. Narrow ridges topped by thousands of delicate spindles lie packed together, resembling the most ethereal, golden-pink interpretation of urbanity. It's made absolutely eerie by its lack of emanating sound—it is well worth the short climb down a trail to get a better look.

Following a spur road from Inspiration Point, you'll reach **Paria Viewpoint**. Look down hundreds of feet—and beyond—witnessing the workings of the Paria River. The cliffs that span out from this point are "failing," in geographical terms. Their broken spines have quit trying to shake off the prevailing erosional forces and are quietly, magnificently, being returned to the canyon floor. Luckily, this process takes thousands of years. Nearby is **Bryce Point**, also named after Ebenezer Bryce. Bryce built a road from his canyon-floor ranch to the bottom of these cliffs for the purpose of transporting wood. Folks took to calling the area "Bryce's Canyon," and the name stuck.

Fairview Viewpoint is aptly named. Natural Bridge, Agua Canyon, Ponderosa Canyon, and Yovimpa Point follow, in full splendor.

And then the last stop, **Rainbow Point**. Here is a world-class view—and also a famous pine tree. It is a bristlecone—when you look at this old, gnarled thing, you may wonder why it's noteworthy. This tree and its relatives are among the longest living things on the planet. This particular specimen is about 1,800 years old. It has survived by being tough and frugal with its resources. During drought years, bristlecone pines will actually kill off parts of the tree to save itself. During years of heavy rainfall, they soak up moisture and hold it. The needles on these trees remain for decades.

mesquite. The result is deeply flavorful barbecue ribs, chicken, turkey, and brisket—always augmented by a side order of spicy pinto or baked beans and wonderful potato salad. Breakfasts are traditional country fare. This is no place for the squeamish. With its mounted game heads, the Cowboy's Smokehouse is a veritable museum of natural history. Moose, elk, bear, reindeer, caribou, and even wild boar eye you as the paper towels (napkins don't work well here) pile up on your table. Hours are 7 a.m. to 10 p.m.

Nearby, up Clear Creek Canyon, is **Panguitch Lake**, which sits at an elevation of 8,400 feet. The lake has almost ten miles of shoreline and bounteous fishing year-round. Rent a boat and relax in the heart of the **Dixie National Forest**, or try to catch some of the biggest rainbow trout in Utah. Winter offers plenty of scenic cross-country skiing, as well as ice fishing.

By the look of the rock formations along the west end of Highway 12, you may wonder if you've arrived at Bryce Canyon National Park. Well, you haven't. But who cares? This is Red Canyon and, with far fewer visitors and no theme-park atmosphere, it's a better place than Bryce Canyon to go exploring anyway. Red Canyon's vermilion-colored hoodoos (the name of the rock spires) are part of the same Claron Formation jutting out of the ground in Bryce Canyon. Take the time here to do some hiking, mountain biking, or cross-country skiing. Leave Bryce for the drive-through. Stop in at the Red Canyon Visitor Center on Highway 12, and learn all your options for hiking in the canyon. But note that the visitor center closes from Labor Day to Memorial Day. In that case stop at the Red Canyon Trailhead Kiosk as you enter the border of the National Forest. From the kiosk you can access five trails. Look for the Losee Canyon Trail, a rugged 3-mile trail through what's known in the area as "the crown jewels." Another option is the Tunnel Trail, beginning just west of the two tunnels on Highway 12. The trail ascends 300 feet along a ridge, providing a great view of the canyon in a less than 2-mile round-trip hike. If you're interested in horseback riding, mountain biking, or cross-country skiing in Red Canyon, ask at **Ruby's Inn** (435-834-5341 or 866-782-0002) at the entrance to Bryce Canyon National Park about rentals, guided trips, and shuttles.

Turnoffs are spectacular, but to get the feel of Bryce, take a hike down into the canyon and surround yourself with rock formations. There are about twenty-three self-guided walking trails. Bring snacks and water along in a day pack, and take it easy. Bryce's elevation is about 8,000 feet, and the thin air can leave you breathless. One more word of caution: the trails are carved from the surrounding rock, and they are often sprinkled by tiny stones that can act as ball bearings for human feet. The drop-offs from many of the trails are sheer cliffs, so be careful.

If you don't have all day, two good hikes to choose are **Navajo Loop** and **Queen's Garden Trail**. Navajo Loop travels 1½ miles past some of Bryce's more famous landmarks. You've probably seen pictures of Thor's Hammer (next to Delicate Arch in Arches National Park, perhaps the most photographed piece of stone in Utah), and if so, you'll recognize it on this trail. Look for The Pope, Two Bridges, and the wedded pine trees. The trail takes you up a steep set of switchbacks. A short side trail leads to a view of Silent City, which is described above.

Queen's Garden Trail is 1½ miles or so down and back up the canyon, courtesy of a self-guided, signpost-marked tour. This trail begins at Sunrise

Point and ends at Queen's garden, named after the big stone face of Queen Victoria that peers from on high. There are rest benches here, which you may want to use before you turn around and head back out and up this non-loop trail.

If you do have all day and you are feeling adventurous, you might want to try the ***Rim Trail***, which travels 11 miles (yes, 11, but the trail is fairly level and this hike is rated easy-to-moderate) from Fairyland Point to Bryce Point. Take a lot of food and water and prepare for much picture taking on this most-scenic hike. If you get tired along the way, you can always veer off at any of the car park view points, and figure out a way to get back to your own automobile.

Another suggestion is tackling a section of the ***Under-the-Rim Trail***, which travels the entire length of the canyon for 22½ miles. Consider coming back for another visit and backpacking the entire rim trail, which takes two to three days to complete and requires a heavy backpack and a lot of steep up-and-downs. Information on permits, water, and campsites is found at the visitor center.

A good rule of thumb is to hike in the park early in the morning. One reason is that Bryce is a south-facing canyon and the morning light is spectacular. If you get to Sunrise Point at sunrise, clouds permitting, you'll have an unforgettable experience. Bryce's high elevation makes for snowy, cold winters—and few visitors. A workable plan is to get up early, hike a few miles, then have breakfast at beautiful Bryce Canyon Lodge, which is located inside the park, and then take the loop drive—stop and look often.

Although officially part of Bryce Canyon National Park, ***Mossy Cave*** is well outside the park's borders, leaving it mostly free of people. The ⁴⁄₁₀-mile

Utah Folk Live Longer . . . and Love Children

Not only is Utah a unique, gorgeous state, it's also a healthy place to live! Apparently, all that fresh mountain air, desert wind, great skiing, and clean living are paying off.

The population of Utah is younger (lots of children), lives longer, and has more persons per household than the rest of the nation. With the highest birth rate and the second lowest death rate in the nation, Utah is a state with big families and young children.

While traveling with children, this family-oriented culture gives unique advantages. It doesn't take long to find a lovely park, an ice-cream stand, or a playground in any Utah city or town. You're also likely to find a child-friendly environment just about everywhere.

Pictographs and Petroglyphs

Rock art is haunting evidence of a people and a way of life now past. Rock art is common throughout most of Southern and Eastern Utah. Pictographs were painted with blood, ground minerals, ground or crushed plant materials, ash, or charcoal. Depending on what the artist was trying to say, the word was drawn or carved. Such art spoke of life as it was and of changes that occurred.

Let the rock art wash over you in some grand way—take it in with long, thirsty glances. Absorb each piece individually, dissecting each image. It's an outdoor Louvre without crowds.

Perhaps you'll see a mountain lion and a bighorn, or a man with a spear. Another panel might show a man with large feet, possibly suggesting that he has walked a long way. Everything is sacred and each image and group of images has a meaning. These were, you soon discover, an intelligent people.

Most extant rock art is in areas protected from the wind and harsher buffets of the elements. Several good places to start are Dry Fork Canyon on the McConkie Ranch, near Vernal, Barrier Canyon, Canyonlands National Park, Nine-Mile Canyon, and San Rafael Swell, among several dozen other places (including most of the national parks).

walk is full of the red rock that makes the park famous, and it terminates in a waterfall and a cool damp cave hung with moss. Travel east on Highway 12 past the turnoff for Bryce Canyon and Ruby's Inn and continue into Water Canyon. Just inside, the trailhead is marked by a small parking lot.

There are many amazing views in Utah, but the one from Powell Point may just be one of the most fantastic, and one for which you'll need to labor. *Powell Point* sits at the edge of the highest plateau in North America, the *Table Cliff* (an extension of the Aquarius Plateau). Standing at an elevation of 10,188 feet and with a drop-off of 2,000 feet, you can see more than 100 miles across most of Southern Utah and Northern Arizona. Below are more of the *Claron Formation hoodoos* found also at Bryce and Red Canyons. There are certain variables you need to pay attention to if you plan on going to Powell Point. First, forget it if there's a threat of a thunderstorm. Lightning-scarred bristlecone pines here are sufficient warning of the dangers of getting struck. Second, be prepared to do some hiking or mountain biking. There's no promenade to the lookout. Getting there is a little difficult and virtually impossible when there's snow on the ground or when it's raining. From Highway 12, drive north on Highway 22 for about 11 miles. Follow the signs east to Pine Lake Table Cliff Plateau. At the lake junction, stay left on the northernmost road that leads to Powell Point. The dirt road is negotiable for most cars with good clearance until you reach the final turnoff for Powell Point, about 5 miles from the overlook. High-clearance 4WD vehicles with experienced off-road drivers at the helm should be able to get to within a mile. Contact the Escalante Interagency Office at (435) 355-7382 or 755 W. Main St., P.O. Box 225, Escalante 84726 if you're unsure about road conditions.

If you want to stay in the area of Bryce National Park, there aren't many good alternatives to the run-of-the-mill motel accommodations. But there are a couple places a few miles below the park in a little rancher town called **Tropic**. In a town the size of Tropic (about 200), you wouldn't expect to find more than one bed-and-breakfast. But the folks in town know what kind of advantage they have being situated under Bryce Canyon's rim in the heart of Southern Utah.

Kodachrome Basin State Park became a state park in 1963. The park got its name from the film that captures as many colors as the strange-colored rock formations throughout the park. Nowhere else in the world will you find these rock formations, called chimneys. This may be a good thing, at least for the sake of decency. Depending on the kind of mind's eye you have, you might see a resemblance between the chimneys and a certain part of the male anatomy. You would almost expect the park to draw multitudes of pagan worshipers, especially to "Big Stoney," the most explicit of the park's chimneys, proudly standing at attention above the campground.

The chimneys, about sixty-seven of them in the park and surrounding areas, are the remnants of dried-up geysers. Geologists surmise that the area's geological activity was, at one time, quite similar to that of Yellowstone today.

Hey Daddy, Are Those Dino Tracks?

While hiking in Southern Utah with the kids, don't be surprised if your four-year-old shouts, "Hey Daddy, are those dino tracks?" There are horse and cow tracks all over the place, but your kid may not be that far off.

In the last few years, a number of dinosaur track sites in the **Grand Staircase–Escalante National Monument** area have been documented.

Millions of years ago, Southern Utah was literally covered with dinosaur tracks. Such creatures of old left their famous footsteps in sediments that have been preserved for us today. The wet sands during the Jurassic period made such footprint preservation possible.

In the Escalante Monument area, for example, there is one site where more than thirty big meat-eating types have graciously left more than 200 footprints for scientists to study. Maybe your kid will actually discover the next set of dinosaur tracks.

climatefastfacts

Southwestern Utah's climate

winter, 29 to 55 degrees

summer 68 to 102 degrees

about 10 inches of precipitation

The geysers at Kodachrome were filled in with sediment and various binding minerals. In time, surrounding sandstone eroded away, leaving the filled-in springs standing at heights now ranging from 6½ to 170 feet. There are several short hikes through the park, the most informative certainly being the Nature Trail—a short walk meant to be done with the accompaniment of an interpretive guide you pick up at the trailhead.

If you want more information or would like to reserve a campsite, call (435) 679-8562. The park has an attractive campground and would probably be a better choice than trying to camp in or around Bryce. To get to Kodachrome follow the signs along Highway 12, and head southeast once you enter Cannonville. The park is about 7 miles from the highway along paved roads.

If you have the time and feel like seeing more of the area, continue down the road about 10 miles past Kodachrome to **Grosvenor Arch**, another site visited and named by the National Geographic Society, this time in honor of the expedition's president. The arch is unusual because it is actually a double arch, the larger of the two spanning about 99 feet. The drive, on a dirt road that's manageable by two-wheel-drive cars in good weather, takes you through Cottonwood Canyon and the upper reaches of Cottonwood Creek, a tributary of the Paria River. The road lets out on Highway 89, about 35 miles east of Kanab. The land is rugged and beautiful and, for all intents and purposes, still wilderness. The views take in, among other things, Bryce Canyon and the upper sections of Zion National Park.

Places to Stay in Southwestern Utah

CEDAR CITY

Abbey Inn
940 W. 200 North
(435) 586-9966
Moderate

Bard's Inn Bed and Breakfast
150 S. 100 West
(435) 586-6612
Moderately expensive

Big Yellow Inn Bed and Breakfast
234 S. 300 West
(435) 586-0960
Pretty expensive

Garden Cottage Bed and Breakfast
16 N. 200 West
(435) 586-4919
Moderately expensive

TOP ANNUAL EVENTS IN UTAH

JUNE–OCTOBER

Utah Shakespearean Festival
Cedar City
(435) 586-7878

AUGUST

Garfield County Fair
Panguitch
(800) 444-6689

Washington County Fair
Hurricane
(435) 652-5899

Iron County Fair
Parowan
(435) 477-8380

SEPTEMBER
R'Oktoberfest
Brian Head
(435) 677-2035

DECEMBER
Audubon Christmas Bird Count
Various locations

GLENDALE

Historic Smith Hotel Bed and Breakfast
295 N. Main St.
(435) 648-2156
Moderate

HURRICANE

Travelodge
280 W. State St.
(435) 635-4647
Moderate

KANAB

Holiday Inn Express
217 S. 100 East
(435) 644-3100
Moderate

Kanab Mission Inn
386 E. 300 South
(435) 644-5373
Inexpensive

Parry Lodge
89 E. Center St.
(435) 644-2601
Moderate

Quail Park Lodge
125 N. 300 West
(435) 215-1447
Inexpensive

MT. CARMEL

Thunderbird Best Western
Junction of Hwys 9 and 89
P.O. Box 5536
(435) 648-2203
Moderately expensive

SPRINGDALE

Harvest House Bed and Breakfast
29 Canyon View Dr.
(435) 772-3880 or
(800) 719-7501
harvesthouse.net
Moderately expensive

Under the Eaves
980 Zion Park Blvd.
(435) 772-3457
otooles.com
Moderately expensive

ST. GEORGE

Best Western Travel Inn
316 E. St. George Blvd.
(435) 673-3541
Moderate

Seven Wives Inn
217 N. 100 West
(435) 628-3737 or
(800) 600-3737
sevenwivesinn.com
Pretty expensive

Places to Eat in Southwestern Utah

CEDAR CITY

Brad's Food Hut
546 N. Main St.
(435) 586-6358
Inexpensive

FOR MORE INFORMATION ABOUT SOUTHWESTERN UTAH

TRAVEL COUNCILS

Canyonlands Travel Region
Grand County Travel Council
P.O. Box 550
40 N. 100 East
Moab 84532
(435) 259-1370 or
(800) 635-6622
Fax (435) 259-2425

Road Conditions
(800) 492-2400

Rusty's Ranch House
2275 E. Hwy 14
(435) 586-3839
Moderate

The Pastry Pub
86 W. Center St.
(435) 867-1400
Inexpensive

The Pizza Factory
131 S. Main St.
(435) 586-3900
Inexpensive

KANAB

Escobar's Mexican Restaurant
373 E. 300 South
(435) 644-3739
Inexpensive

Nedra's Too
310 S. 100 East
(435) 644-2030
Inexpensive

Rocking V Cafe
97 W. Center St.
(435) 644-8001
Moderately expensive

PANGUITCH

Cowboy's Smokehouse Cafe
95 N. Main St.
(435) 676-8030
Moderate

SPRINGDALE

Bit & Spur Saloon
1212 Zion Park Blvd.
(435) 772-3498
Moderately expensive

Spotted Dog Cafe
428 Zion Park Blvd.
(435) 772-0700
Moderately expensive

Zion Lodge Red Rock Grill
Zion National Park
(435) 772-7760
Moderately expensive

ST. GEORGE

China Palace
195 S. Bluff St.
(435) 673-0068
Inexpensive

The Palms at the Holiday Inn
850 S. Bluff St.
(435) 628-4235
Moderately expensive

Southeastern Utah

Water, wind, and ice laid down layers of sediment over a period ending fifty million years ago, when powerful forces within the earth created an upheaval. While the earth's crust was being pushed up, the Colorado and Green Rivers started to flow, taking sediment on their downward, ever-eroding, ever-sculpting course. Recently (geologically speaking), molten material swelled up through the sedimentary rock, soaring to heights of 9,000 to 12,000 feet and then cooling. These magma protrusions—referred to as the La Sal, Henry, Abajo, and Navajo Mountains—now cap the landscape, offering an alpine climate, flora, and fauna that are strikingly different from the hot sandstone desert below.

Embrace the isolation as you wander among the canyons, mountains, buttes, and bluffs of the Colorado Plateau, where it seems every route, no matter how short, is fraught with adventure and mind-bending scenery. There are few places left in the lower forty-eight states that are as solitary. There are only a handful of towns, few with a population over 5,000. When you visit Southeastern Utah, you may wonder how an Anglo population of any size managed to settle this region. It is beautiful but, at the same time, inhospitable.

SOUTHEASTERN UTAH

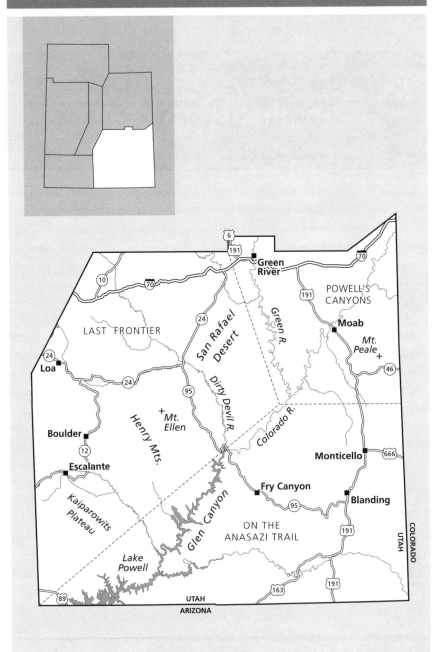

POWELL'S
CANYONS

Green
River

LAST FRONTIER

San Rafael
Desert

Green R.

Moab

Mt.
Peale
+

Loa

Dirty Devil R.

Mt.
Ellen
+

Henry Mts.

Colorado R.

Boulder

Escalante

Monticello

Fry Canyon

Blanding

Kaiparowits
Plateau

Glen Canyon

ON THE
ANASAZI TRAIL

Lake
Powell

UTAH
COLORADO

UTAH
ARIZONA

N

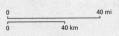

0   40 mi

0   40 km

This region has supported humans for thousands of years. Nomadic hunters and gatherers—sometimes referred to as the Archaic Culture—wandered these splendid canyons for thousands of years. Around AD 750 the Ancestral Puebloans (somes referred to as the Ancient Ones or Anaszi), moved into the southern portion of the region, while the Fremonts settled to the north. Both cultures left their marks in the form of figures etched (petroglyphs) or painted (pictographs) on canyon walls.

Beginning around 1300, groups of nomadic Utes and Paiutes passed through the region. Navajos, members of the Athapascan linguistic family in western Canada, made their way to the Southwest sometime around 1500. After a failed American attempt at "civilizing" the Navajos at a fort in New Mexico, the nation received its own reservation, which now spans the four-corner states. With more than 172,000 members, the Navajos count themselves as the largest tribe in America.

Last Frontier

The town of *Escalante* and the river running south of it are named for Father Escalante, leader of the first European expedition to explore the Colorado Plateau. But this factual tidbit hardly helps in making sense of this general area, referred to as Escalante. It is some of the most awesome scenery that Utah has to offer and some of its most untouched, inaccessibility being the reason. If you want to venture into the canyons of the Escalante River and its tributaries, it takes some perseverance, something the *San Juan Mission* would have wholeheartedly confirmed.

AUTHOR'S FAVORITES IN SOUTHEASTERN UTAH

Canyonlands National Park, southwest of Moab	Newspaper Rock, northwest of Monticello
Arches, Moab	Dead Horse Point, southwest of Moab
Goblin Valley State Park, south of Green River	Hovenweep National Monument, southeast of Blanding
Barrier Canyon, Canyonlands National Park	Capitol Reef National Park, northeast of Torrey
Burr Trail, Lake Powell	
Downtown Moab, Moab	

Hole-in-the-Rock Trail is the result of the faith and audacity that possessed the San Juan Mission, the Mormon pioneering party that blazed this tortuous trail to the southeast corner of Utah. There they hoped to establish peaceful contact with the Navajo Indians and begin a settlement. Two hundred people, eighty-three wagons, 350 horses, and 1,000 head of cattle took six months to make their way 290 miles across the sun-baked landscape. The few miles through and beyond Hole-in-the-Rock, a narrow V-slot in one of the Colorado River cliffs, were the most daunting. A 45-foot drop was beyond the slot, as was nearly a mile of steep slickrock. Three crews went to work, blasting and carving a wagon road down the incline and then back up the cliffs on the other side of the river. After a six-week delay, the party continued, slowly making its way down the precipitous trail to the Colorado River, where it was ferried across. Every person, animal, and wagon made it uninjured.

Today you can follow the same trail the San Juan Mission took back in 1879, but in the luxury of your car. The unpaved road isn't much more forgiving than it was more than a hundred years ago. The road stretches 60 miles from the town of Escalante to Hole-in-the-Rock, perched above what are now the dammed waters of the Colorado—Lake Powell. Most of the road is manageable for low-clearance cars, except for the last 10 miles, which should be negotiated by high-clearance, 4WD vehicles with experienced backroads drivers at the wheel. (Remember: Just because you have a 4WD doesn't mean you have all that it takes to negotiate these tricky roads. Experience at backcountry driving is necessary and can save you a hefty tow fee.) Before you attempt to drive down Hole-in-the-Rock, check road conditions at the Interagency Visitor Center (435) 335-7382 in Escalante at 755 West Main. You can also discuss your hiking and backpacking options here with the knowledgeable staff.

You can access several great hikes into the canyons of the Escalante from Hole-in-the-Rock Trail, as well as see some interesting sights along the way, such as Devil's Garden, a mélange of cream-and-red rock spires, thrusting out of the landscape and tilting in all sorts of chaotic directions. There are no trails but plenty of slickrock and washes. So go ahead and just wander, but look out for cow patties. The turnoff to the garden is 16½ miles from Highway 12 in Escalante and a half mile down the hill.

Farther down the road, 14³⁄₁₀ miles from Devil's Garden, are Peek-a-boo and Spooky, two narrow slot canyons that make for thrilling exploration. Look for a turnoff on your left, posted as Dry Fork Coyote. Stay to the left at the fork and go ¼ mile to the road's end, where you'll see a parking area at the canyon rim. Descend by way of the draw into Dry Fork Coyote Gulch. Once you are down in the gulch, look downstream for Peek-a-boo's mouth, entering from the north.

Evidence of the "Ancient Ones"

The Colorado Plateau is rich in Native American history. Thousands of years before white men came to red-rock country, ancient peoples roamed the plateau region.

We don't know as much as we'd like about these early civilizations, but we do have archaeological evidence of their culture. Several draw a great deal of attention, including a group of Indians known as The People.

In addition to artifacts and dwellings, we have wonderful reminders in the form of pictographs and petroglyphs. The Fremont and Ancestral Puebloans evolved from hunter-gatherer clans into farming and herding civilizations, leaving their expressive artwork on canyon walls.

Many of these ancient peoples lived in the canyons and later in cliff dwellings to protect themselves from roaming bands of tribes. Moqui houses, or stone huts, can still be seen from the road near Escalante. The remains of these cultures are a silent, reverent reminder of those who came before us. Enjoy with your eyes, but leave remains and rock art where you've found them.

Downstream from Peek-a-boo is Spooky, also entering from the north. Follow these slot canyons in as far as you like, but have plenty of water with you. It is not a good idea to be in them if thundershowers are threatening. (Check weather conditions at the Interagency Visitor Center before you head out.)

Forty-two miles down Hole-in-the-Rock is Dance Hall Rock, near where the San Juan Mission was held up for three months, waiting to proceed. This solid-stone, natural amphitheater was the site for morale-boosting fiddle dances during the first trek. People from the area have kept the tradition alive.

There are two ways of traveling between Escalante and Boulder; both routes are equally dramatic. One is to continue along Highway 12 through the Escalante River Drainage. Scenic byways in Utah don't get more intensely beautiful than this section of Highway 12. Inexhaustible views of Escalante's canyon maze line the road.

An excellent opportunity for a day hike awaits along Highway 12 at **Calf Creek Recreation Area**. The hike to **Lower Calf Creek Falls** is a trip through a fertile and diverse ecosystem, a spectrum of colors (from Navajo red to chalk white), and daunting geological formations. The hike is like walking the lengths of a great cathedral, its altar being the 126-foot-high waterfall, dropping into a limpid pool at trail's end. It's a popular hike, but that shouldn't distract you from the beauty of this place. Pick up an interpretive brochure at the trailhead. It points out twenty-four different natural and man-made features in the canyon, including an Indian granary and some 1,000-year-old

Fremont petroglyphs. The hike is 5½ miles round-trip, with very little change in elevation.

From Calf Creek Campground, Highway 12 begins its ascent along one of the most unbelievable stretches of road ever built. The road floats between drop-offs of 1,000 feet or more. The Civilian Conservation Corps completed this "Million Dollar Road" in 1940, allowing Boulder to receive year-round mail service for the first time. In fact, Boulder was the last town in the lower forty-eight states to receive its mail and supplies by mules and packhorses, which came from Escalante via Hell's Backbone Road.

While driving along Hell's Backbone Road, remember that milk and cream that mules used to carry across this road often turned to butter. This 38-mile gravel and dirt road, your other option for driving between Boulder and Escalante, winds and cuts through alpine forests of aspens and ponderosa pines, reaching an elevation of 9,200 feet. You'll cross a bridge fortifying the route along Hell's Backbone, the name for the ridge emerging out of Box Death Hollow. The bridge was also built by the Civilian Conservation Corps in 1935, allowing vehicles to enter Boulder for the first time. Before the bridge's construction, mule teams inched their way between Hell's Backbone's hair-raising drop-offs. The name for the ridge hits home when you look down into Box Death Hollow. The road is generally fine for two-wheel-drives when it's dry, usually from late May until the first snow falls in autumn. Check with the Interagency Visitor Center in Escalante before you attempt it.

At the southern foot of Boulder Mountain and on the northern rim of Escalante's canyons, the tiny town of **Boulder** is socked in by its surrounding landscape. Boulder was "settled" in 1889 by Amasa and Roseanna Lyman, who had to cut down trees and remove huge boulders in blazing a trail to this isolated territory. With a population of 150 in such a remote location, Boulder, Utah, can claim a ruggedness that Boulder, Colorado, forfeited long ago.

Besides its proximity to so much natural beauty, Boulder really has nothing going for it that would make people think of it as a destination, which is perfectly fine with its inhabitants. But the reason most people stop in Boulder on their way elsewhere is the **Anasazi State Park** (460 N. Hwy 12; 435-335-7308). University of Utah's excavation of the site and its eighty-seven rooms uncovered so many artifacts that a museum had to be built to exhibit them all. The self-guided tour takes you through the ruins and introduces a variety of Ancestral Puebloans building styles. A replica of an Ancestral Puebloan dwelling gives you an idea of what the ruins may have looked like in their original state. Hours are 9 a.m. to 5 p.m., daily.

The designer and builder of the **Boulder Mountain Lodge** had a fairly good idea about how to achieve a symbiotic relationship between architecture and the environment. The four sandstone-colored structures that make up Boulder Mountain Lodge meld with the landscape and mirror early Mormon architecture, which seems to have had the greatest of influences on the designs. In sync with the lodge's rural location, the builder chemically dyed the sheet-metal roofs to give them a rusted, sun-baked appearance. If Boulder Mountain Lodge seems a little familiar, then you won't be surprised to know that the same person designed and built the Bit & Spur Saloon in Springdale and the Santa Fe Restaurant in Salt Lake City.

Two of the lodge's buildings sit on the edge of wetlands, which have been designated a bird refuge. An ornithologist who stayed at the lodge counted eighty-three species. From May through Dec 1, *Hell's Backbone Grill*, on the grounds, serves a good breakfast (7 to 11 a.m.), lunch (11 a.m. to 2 p.m.), and dinner (5 to 9 p.m.). To make reservations call (435) 335-7460.

There aren't many roads left in the United States that have signs posted at the beginning of them that say "Next Service 67 miles." The *Burr Trail*, connecting Boulder and Bullfrog Marina on Lake Powell, can claim such a sign and a lot of mind-bending beauty to go along with it. In Boulder the Burr Trail sets out among the sandstone sand dunes, petrified into round domes and hills, then dips into *Long Canyon*, where enormous embedded arches and alcoves have eroded from the Wingate sandstone walls. The road stretches through the length of the gulch and reveals its spectrum of colors, ranging from red to white to black desert varnish. (The 7 paved miles through Long Canyon make for an excellent bike ride.) The road continues past the Circle Cliffs and into *Capitol Reef National Park*, where the pavement ends and dirt road begins.

The Burr Trail is your backdoor access to the park, providing the best opportunities for exploring the area undisturbed. Beginning a few miles east of the park boundary, Lower Muley Twist Canyon trail follows sandy washes that weave through the Waterpocket Fold, past eerie skull-like sculptures formed

The 4WD Mystique

It's traditional to drive a 4WD vehicle in the rugged desert country—especially around the Arches–Canyonlands area. In fact, Moab is the home of the *Utah Jeep Safari*, an event not to be missed if you're in the area around Easter.

Off-road is the best way to see country you won't see otherwise. There are hundreds and hundreds of miles of dirt roads for everyone to play on—from the rank amateur to the hard-core rock banger. And if you don't have an off-road vehicle, don't worry. There are several rental agencies throughout the area where you can select the 4WD of your choice.

out of the cliffs, and over plenty of slickrock. An old rancher once remarked that this canyon was so narrow and sinuous that it would twist a mule to get through it. After 4 miles down the stream bed, you have the options of turning back, continuing to Halls Creek (8 miles farther on), or veering east to the Post Trailhead, near the junction of the Burr Trail and Notom Road. The Post is 2⅓ difficult miles from Lower Muley Twist Trailhead. This strenuous 9-mile loop is definitely not for the unfit. Remember to wear a hat and bring plenty of water.

As most scenic byways in Utah go, the Burr Trail is not without its section of mad switchbacks clinging to an escarpment. In this case the escarpment belongs to the **Waterpocket Fold**, Capitol Reef's most treasured feature. The Waterpocket Fold is perhaps America's finest example of a monocline, a geological term referring to a buckling in the earth's crust. John Wesley Powell named this fold in the strata as such because it contains scores of shallow depressions in the rock surface, holding rainwater over long periods of time. Although only a few miles wide, this fortified wall of rock runs 100 miles north and south. All along it are dizzying displays of rock jutting out at crazy angles. In addition, stripes of yellow, orange, red, and lavender come together in a remarkable band of colors.

Either way you turn at the junction of Burr Trail and Notom Road (36 miles from Boulder) is a good choice. Both roads run parallel to the fold and allow you to see it in all its crazy glory. Turn right (south) to continue on the Burr Trail, which drifts to the southeast into BLM land and then into **Glen Canyon National Recreation Area**. You can do a short hike into one of the Fold's twisting canyons, called Surprise Canyon. Its trailhead begins a few miles south

Capitol Reef National Park: In More Detail

How was this park named? *Capitol* comes from huge rocks shaped like the capitol building in Washington, D.C. *Reef* comes from early Anglo explorers who had seafaring backgrounds—reef provided an impenetrable barrier to travel, just as a coral reef in the ocean. The most-visited sections of the park extend from the visitor center. Directions to all Capitol Reef hikes and drives can be found here, as well as books, maps, exhibits, and a short film. There are bathrooms, drinking water, and a campground by the Fremont River. Campsites can be reserved from Mar 1 to Oct 31. Visit recreation.gov to make a reservation. Reservations are accepted 6 months in advance. From Nov 1 to Feb 28, all campsites are first come, first served. In the fall, visitors are invited to pick fruit for their own use, for a small fee. A brochure in the visitor center will give you more information about this attraction.

of the junction. The Burr Trail finally connects with Highway 276 just north of Bullfrog, 28 desert miles from the Notom Road junction.

Capitol Reef is a hidden prize—it's literally a wrinkle in the earth—filled with canyons and cliffs, accented by bridges and domes. The rock formation is called **Waterpocket Fold**, a big ridge (100 miles long) that was thrust higher than its surroundings seventy million years ago. The opposite side has gradual decline. The term comes from the erosion-formed depressions in the fold, which are now the natural holding tanks for water after a storm.

The area called **Fruita** is a favorite haunt. The Freemont River runs through an oasis in the red-rock desert. A hundred years ago settlers established a township, planting hundreds of fruit trees. The original orchards are still maintained. One roadside exhibit features an old blacksmith shop. Press a button and the blacksmith will tell you his story. The same device is used at the tiny, one-room, log schoolhouse, where Mrs. Torgerson tells us her true-life teaching experiences. The school was built in the 1890s and used until the 1940s. While you're here, think how the world has changed—not that long ago children sat in this school and learned to read! You might recognize the beautifully restored hay barn. Its photograph graces some of the park publications. Fruita has a large grassy area that is perfect for a picnic, a game of Frisbee, or an afternoon nap. You will probably notice the abundance of deer in the area, many of which are extremely tame.

When your family is ready for a hike, grab a **Hickman Trail** pamphlet at the visitor center, so you will be able to interpret each of the eighteen markers along the way. This relatively easy 2-mile round-trip hike is probably the most popular in the park, and deservedly so. It features 125-foot **Hickman Bridge**, a spectacular stone arch. Try to be the first one to spot Hickman, as it is camouflaged quite cleverly. On the way you will pass the foundation of an ancient pit house and granary probably built by the Freemont Indians. There are all sorts of rock hiding places along the trail, including small fins and cliffside depressions. Once you reach the bridge, continue on the path. You will loop back around to the original path, but first treat yourself to a long look at Fruita.

Grand Wash is another great hike. This ancient riverbed makes for an easy stroll through a magnificent rock canyon. Caution: if it looks like rain you will want to make other plans. This is not a good place to be during a flash flood. A one-way trip through Grand Wash is 2.4 miles. You can start in two places—a marked pull off a few miles south of the visitor center or a marked side road on the Scenic Drive. Whichever way you begin you might want to arrange for a car to pick you up at the other end. You'll squeeze through narrow cliff passages. See the arches and the smooth river stones of every possible color and feel the power of the canyon walls surrounding you.

Take the turnoff to **Panorama Point**. Just before dusk, try heading to **Sunset Point Trail,** which is an excellent place to be during a sunset. You might want to take refreshments and make a dinner party out of your visit. From Panorama Point, take the short walk to **Gooseneck Point**. Stop and gaze down in wonder at the path of Sulphur Creek. Then continue for a half mile to Sunset Point, looking east with the sun at your back. You'll get a good view of the Waterpocket Fold and the pink and orange world beyond.

A scenic drive begins at the visitor center, passes through the picnic area and national park campground, and then heads into desert country. There is a free pamphlet available at the visitor center that is helpful in interpreting your surroundings. This is a narrow, twisty road at times, with plenty of pullouts and short hikes. Eight or so miles into the scenic drive, you'll see the sign for **Capitol Gorge.** Weather permitting, this turnoff onto a graded dirt road is easily managed in a passenger car. There are picnic tables and displays at the trailhead inside Capitol Gorge—this was the main road from Hanksville to Torrey for many years. Some of the trials and tribulations of maintaining the road are documented. There is an easy, 1-mile hike deeper into the narrowness of Capitol Gorge—look for the **Pioneer Register,** where pioneers signed their names on the rocks and the natural water tanks.

The **Cathedral Valley district** of the park is a half-day drive on a bumpy road. Ask for directions and road conditions at the visitor center. This road requires a high-clearance vehicle, some driving skill, and is not for everybody. The valley is beautiful—with several unmatched viewpoints—especially memorable are the Temple of the Sun and Moon monoliths. Cathedral Valley is named for its many-spired formations that resemble church architecture and also inspire spiritual thoughts.

Turn left (north) at the junction to begin your trek along Notom Road, which goes 34 miles until it ends at Highway 24, just east of Capitol Reef National Park. Several more hikes into the Waterpocket Fold can be accessed from the Notom Road, including Red Canyon Trail, which begins at the **Cedar Mesa Campground** (12 miles from Burr Trail junction and 22 miles from Highway 24). This 4-mile round-trip hike goes into an enormous box canyon sliced out of the fold.

An excellent 108-mile-loop tour of Capitol Reef National Park and its surrounding landscape is the following route: Burr Trail to Notom Road to Highway 24 to Highway 12 (or vice versa). Check road and weather conditions at Capitol Reef Visitors Center in Torrey (435) 425-3791 before you attempt the Burr Trail (which is only paved between Boulder and the boundary of Capitol Reef) or Notom Road (which isn't paved at all). If the roads are wet, even 4WDs could get stuck in the sticky surfaces.

Part of the loop includes a section that passes over **Boulder Mountain**, bulging up between Boulder and Torrey. This scenic alpine section of Highway 12 provides an excellent display of the kind of geological forces at work in the region. Boulder Mountain sits on top of the Aquarius Plateau. Reaching an altitude of 11,300 feet, it is the highest plateau in North America and an excellent place to look down onto the Colorado Plateau. Stunning views of Capitol Reef, the Waterpocket Fold, the Henry Mountains, Navajo Mountain, and the San Rafael Swell are all at hand. Hiking, cross-country skiing, and mountain-biking trails also abound on Boulder Mountain. (Highway 12 occasionally closes in the winter after heavy snowstorms.)

As "the Gateway to Capitol Reef National Park," **Torrey** attracts a fair number of tourists each summer who use the town as a base for seeing the park and all the great surrounding areas. Nearly 7,000 feet above sea level, Torrey and the Capitol Reef area maintain surprisingly comfortable temperatures in the middle of the summer, so they shouldn't be overlooked when planning a trip to Southern Utah. Enjoy the pioneer homes and a group of downright friendly people. Torrey quickly begins to grow on you, especially if you have the opportunity to stay at SkyRidge Bed and Breakfast Inn.

SkyRidge Bed and Breakfast Inn perches on top of a hill at the edge of Capitol Reef with a panoramic view. The inn has been recognized by *National Geographic Traveler* and *Sunset Magazines* as one of the best lodges or bed-and-breakfasts near Capitol Reef National Park. Breakfast is enjoyed each morning. Call (435) 425-3222 or visit skyridgeinn.com for further information. The house is located 1 mile from Torrey on Highway 24, 1012 East Highway 24.

Because so much of this region is inaccessible to two-wheel-drive vehicles, consider renting a 4WD, a bike, or an ATV. **Hondoo Rivers and Trails** (90 E. Main St.) offers wildlife expeditions, a working cowboy experience in a cattle roundup, and Indian rock art seminars with Jeep tours into remote canyons. With Hondoo you can also raft down the Green River or go on a horseback ride with the support of a chuckwagon. Call them at (435) 425-3519.

For a good meal visit the **Capitol Reef Inn and Cafe** (360 W. Main St.; 435-425-3271). Open daily from 7 a.m. to 9 p.m. The comfortable rooms come with handmade furniture and Southwestern bedspreads. Visit capitolreefinn .com for more information.

Luxury-minded people should check out the **Lodge at Red River Ranch** (435-425-3322 or 800-205-6343), a few miles west of Torrey just off Highway 24. The Western atmosphere doesn't get much more grandiose than here. This log mansion sits in the shadow of enormous sandstone cliffs on the banks of the **Fremont River**, 5 miles of which run through Red River's property. Guests are free to fly-fish in the river or just wander across the 2,000 acres that make

Erosion Is the Architect of the Colorado Plateau

The Colorado Plateau was formed by nature's splendid architect: erosion.

The breathtaking landscape of Utah's national parks and surrounding areas have been sculpted from layers of colorful limestone and sandstone.

Such rock was originally in sand dunes or silt—or mud from the floors of primeval seas. Over the years, rock has been pushed up, "uplifted." As this was occurring, wind, water, and frost etched and carved the wonderful designs we're now enjoying.

Mountains on the plateau were formed when molten lava raised the crust of the earth into domes, which have since been eroded into the rock art we see today.

This rugged landscape is in a state of constant change, even if the geologic clock does tick rather slowly.

up this working ranch. Each of the fifteen rooms comes with its own fireplace, balcony, or patio, and its themed décor that ranges from Ancestral Puebloans to African. Called "Safari," the room with the African motif has the heads of a wildebeest and an impala hanging on its walls. Downstairs in the Great Room (commons area), you'll find a cozy, rock-slate fireplace and a Navajo rug draped on one of the walls. The lodge restaurant serves breakfast from 7 a.m. to 9:30 a.m. Sack lunches are available upon request, but you must order the night before. Catered dinners are available by prearrangement. For more details, see redriverranch.com.

Cathedral Valley in the northern section of Capitol Reef National Park takes its name from the sandstone monoliths that emerge from the desert floor and soar to heights of 500 feet. But measurement means little when you stand next to one of these pinnacles set in its lunar-like surroundings. Unless you have a high-clearance 4WD, getting to Cathedral Valley can be a problem. One option is to forget the car and head out on a mountain bike, which you can rent at *Capitol Reef Resort* (2600 E. Hwy 24; 435-425-3761) in Torrey. Taking one of Hondoo's Jeep tours (see page 125) is another option. If you have a high-clearance 4WD, then take the loop tour through Cathedral Valley, starting on Highway 24 just east of the park boundary. But check road conditions at the Capitol Reef Visitors Center (435) 425-3791 before you attempt it.

There is a way of getting at least a view of Cathedral Valley in your regular passenger car: by entering from the west via Highway 72. About 7 miles north of Fremont, take a right (east) onto a dirt road marked as Elkhorn Campground. Follow the road up Thousand Lake Mountain, and stay to the left when the road forks, about 4 miles from the highway. The road goes up to Baker Ranch and drops into Capitol Reef National Park from the north, where the road is accessible by 4WD only. But you'll still get plenty of amazing views of the valley and its must-see pinnacles. The road is passable only in summer and early fall. Check at the National Forest office (435) 836-2811 at 138 South Main in Loa for road conditions.

In *Hanksville* take a look at the *Wolverton Mill*. It was built by E. T. Wolverton in the 1920s at his gold-mining claim in the Henry Mountains. The BLM moved the pieces to Hanksville and rebuilt it outside the BLM office, where it stands in all its glory today. You can take a self-guided tour inside the mill and see the ore grinder and sawmill, both hand-built by Wolverton and powered by the 20-foot waterwheel.

Formed by wind and water erosion, the provocative rock formations balanced on their natural pedestals at *Goblin Valley State Park* evoke all kinds of comparisons, from fairy-tale figures to Middle Earth. The first Anglo to discover the formations thought they looked like mushrooms, so they called it Mushroom Valley. But you be the judge of what they resemble when you wander through them. The park is in a wonderfully remote setting, making it a popular place to camp. There are plenty of facilities, including restrooms and showers. Call (800) 322-3770 to make a reservation for a campsite. Look for the sign to Goblin Valley, 21 miles north of Hanksville and 24 miles south of Green River along Highway 24. Take a left (west) onto a paved road and follow it 5 or so miles until you see the turnoff for Goblin Valley, located another 15 miles south on good gravel road.

To the west of Goblin Valley, you'll see an emergence of white sandstone running north and south and tilting at crazy angles. This is the *San Rafael Reef*, also known as the flat irons. The San Rafael Reef marks the eastern edge of the *San Rafael Swell*, one of America's least-trodden wilderness areas. The most ardent of isolation seekers will find their paradise here. Take the Goblin Valley exit on Highway 24 and continue past the turnoff for Goblin Valley. You'll head into one of the San Rafael's canyons, where the pavement ends and a good dirt road begins. This road leads through the Swell and accesses scores of hikes before it intersects with Interstate 70 at Ranch Exit 129, 19 miles west of Green River. (If you hike, please stay on trails, slickrock, or washes so as not to destroy the fragile desert vegetation.)

As you enter through San Rafael Reef you'll pass the high pinnacles of *Temple Mountain*, named for its resemblance to the Mormon temple in Manti. Miners scoured this mountain for uranium and radium. Legend has it that Madame Curie experimented with radium from these mines. You can still see several of the old mine portals and deserted sandstone dwellings along a road that forks off the main road (6⁷⁄₁₀ miles from Highway 24) and heads up the mountain. (If you go up this road, stay out of the mines, because they are radioactive and unsafe.)

At 15²⁄₁₀ miles and again at 18⁴⁄₁₀ miles you'll see a fork in the road. From either one of these forks you have the option of heading north to I–70 or continuing westward to the 29-mile **Hondoo Arch Loop**. This is a spectacular romp through some of the Swell's most colorful and outlandish topography. A mile beyond the second fork you'll come to yet another fork. This is where the loop comes full circle. The right fork drops into Reds Canyon, where white-knuckled driving again becomes a factor, and veers past Family Butte, notable for its series of pinnacles rising at the foot of it. The road then winds past Tomisch Butte, where old miners' cabins still stand, and veers past Hondoo Arch, perched on top of an enormous butte on the other side of Muddy Creek. About halfway around the loop you'll come across another fork. Keep to the north to stay on the loop or head south through a fertile valley made lush by Muddy Creek. This south-fork road ends at the now-defunct Hidden Splendor Mine, the biggest of the mines in the San Rafael Swell. From there you'll have to backtrack to the loop. At the end of the loop you can either go back to Highway 24 or head north to I–70 through Sinbad Country and past the Sagebrush Bench, where wild horses and burros are often seen roaming. It's a good idea to check road conditions before you attempt this scenic drive. Call the BLM office in Price at (435) 636-3460.

I–70 cuts through the middle of the San Rafael Swell. (See the Northeastern Utah chapter for coverage on the northern half of the Swell.) There are several great viewpoints at rest stops along this section of I–70, between the junctions of Highway 24 and Highway 10.

Powell's Canyons

Traveling through this mind-bending region of Southeastern Utah demands some understanding of the forces that formed, shaped, and carved the landscape. Named after the first madman to lead an expedition down the Green and Colorado Rivers, the **John Wesley Powell River History Museum** (435-564-3427) in the town of **Green River** offers a much-needed orientation to the geology and history of the Colorado Plateau and its rivers. Although the museum does very little in the way of introducing you to the region's first native inhabitants, it does familiarize you with the men who, instead of bypassing this seemingly impassable country, dove straight into it.

The most infamous of these adventurers was, of course, John Wesley Powell, the museum curator from Illinois who first navigated the waters all the way from Green River, Wyoming, down to the Grand Canyon. His first voyage was in 1869. The Utes and Shoshonis called him "Kapurats" (meaning "Arm Off") because Powell was missing his right forearm, the result of a musketball fired at him in the Battle of Shiloh. Even without the arm, Powell made the expedition twice, first in the spirit of discovery and second in the spirit of science.

While perusing the museum, don't miss the first map of the Colorado Plateau, done by Bernardo de Miera, topographer in the Dominguez–Escalante Expedition of 1776. Although it is the first map of the region, the Miera map is surprisingly accurate and quite a work of art to boot. The museum is appropriately located on the banks of the Green River at 900 East Main Street, Green River. Open Mon through Sat, 9 a.m. to 7 p.m., and Sun 12 p.m. to 5 p.m. In the winter, the museum's hours are Tues through Sat, 9 a.m. to 5 p.m.

You will view many spectacular red-rock formations in Utah, but *Arches National Park* is special. This park hosts the largest collection of sandstone arches in the world: colossal sandstone fins, spectacular balanced rocks, looming pinnacles, and spires. It is a must see. The entrance to Arches National Park is 5 miles north of Moab, along Highway 191.

Take at least half a day for this adventure—and bring along a picnic lunch and a lot of water. Go on a few hikes. There are friendly rangers at the visitor center and all sorts of good orientation information. For information, contact the Moab Area Travel Council at (435) 259-8825, Mon through Fri from 8 a.m.

Green River Melons

If you're near **Green River** (just north of Arches and Canyonlands National Parks) anytime from late June to early October, you owe it to yourself to stop and sample the local melons. They'll be world famous one of these days.

Green River melons are a gourmet treat—the sweetest, juiciest melons you'll ever taste. In 1878, the town of Green River was a mail station on the Green River . . . and nothing else. After a few years, a few travel-weary farmers accidentally discovered that melons grew in this veritable desert. Not only did they grow well, but the taste of these melons was something out of this world.

Water from the famous Green River is certainly plentiful, a necessary element in a good melon. The sun is hot and steady. But it is the alkaline soil that makes the melons grow fast and sweet. Besides the watermelon, try some of the local favorites such as the honeyloupe, a hybrid of the honeydew and cantaloupe.

If you visit in mid-September, you can eat melon with the best of them at the soon-to-be-famous Melon Festival.

to 5 p.m., or visit discovermoab.com/contact. You can also contact Arches National Park at (435) 719-2299 or nps.gov/arch/index.htm.

Now you are ready to hit the park's 4-mile loop road. Wind around for a mile to **Park Avenue**, the first stopping spot. The main feature is the vertical slab on your right, which forms a huge "storefront" to the "avenue." Strolling down the avenue is an easy mile if you arrange to get picked up at North Park Avenue. The next stop is another 1½ miles up the road, at **Courthouse Towers**. These monoliths were probably arches at one time. The largest is called Sheep Rock, and you can see the grounds. Look to the left for Baby Arch, and you will have a lesson in how arches are formed. On to **Petrified Dunes**, which, in fact, were real sand dunes a couple of million years ago. You will notice the rock's whiter color. This is Navajo sandstone, which contains a smaller amount of the iron that colors the rocks nearby. About 9 miles from the visitor center is **Balanced Rock**—a perfect example of two varieties of sandstone, with different hardening agents at work against the elements. A huge boulder (about 3,500 tons) sits on top of a smaller boulder, performing one of nature's more precarious balancing acts. This is a good spot to take pictures of the red rock with the green La Sal Mountains courteously making a perfect backdrop.

A short drive down the road brings you to **The Windows**—get out of the car and walk around for an hour or so. Remind your family that nature really did make these arches—they are so whimsical and perfect that it seems Disney might have had something to do with it instead. North and South Windows are so named because both arches provide a perfect frame for the gorgeous scenery beyond. These are formed inside the same huge fin. If you face them directly and back up a couple hundred feet, you will see why they are also known as The Spectacles (as in eyeglasses, not public embarrassments). **Turret Arch** is just across the way, with its castle-like capstone.

Back in the car, it's a few minutes to **Double Arch**. This requires an easy five-minute walk to see its twin image. These arches were formed differently—see if you can tell which was originally a pothole, and which was formed by water and wind beating against its rock fin. Stand at the end of the trail, and you can see the **Parade of Elephants** leading a billion-year-old circus march. Less than 2 miles beyond is **Pothole Arch**, so named because water that once rushed down from above formed a depression in the rock. After time, a hole formed in the cliffside, which wore away to leave this span of stone.

The next stop is **Delicate Arch**—an extraordinary formation. It has become Utah's signature arch, celebrated on license plates and official road signs. You can see Delicate Arch from a roadside turnout, but this is a must-see kind of experience and its 3-mile round trip hike is worth your effort. If you hike this trail in the summer, you will need a lot of water and rest stops. If you visit the area during the cooler months, the hike seems easier and you will need less hydration. Be warned that you are exposed to the full sun for much of this hike. It's officially labeled "moderately strenuous," so plan accordingly.

Just past the trailhead to Delicate Arch are the remains of Wolfe Ranch, where a hardy family lived for twenty years at the turn of the 19th century. Take a moment to marvel at the hardships they must have faced.

climatefastfacts

Southeastern Utah's climate

winter, 21 to 50 degrees

summer, 64 to 100 degrees

about 10 inches of precipitation

Shortly, you'll reach a sandy path, then cross a bouncy bridge. Just past the bridge, look for a side trail on your left. Follow this around the corner for a hundred yards and you'll see a large *Ute Indian Petroglyph Panel*. Continuing on after the switchbacks, the boulder portion of the hike is the most strenuous, as it climbs over rolling slickrock marked by rock cairns. It is hidden from view until the very end. When you turn the final bend, there is a 45-foot arch inside a sandstone bowl the size of a small town. If you are feeling brave, you can hike into the slippery bowl and stand under the arch. Like every good thing, Delicate Arch is unbeatable as a picnic or contemplation spot.

Back in a car, the next pullout point is *Fiery Furnace*. Notice this intense cluster of rock flame-fins before you get there. The Fiery Furnace is so winding and convoluted that a ranger's accompaniment is needed, which requires a sign-up at the visitor center, and often at least a day's notice. There are places where you'll squeeze and jump through narrow places, but it is worth the effort. The naming of the Fiery Furnace is an obvious choice, but if you see this formation at sunset you will view it in its fullest, flaming beauty. Next up is *Sand Dune Arch*. Nature has made a terrific trail—it's in shade for most of the day. If you feel like walking further, you will come to *Broken Arch*, named because it looks broken from for a distance (it really isn't).

Another mile up the road you will pass *Skyline Arch*, on your way to the third, and final, big hike of the day, in *Devil's Garden*. The hike in Devil's Garden can be split up a number of ways. The main trail will take you to *Pine Tree Arch* (a short side trip and well-signed—when you get to the "T" in this trail, go right for a view of Tunnel Arch, left to Pine Tree), Landscape, Navajo, Partition, Double O, and Dark Angel arches. If you make it all the way to Dark Angel you deserve dessert—it's 7⅓ miles round trip. You will be walking on sand for much of the way. After *Landscape Arch*, the trail gets iffy as you are following cairns, and it is just plain tiring. The most popular destination is

Landscape Arch—about a mile in from the trailhead on a well-marked path. Landscape Arch is the longest known natural span in the world, with an inside width of 306 feet. You can hike up the short side trail to Landscape, sit under it, and contemplate man's small place in the universe. The very apparent land restoration going on here is a lesson in what it takes to save an area from being "loved to death."

Near the Devil's Garden parking lot, you will see the ***Devil's Garden Campground***. It has fifty-two sites, many of them clustered with juniper and bordered by big mounds of sandstone. From March through October, weather permitting, the campground has running water. Be aware that this is the only camping possibility in the park, and it is nearly always full. There are many privately owned campgrounds within the 10 miles, however. After an hour or two at Devil's Garden, it's an 18-mile drive back to the visitor center. Activities at Arches include campfire chats every night of the week during the summer. Topics include "Why scorpions live in the parks," "Shaman's paint box," and "Why Arches?"

A few miles south of the bridge you'll begin seeing the jagged edges of ***Fisher Towers*** slicing through the sky. These rock formations are the isolated remnants of a 225-million-year-old floodplain that covered much of this area, known as the ***Richardson Amphitheater***. "Fisher" is actually a corruption of "fissure," a geological term meaning "narrow crack," and the name for this sort of rock formation. The tallest of these towers is Castleton Tower, soaring to a height of 900 feet. A 2⅕-mile trail begins at the campground, located a mile or so from the highway at the end of a bumpy dirt road, which should be negotiable for just about any vehicle. The trail takes you to the base of the towers and to a viewpoint of Onion Creek's chaotic formations. See if you can't pick out the profile of a crocodile in one of the towers.

How Moab Was Discovered

In 1765, about the time of the Stamp Act in Colonial American history, an adventurous sort named Juan Mana de Rivera wandered about present-day Moab looking for a place to cross the Colorado River. Rivera had wandered up from New Mexico and might have been the first European to see this part of Utah.

Ostensibly, he came to add territory and to learn more about the Indians. He also wanted to find out if they were hostile to traders and to discover if the French had come this far south. Mana de Rivera also had dreams of discovering a gold-laden civilization. At the very least, he hoped to find gold and silver mines.

What he found was a rugged land, haunting and forbidding. Gold and silver would have to wait to be discovered.

Southwest of Fisher Tower along Highway 128, you'll see a turnoff for **Castle Valley** and the **La Sal Mountains Loop Road**. The road is an extraordinary trip through two different ecosystems: desert and alpine. The trip begins in Castle Valley, the name of the town and the valley in which it is situated.

Here you'll find superb accommodations at **Castle Valley Inn** (424 Amber Ln.; 435-259-6012 or 888-466-6012). This secluded bed-and-breakfast, thirty minutes from Moab, has everything going for it: stunning views of the towering La Sals and the silhouettes of Castle Rock and the Priest and Nuns; eleven acres, endowed with a fruit orchard and trails; and impeccable, smartly furnished rooms. Obviously, you need to book well in advance for this gem that has turned into a destination for a lot of return guests. Signs for Castle Valley Inn, beginning at the Castle Valley turnoff on Highway 128, point you in the right direction. Visit the website at castlevalleyinn.com.

From Castle Valley the narrow paved road climbs into the high reaches of the La Sals, the second-highest mountain range in Utah and a bold contrast to the red sandstone below. This 35-mile road, which ends up 8 miles south of Moab on Highway 191, offers spectacular views of Canyonlands and Arches National Parks, the Moab Rim, and, of course, Castle Valley. You can gain access to several trailheads by venturing off the paved road and onto some dirt roads that extend farther up into the mountains.

Ever since John Ford began filming his epic Westerns in this part of Utah in the 1920s, filmmakers have continually set their sights on **Moab**, otherwise known as Hollywood East. Set in a fertile valley and encased by sandstone cliffs, Moab has, for the most part, resisted becoming another Aspen or Santa Fe. The town's rough-and-tumble appearance has kept this from happening, much to the relief of its natives. But because of its close proximity to two national parks, the town attracts tourists by the busload, who stay in the gaudy motels lining Main Street. And with its hundreds of miles of slickrock trails, Moab draws mountain bikers from around the globe. The best way to avoid the crowds is, of course, to avoid the busy season, which lasts from late spring to early fall. No one in his right mind would really want to be in Moab in the summer anyway. Temperatures regularly soar above 100 degrees, and the slickrock only radiates more heat.

With the advent of the Cold War, prospectors with "uranium on the cranium" flooded Moab, scouring the surrounding desert canyons in search of the metal for which the US government was willing to pay top dollar. By 1952 Moab had become "the uranium capital of the world," and within three years the population tripled in size. Many died out in the inhospitable desert, and some struck it rich, such as Charlie Steen, who became a multimillionaire overnight. In a show of ostentation, he built a large mansion (now the Sunset Grill) on a hill high above Moab. But as the bottom fell out from under the uranium market, so went Steen and all the others making their living on this metal that fed the Cold War. All that remains now of the uranium boom are thousands of miles of Jeep trails crisscrossing the desert landscape.

A good starting place to get your bearings on the geology, archaeology, and history of the Moab region is the ***Moab Museum*** (118 E. Center St.; 435-259-7985). The museum recently underwent a large-scale remodeling of both floors to increase the space for their collection and growing library/archive. They reopened to the public in the Fall of 2019 with an entirely new visitor experience. Check it out!

Moab has a number of bed-and-breakfasts. ***Sunflower Hill Bed and Breakfast Inn*** (185 N. 300 East; 435-259-2974 or 800-662-2786) with its bright and cheerful decor allows for maximum amounts of sunlight to enter the rooms. The main house and cottage are set on an acre or so of gardens and lawn, inviting you to read or snooze underneath one of the big trees. Sunflower Hill has an excellent location on the very edge of town, which doesn't mean it isn't within walking distance of downtown. It is. See the location at sunflowerhill.com.

A gaggle of possible tours besets unsuspecting travelers who enter Moab. Tours by boat, bike, and Jeep are all at hand. ***Adrift Adventures*** (378 N. Main St.; 435-259-8594) offers a number of combination trips, including mother/daughter and father/son trips that can last as many as six days. Options include river rafting, Jeep tours, and mountain-bike tours. Or you can settle for a day trip by raft through Cataract, Gray, or Desolation Canyon, or by Jeep through the Needles or Maze district of Canyonlands National Park. For more details, visit adrift.net. ***Sheri Griffith Expeditions*** (2231 S. Hwy 191; 435-259-8229 or 800-332-2439) allows you to design your own river trips or, if you are a woman, go on a women-only tour. Sheri Griffith also provides bike tours, educational programs, 4WD trips, and horseback trail rides. Visit the website at griffithexp.com.

You can see a lot from the road. But resist the temptation of staying inside your vehicle. Take a few hikes. Highway 279, forking off Highway 191 a mile north of Moab, offers several opportunities for you to get out and breathe air that isn't conditioned. The road, following the Colorado River through one of its deep gorges, goes past a number of "Indian Writing" interpretive signs, pointing out several petroglyphs, Indian ruins, and even a pair of dinosaur tracks. From the road you can venture out on some hiking trails, such as the 1½-mile hike to Corona and Bowtie Arches, beginning at a designated trailhead 10 miles from the Highway 191 turnoff. Rock cairns mark the way across the slickrock terrain and point you in the direction of the two arches. Besides

Corona and Bowtie, the trail winds past a third arch—Pinto Arch. If you're mainly interested in seeing these unique formations, this short hike is an excellent alternative to Arches National Park.

Thanks to the hundreds of miles of Jeep trails that uranium prospectors laid down, Canyonlands National Park is an excellent place for bike and Jeep tours and for experiencing wilderness at its wildest. Most of the roads, however, are 4WD only. One is White Rim Road, a 100-mile route across Canyonlands' basin. You will venture beneath towering mesas and above the canyons carved out by the Green and Colorado Rivers. Plan on several days; A backcountry permit is required for overnight trips. If you are lucky, you'll spot some desert bighorn sheep.

The **Shafer Trail Road** is definitely not for those suffering even mildly from acrophobia. The switchbacks cling to the mesa escarpment and twist a whopping 1,200 feet to the top of the mesa. With no guardrail and severe exposure to the heights, the Shafer Road may give new meaning to white-knuckle driving. Branching off Highway 313 just after you enter the park gate, the Shafer Road is manageable for a low-clearance, two-wheel-drive vehicle until the road begins to switchback down the canyon (or "the Neck," as it's known here). From there on, the road is designated 4WD. Check with the ranger at the gate for road conditions. Depending on recent-past or current weather conditions, the ranger may tell you that all of Shafer Trail is open to two-wheel-drives. In that case (or if you do have a 4WD), take Shafer Road as an alternative route back to Moab. The road connects with Potash Road and Highway 279. If you decide to go the opposite direction and go up Shafer Trail, call park headquarters at (435) 719-2313 for road conditions. An excellent loop tour of the canyons, mesas, and slickrock west of Moab would be the following route: Highway 191 to Highway 313 to Shafer Trail Road to Potash Road to Highway 279 (or vice versa). Plan on three to four hours of driving time for this tour.

If you thought that cliff-dwelling was a thing of the past, think again. **Hole 'N the Rock** (11037 S. Hwy 191; 435-686-2250) is a home set inside a sandstone cliff. With 5,000 square feet and fourteen rooms, this home is no pueblo. In fact, it goes further than the creators of the Flintstones could have imagined. The rooms are more like alcoves, or separate caves. The fireplace, with a 65-foot chimney drilled to the surface of the cliff, is for all practical purposes unnecessary because the temperature stays between 65 and 72 degrees year-round, without the help of any heating or cooling mechanism. After all, the home does have the best possible insulation you could imagine.

It took Albert Christensen twelve years to excavate the hole he would live in for five years. He died in 1957, but his wife, Gladys, continued to develop the home, which wasn't completed until twenty years after excavation had begun. An apparent jack-of-all-trades, Christensen was a painter, sculptor, and amateur taxidermist. The ten-minute tour of the home features Harry, his favorite donkey and first attempt at taxidermy. Christensen revered Franklin D. Roosevelt. He sculpted FDR's face on the front of the cliff. Tours are conducted seven days a week, every ten to fifteen minutes. The house is open from 8 a.m. to 8 p.m. from Memorial Day to Labor Day, and from 9 a.m. to 5 p.m. the rest of the year. You can't miss the home if you're traveling 15 miles south of Moab on Highway 191. *Hole 'N the Rock* is whitewashed in gigantic letters on both sides of the cliff/home. Even though it looks a little gimmicky, don't be turned off. It's a hoot.

Canyonlands National Park, near Moab, is so large it's split into four sections: 1. The Maze; 2. The Needles; 3. Island in the Sky; and 4. Horseshoe Canyon. These areas adjoin but are neatly trisected by the Colorado and Green Rivers and must be reached from different entry points.

Canyonlands' vast expanse dwarfs Arches National Park and makes Arches, with its paved roads and signed trails, seem almost tame. This is not the place to fool around with Mother Nature. Get directions, have provisions on hand, and be careful. Throughout Canyonlands National Park backcountry camping, accessed by backpackers and four-wheelers, is allowed. This area is remote and rugged. Some parts can only be accessed by 4WD, ATV, motorcycles, or mountain bikes. Reservations and permits for camping can be arranged at park visitor centers, by calling (435) 259-4351, or on the park's website.

The Maze is known as one of the most remote places on earth—not in terms of distance but the tons of sandstone between you and others. Once you enter this 30-square-mile tangle of rock wilderness you'll truly be away from it all. If you're extremely hardy, you might make it all the way to the *Doll's House*, 40 miles on a dirt road. You'll be rewarded by colorful rock formations and a stunning view of the Colorado River. Accessible by Utah highways 24 or 95, this area is accessible by 4WD, ATV, or mountain bike.

The Needles section of the park is named for its predominant red-rock spires. It is an hour-and-a-half drive from Moab. About 20 miles in, you'll pass *Newspaper Rock*—a worthwhile stop. From prehistory through frontier days, people felt the need to make their mark. The result is a crowded mix of messages on a huge rock wall. Perhaps it was the black oxide surface—which makes carving easy and distinct—or perhaps it was its location as an ancient trail. Newspaper Rock is an amazing amalgam of history. Moving about 25 more miles, you'll arrive at The Needles. Here you will find a visitor center with artifacts, displays, a short film, and a book shop.

Squaw Flats Campground has 26 individual sites, plus 3 group sites in different locations around the Needles district. Twelve of the sites can be reserved in spring and fall. Make reservations online at Recreation.gov or by calling (877) 444-6777. Other times of the year, individual sites are first-come, first-served. Sites fill quickly in spring and fall. You can also reserve group sites for nights between mid-March and mid-November. There are toilets, picnic tables, and fire rings in the campground. Running water is available during the warm weather.

Back on the road, look for the ***Wooden Shoe formation***. When you spot it, you will definitely know what you're looking at. Two excellent hikes in this area are recommended. ***Roadside Ruin*** is a short, easy, loop trail. Pick up the interpretive pamphlet for this hike at the visitor center, so you can identify the flora and fauna along the way. This area was occupied a century ago by Indians who used this same flora and fauna for sustenance. One of their better-preserved storage houses constitute the "ruin" on this hike. Just down the road is the pullout parking area for the ***Cave Spring Trail***, a ⁶⁄₁₀ mile loop. This hike includes climbing ladders, viewing an old cowboy camp, and finding Indian markings on boulders.

If you have a four-wheel-drive vehicle, continue on the Cave Spring dirt road to ***Paul Bunyan's Potty***, the fodder for many jokes. This giant rock formation could be described, but you probably get the idea. Major attractions in Needles are ***Chesler Park***, the confluence of the Green and Colorado rivers, and ***Angel Arch***. However, all three of these natural phenomena are hard to reach. The access roads are classified for difficulty. They require not just a 4WD vehicle, but an experienced driver. The trade-off is that this area provides high adventure and solitude. Ask a ranger before you head out.

Chesler Park is a huge, scrub-grass meadow rimmed by needle-shaped rocks for which this park is named. You get a sense of how the needles were formed and their size and shape.

To view the confluence of the Green and Colorado Rivers, follow the road to the ***Big Spring Canyon Overlook***, and then set out on dirt for a hefty four-wheel drive. Park at the sign and hike the last mile or so of this trail. When you reach the terminus, your reward will be a heart-stopping view, straight down—the two mighty rivers join. *Colorado* is a Spanish word for "red," you know what green is. When they join they turn a third, marvelous color. This is not for the vertigo-impaired. You'll probably see pictures of Angel Arch in the visitor center. Again, this trail follows a long 4WD route into Salt Creek Canyon and requires a strenuous hike. But this 150-foot high-winged arch is simply breathtaking.

Island in the Sky is not about rock scrambling, hidden picnic spots, or dirt roads. It is a vivid contrast to The Needles and The Maze. This lofty perch offers sweeping mesas and an eagle's eye view of the world. Bonus—the road is paved almost the entire way. There are restrooms and water in the visitors center, as well as a bookstore and a theater showing films that describe the area. It is recommended that you bring plenty of water along on your visit; there are no water stations on Island in the Sky. After a short drive out onto this section of the park it becomes apparent how the Island got its name. This high peninsula towers above the winding river below, offering fabulous viewpoints from the pullouts that dot its scenic route. You'll see canyon after canyon rolling into the far distance. Three mountain ranges rim the horizon—they catch all of the water that would fall here, which is one reason why the mountains are blue-green in the distance but the closer view is of barren red rock. The Henry Mountains are to the southwest, the Abajos Mountains (a Navajo word for blue) are to the south, and the La Sal Mountains are to the east. The closest mesa you'll see is the massive White Rim, which runs almost continuously below the Island.

You'll also view both The Needles and The Maze from this elevated point in space.

There are a couple of easy hikes on the Island. The **Mesa Arch Trail** is a short route looping across a piñon and juniper plain to the edge of the mesa. The arch here is perfect frame for the La Sal Mountains in the distance. Pick up a guide to the geology and plant life of this trail at the visitor center. The **Upheaval Dome Crater View Trail** leads just 500 yards to the remains of an incredibly turbulent geologic event. Tons of layers of rock were pushed up, and others fell down—and the result is a big bowl of rock. **Buck Canyon Overlook** and **Grand View Point Overlook** complete the scenic drive.

Horseshoe Canyon requires a hike. There are two ways of getting to Horseshoe Canyon. One is to turn east off Highway 24 just before the Goblin Valley exit, 21 miles north of Hanksville. Follow signs to the Horseshoe Canyon trailhead, 30 miles from Highway 24. A more scenic but longer way is from Green River. Take Airport Road for 47 miles (stay left at the fork), until you see the sign to the Horseshoe Canyon trailhead. Road conditions depend on the weather and the last time the county scraped the road. Generally, it's fine for regular passenger cars, but check at the ranger station (435) 542-3461 in Hanksville.

You will drive through the **San Rafael Desert**. It gives you a feeling that compounds once you enter the canyon. The trail begins at the western rim of Horseshoe Canyon and descends about a mile. At the bottom of the canyon turn right and continue below the immense cliffs and desert-tarnished mosaics. Keep an eye out for panels of Indian pictographs, known as the "Great Gallery," when you're down in the canyon. This rock art is an excellent example of the Barrier Canyon style practiced by the Archaic Tribe, who roamed this

Utah Trivia

The Henry Mountains were named by a member of the Powell Expedition, in honor of the secretary of the Smithsonian Institution, Joseph Henry.

Mexican Hat is a tiny town named for the sombrero-like rock formation located several miles northeast of the town.

As you study Native American petroglyphs, remember this is not graffiti and there is no such thing as swearing in the Indian culture.

Utah's Colorado Plateau covers nearly half the state (in the south and east).

All of Utah's national parks are found on the Colorado Plateau.

The Rocky Mountain elk became the official state animal in 1971.

The same year the Declaration of Independence was signed, Fathers Dominguez and Escalante, two Franciscan priest-explorers, journeyed across much of the state.

Utah is one of the most popular states for filming movies.

The rugged San Rafael Swell region was nearly untouched by white men until the Cold War uranium prospectors wandered its canyons with Geiger counters.

region from around 8000 BC to AD 450. Also watch for Fremont and Ancestral Puebloan petroglyphs along the way. Please do not touch the rock art. It is extremely fragile, and oils from your hand will remove the paint. Get plenty of water and a tank full of gas before you make the drive out to Horseshoe Canyon. You won't find any conveniences there or anywhere else along the dirt road. Even if the temperature is comfortable, you'll be surprised how quickly the parched air and beating sun lift moisture from your body. You can find yourself dehydrated even before thirst sets in. Free ranger-led tours of Horseshoe Canyon are available by calling (435) 259-2652.

The *Mt. Peale Animal Sanctuary and Healing Center* is nestled on ten acres in the middle of the La Sal Mountains. The rooms are beautifully appointed, and the dining room, serviced by a commercial kitchen and chef, offers a panoramic view of the terrain. Visitors are invited to relax by the fireplace in the front room after a long day of hiking, cross-country skiing, or snowshoeing. Or you can take a dip in the hot tub on the outdoor deck or get a mud bath at the spa. The inn also has several cabins. Contact the inn at (435) 686-2284, (888) 687-3253, or visit the website at mtpeale.com.

Canyon Rim Recreation Area is perhaps your best alternative to Island in the Sky at Canyonlands National Park. The area sits on the rim of the mesa, offering views similar to the ones you'll find at Canyonlands. And because it's

BLM property, you'll find less of a crowd. The paved road through the recreation area branches off Highway 191, 32 miles south of Moab, and ends up 22 miles west of the highway at Needles Overlook, providing another aerial view of the basin floors and the canyons carved out by the Colorado River. **Dead Horse Point** is spectacular—a world class destination. Be sure to include it in your plans. Take a few minutes and stop at the visitors center. Better yet, bring a picnic, and absorb the Utah wonder. The overlook, perched 1,600 feet above the Colorado River, takes in Kane Creek Anticline and its contorted rock formations, as well as more of the Colorado's sinuous canyons. The 17-mile road forks off the main paved road, 15 miles from Highway 191. Avoid the overlooks when lightning threatens, or you might get shocked by more than just the views.

On the Anasazi Trail

When the first pioneers came to the east foot of the **Abajo** (pronounced u-BAH-hoe) **Mountains**, they were reminded of Thomas Jefferson's lush "little mountain" in Virginia. The sight was an oasis compared with the inhospitable desert they had just sweated through. Just how many of the pioneers had actually been to the site of Jefferson's home in Virginia is questionable, but they named the town Monticello anyway (pronouncing it mon-ti-SELL-o).

The incentive for driving up through the 11,000-foot Abajo Mountains is a panoramic view of a great section of the Four Corners region, including the La Sal Mountains to the north, Needles District of Canyonlands National Park to the northwest, Henry Mountains to the west, Monument Valley and the Chuska Mountains of Arizona to the south, and Shiprock in New Mexico to the southeast.

From Monticello head a mile west on 200 South from Highway 191. Take a left on South Creek Road and go 8 or so miles until the pavement runs out. A scenic loop would be to head north from Canyonlands Overlook (near the pavement's end) and follow another paved road down to Highway 211, where you come out near Newspaper Rock. This scenic tour beginning (or ending) in Monticello climbs though the cool forests and summer wildflowers of the Abajos and lets out in the red sandstone desert. The distance from Monticello to Newspaper Rock is 14 miles, but the road is open from late April or early May until late October, or whenever the snow begins to pile up. Then it becomes a paradise for cross-country skiers and snowmobilers.

Although **Blanding** could probably use a flashier name for luring tourists, it does suffice as a good base for exploring the **Four Corners region**. Between 1905 and 1915, the town went through three names—Sidon, Grayson, and, finally, Blanding. In 1915 the rich, egocentric Thomas W. Bicknell offered any town in Utah a free library if the town agreed to change its name to Bicknell. Grayson (as the town was known then) bit, but so did the town of Thurber in central Utah. Mr. Bicknell decided to split the library between the two towns. But you couldn't have two towns in Utah with the same name, despite what Mr. Bicknell probably desired. So Thurber became Bicknell. And Grayson? It got the short end of the stick, having to take Mrs. Bicknell's maiden name of Blanding.

Despite the name, the people of Blanding can be proud of the museum located here. ***Edge of the Cedars State Park*** (660 W. 400 North; 435-678-2238) culls its fame from the small Ancestral Puebloan village that was occupied on the site from roughly AD 750 to 1220. Although excavation is ongoing, you can see six separate habitation and ceremonial complexes. The museum allows you to get up close and personal with the remains (as long you don't climb on the walls), which give you a good idea of how the tribe conducted its daily affairs. You can descend a ladder and enter one of the kivas, all of which are completely original except for the restored roof. On the second floor is one of the finest collections of Ancestral Puebloan pottery found anywhere. Sandals, tools, baskets, and jewelry offer deeper insight into the culture and further evidence of the culture's special artistry and craftsmanship. In addition to the Ancestral Puebloan displays and artifacts, you'll see exhibits on Utes, Navajos, and early Anglo settlers. The museum opens at 9 a.m. and closes at 5 p.m. daily.

Continuing in the tradition of Ancestral Puebloan potters, the Navajo and Ute painters at ***Cedar Mesa Pottery*** in Blanding (435-678-2241) lend their creative, steady-handed talents to each of the pieces that come out of the factory. A free tour takes you through the steps of mixing and casting the clay and then introduces you to the painters, who can turn out as many as sixty pieces a day in their own signature style. Of course, the incentive for showing you around is that you'll be tempted to buy something from the gift shop, which sells Navajo rugs, sand paintings, and jewelry, all in addition to the factory's pottery. Tours at Cedar Mesa, located at 330 South Main Street, are conducted from 9 a.m. to 6 p.m., Mon through Sat.

If the Indian ruins at Edge of the Cedars have got your interest piqued, then try the "Trail of the Ancients" tour, beginning at Edge of the Cedars in Blanding, continuing south on Highway 191, heading west on Highway 95, south on Highway 261, east on Highway 163, and north on Highway 191 (or vice versa). The majority of Indian ruins and other attractions found along this route are discussed here. Getting to many of the attractions requires side trips from the highways along paved or dirt roads. The time it takes to complete this loop through the Four Corners area of Utah depends on how long you decide to linger at each of the sites. You can do it in a day, if you so choose.

Butler Wash Ruin is in pretty good shape for being 700 years old. Like the cliff dwellings at Hovenweep (see page 158), it sits at the head of a canyon underneath a rock overhang, where water spills down across the front of the dwellings. From the overlook, established on the other side of the canyon, you can get a good look at a kiva and some other dwellings perched high above the canyon floor. The overlook is a pleasant ½-mile walk through a piñon and juniper forest. You'll see a sign for Butler Wash on Highway 95, 10 miles from the Highway 191 junction.

From Butler Wash the road continues up and over a monocline called ***Comb Ridge***, a jagged rock wall stretching 80 miles north and south from the Abajo Mountains to Kayenta, Arizona. Another feat performed by the Utah Division of Transportation, the highway squeezes through a narrow slot blasted through the ridge. It was in this area of Comb Ridge that the last Indian war in the West occurred. For fifty years Mormon encroachment on Ute territory and Ute theft of Mormon cattle had been feeding a growing resentment between the two cultures. In 1923 the resentment erupted into bloodshed after a Ute named Joe Bishop was tried and found guilty of stealing a local rancher's cattle. Chief Posey, a well-respected Paiute who married into the Ute tribe, waited outside the courtroom with horses, and the Utes escaped into Comb Ridge. A posse from Blanding chased the group, eventually catching up with them. The Utes surrendered after the posse shot and killed Joe Bishop's son. Chief Posey, however, managed to escape deeper into the canyons of Comb Ridge. His body was later found in a cave, where he apparently died of a gunshot wound to his hip. A nationwide furor over the incident ensued, raising awareness of the Utes' quandary and paving the way for the establishment of White Mesa Indian Reservation south of Blanding.

More Ancestral Puebloan ruins await at the ***Arch Canyon Overlook***, an amazing view of the convoluted sandstone formations that emerge out of the depths of Arch Canyon. To the left of the overlook are a series of granaries that were used to store corn harvests. Coming down from Comb Ridge, take a right (north) where the sign says "Texas Flat." Go 2²⁄₁₀ miles along a good dirt road. Park just before you see a Jeep trail that forks off to the right and heads up the hill. Go up the trail ¼ mile to reach the canyon rim. (There are no guardrails, so be careful.)

Three of the seven 900-year-old ***Cave Towers*** are still standing, giving testament to the kind of masonry the Ancestral Puebloans were capable of. The location, at the head of a canyon, speaks again of where the later Ancestral

Puebloans liked to build their fortifications. Turn south on an undesignated dirt road between Mileposts 102 and 103 and go through a gate. The ruins are less than a mile down the road, but park your car just inside the gate and walk the rest of the way. The road is too rough for passenger cars. (The towers are not supported, which means they can easily topple over if you attempt to climb on or around them. So please stay at a distance and don't touch.)

One of the most gratifying hiking or backpacking trips you can take in this part of Utah is through *Grand Gulch*, a narrow and sinuous canyon sliced through Cedar Mesa. The sandstone, the remains of a sea that flooded the area 250 million years ago, appears in gray, red, and orange, as well as black—the result of iron-manganese that "tarnishes" the rock. Arches, bridges, and alcoves have formed in the cliffs, which can reach as high as 600 feet. Aspen trees, a rare find at this low elevation, grow out of the lush canyon floor amid tamarisk and scrub bush. The canyon also has a rich concentration of Ancestral Puebloan dwellings, rock art, and artifacts.

Because of its archaeological significance, Grand Gulch is a delicate area, one that demands protocol of its visitors, who can cause destruction without even knowing it. Before setting out, read all the information available at the Kane Gulch Trailhead regarding the stipulations of visiting Grand Gulch. Or, if the ranger is in, ask for a handout that explains the archaeological features of the canyon and all the precautions you need to take in seeing it.

One feature that hikers or backpackers should be aware of are middens—charcoal-stained soil that is the remains of prehistoric trash heaps. The soil contains evidence of daily activities and reveals changing preferences in pottery, food, tools, and even treatment of the dead. Note: Avoid middens areas, which are usually found immediately downslope of an alcove or cliff-dwelling site. As usual, don't disturb any of the ruins, artifacts, or bones you might see along the way and don't touch any of the petroglyphs or pictographs. (Federal laws prohibit it.) Don't lessen the chance that future generations will have the good fortune to behold these ancient ways of expression.

Fat-tire Biking

Southeastern Utah has become a hot spot for cyclists from all over the country. The rich landscape and the hundreds of miles of dirt roads attract scores of fat-tire bikers.

There are roads, rocks, and hill climbs for every skill level. If you didn't bring your bike, you can rent one in most towns. (Take along an extra water bottle, a tube, and a few tools.) Pedaling is a clean, natural way to enjoy the scenic beauty.

The trail to Grand Gulch begins at **Kane Gulch Trailhead**, located at the Kane Gulch Ranger Station on Highway 261, about 6 miles from the Highway 95 junction. The trail extends 23 miles from Kane Gulch, through Grand Gulch, and to the head of Bullet Canyon. Four days are recommended to complete this loop, which requires a ride from Bullet Canyon trailhead back to Kane Gulch trailhead. (Check at the Kane Gulch Ranger Station if there are any shuttle services operating at the time of your stay. You'll have to obtain a $5 permit there, anyway, if you intend on staying overnight.) If you're interested in doing a day hike, try the strenuous 10-mile round-trip to **Stimper Arch** and back. Remember to bring as much water as is necessary for the time of year. Call the Monticello Field Office at (435) 587-1500 for more information.

Just a few miles from Grand Gulch on Highway 261, **Natural Bridges National Monument** contains three cedar mesa sandstone bridges. All the bridges can be seen along a 9-mile paved loop, or by walking a trail that allows you to get close to the bridges. These bridges started forming during the age of the dinosaurs. Hard stone sedimented over softer stone, which eroded, leaving hard stone bridges. You may notice that all the electricity here is generated by solar panels. In fact, this monument was chosen to test the use of solar energy in the 1980s. At the time, this test base was the largest sun-powered plant in the world.

Bears Ears National Monument

Our newest national monument is up close and personal, but from a distance, the two twin buttes look like bear ears. My favorite view is on State Route 261 going north towards Highway 95.

It is said that Bears Ears is a monument of layers—layers of geology, cultures, and life. There are juniper forests, plateaus, and Native American artifacts. Because it's new, the "use plan" is not fully developed. There are fewer amenities or services. Bears Ears feels a bit rugged and remote—which is delightful. This means you'll need to be a little better prepared.

Remember to "Respect and Protect." There are a number of delicate ecosystems, as well as a stunning number of artifacts in the monument area. Take pictures and enjoy the archaeological and paleontological wonders you find, but leave them undisturbed. The cliff dwellings are fascinating—built with adobe mortar and stones into the sides of mesas, mountains and caves. They were probably used to store grains and seeds.

As an aside, The Indian Creek unit of Bears Ears is known as a rock climbing mecca. There are campsites. Bears Ears is open year-round, but the best times are March through early June and September through October.

The trail to **Sipapu Bridge** is challenging but breathtaking, including a 600-foot descent on wooden ladders and steel stairs. **Kachina Bridge**, the second and largest bridge on the route, is named for the prehistoric drawings on it that resemble kachina dolls. **Owachomo Bridge**, smallest of the bridges, is 106 feet high. For more information about hiking, camping, or sight-seeing, call (435) 692-1234, or write HC60 Box 1, Lake Powell 84533.

You already know that Utah is chock-full of spectacular views. But **Muley Point Overlook** ranks near the top of the list. From here you look across an expanse featuring all the Four Corners states, Monument Valley, scores of mountain peaks, and the canyons of the San Juan River, meandering 2,100 feet below Muley Point. At the top of the **Moki Dugway** switchbacks, take a right (southwest) and head 5³⁄₁₀ miles on a gravel road. Hopefully, the view from Muley Point will help you prepare (or relax, if you've already come up the switchbacks) for the 1,100-foot descent of Moki Dugway. Clutching the side of the cliff, the gravel road is fine for two-wheel-drives, but not for acrophobics, who should think twice about going down or coming up the escarpment.

While you have the aerial advantage at the top of Moki Dugway, take a mental note of the house squatting on the valley floor directly below. Try to imagine this: This bed-and-breakfast is the only house standing on the 36,000 acres of the Cedar Mesa Cultural and Recreational Area. There is a splendid view of all four states from the front porch; there is no man-made structure in sight. The place has a powerful feeling, to say the least. Looming behind the house are the 1,100-foot cliffs of Cedar Mesa, and out in the distance rise the sandstone monoliths of **Valley of the Gods**, the only apt name for such a magnificent landscape. Monument Valley sits on the horizon, as do the snow-capped peaks of mountains in Colorado, New Mexico, and Arizona.

The Valley of the Gods Bed & Breakfast fills up months in advance, turning away many more people than they can book. In fact, you should call ahead at least five months in advance, (970) 749-1164, to book one of the four rooms, including the root-cellar suite. There are no phone or electrical lines. Everything is solar-powered, and water has to be shipped in. Yes, remote is the keyword. The home is located a half mile from Highway 261. You'll see the sign 6½ miles from the junction of Highways 261 and 163. View the location at valleyofthegodsbandb.com.

The bed-and-breakfast sits at one end of a 17-mile dirt road leading through Valley of the Gods, a smaller, hassle-free version of Monument Valley. Managed by the BLM and attracting nary a large crowd, Valley of the Gods contains scores of gothic sandstone monoliths and spires rising out of a flat desert expanse. Susceptible to stunning sunsets, the valley is cast in red, its hues dependent on the sun's position. With no restrictions on where you can and can't go, Valley of the Gods is the kind of place where it's hard to resist unleashing the barbarian in yourself. The road meanders past the monuments, sometimes through sandy washes, and lets out on Highway 163, 7½ miles northeast of Mexican Hat and 15 miles southwest of Bluff. Its condition depends on the weather and the last time the county took a scraper to it. Generally, you'll be able to get your low-clearance, two-wheel-drive across it—that is, if it isn't raining.

Goosenecks State Park perches 1,000 feet above the San Juan River and its twisting channels, carved through the valley floor. The park's name refers to the tight bends of this section of the river, giving the canyons a gooseneck-like appearance. This is one of the best examples of entrenched river meanders you'll find. So meandering is the river that it takes 6 miles for the river to cover an air distance of 1½ miles. Interpretive signs at the overlook give you a geological explanation of what's below. Head southwest on Highway 316, which branches off Highway 261 less than a mile from the Highway 163 junction. Follow the road 3 miles to its end.

Scraping out an existence in the middle of the desert on the banks of the San Juan, *Mexican Hat* (population 38) is a bare-bones kind of place. The location really hasn't sufficed for any endeavors that its residents have engaged in, such as farming, oil drilling, or gold and uranium mining. By virtue of its existence, the tiny town is now a small trade and tourism center, not to mention a good put-in for rafts and canoes along the San Juan River. The town gets its name from the most prominent of rock formations sticking out above the town. If you look at it upside down, *Mexican Hat Rock* looks like a sombrero. As the story goes, a Mexican vaquero was wooing a young Indian girl near the river. But the girl was married to an old, evil medicine man who, upon hearing of his wife's infidelity, turned the vaquero to stone. The poor vaquero now goes by the name of Mexican Hat Rock.

After six months of traipsing through some of Utah's most inhospitable and dangerous land during the late 1880s, members of the Mormon Hole-in-the-Rock wagon train were too exhausted to continue. So they settled where they stood in a canyon of the San Juan River, and under the shadows of convoluted rock formations, at what is today known as *Bluff*. The town's appearance has retained much of the original pioneering character, which was surprisingly urbane—as indicated by scores of ornate Victorian stone houses standing on Bluff's backstreets. Pick up a Historic Bluff City brochure at any of the businesses around town and take the "Bluff City Historic Loop." The brochure explains the history of each of the fourteen featured homes and guides you to all the Indian remains and rock art found around town.

The Old Spanish Slave Trail

Before white men entered the Southwest, the Paiute Indians lived in small bands, hunting and gathering. Paiutes were protective of their land, which stretched from Southern Utah (north of Navajo land) to the edge of Utah Lake in Utah County.

Early explorers and settlers took their lives in their hands when they entered Paiute country. In 1776 the great explorer Father Silvestre Vélez de Escalante was looking for the best route to California. A Spanish priest, Escalante was the first white man to record his adventures and travels in this region. As a result of his exploration, others followed.

By 1800 the *Old Spanish Trail* was established. It became a major travel artery and trade route. The unsavory practice of trading horses for Indian slaves gave it the name "The Slave Trail."

The trail was later used by fur trappers and traders. In 1844 John Fremont wrote that the trail was well used and nice to travel on—except for vicious Paiutes protecting their home turf.

You can visit the austere, hilltop *Pioneer Cemetery*, where many of the original Bluff residents are buried. (Turn north on Third East, take a left at Mulberry Avenue, and follow the paved road to the top.) The first pioneer to die in Bluff, Roswell Stevens, rested at a different site until the residents decided to move his body and casket to the top of the hill, the only place in town where the wind was apparently not strong enough to blow the dirt off the top of his grave. The hill is also the site of an Ancestral Puebloan pueblo, built between 1050 and 1250, which consists of structures known as Great House and Great Kiva. You can also get a nice bird's-eye view of the town.

You can view many more marks left by the Ancestral Puebloans, not to mention the Navajos and Utes, in and around Bluff. Large panels of petroglyphs hang at *Sand Island Campground*, just west of Bluff on Highway 163. Several designs of *Kokopelli*, the mythological Ancestral Puebloan flute player you've seen in perhaps every gift shop in Southern Utah, dance across one of the panels.

Fourteen Window Ruin, the site of an Ancestral Puebloan cliff dwelling, can be reached by crossing over the San Juan River on a suspension bridge beyond the St. Christopher's Episcopal Mission (2 miles east of town on Highway 163). Take a right (south) 1³⁄₁₀ miles east of the mission onto a dirt road. Stay right at the fork and drive another half mile to the bridge. The walk is a leisurely 2 miles round-trip. Please don't disturb any of the fragile remains. And don't go into the rooms.

The abundance of Indian ruins and geological formations found along the San Juan River demands some expert guidance, which ***Wild Rivers Expeditions*** (435-672-2244) certainly provides. Archaeologists and geologists offer interpretive tours down the San Juan that can last from a day to a week. You'll find Wild Rivers on Highway 191 at the center of Bluff. Write them at 101 Main Street, Box 118, Bluff 84512, or at riversandruins.com.

Your best bet for accommodations in Bluff is ***Recapture Lodge*** on Highway 191, made famous by Tony Hillerman in *A Thief of Time.* You can stay either in the main lodge's motel rooms or in the Pioneer House, otherwise known as ***the J. B. Decker House*** (built in 1898 and listed on the National Register of Historic Places), reasonable rates. The rooms are comfortable, most with fully equipped kitchens. Self-guided walking and mountain bike trails take visitors from the lodge to the San Juan River. During the high season, the lodge's proprietors give informational slide shows of the area in the evenings. Call (435) 672-2281 or visit recapturelodge.com for more information.

Underneath Bluff's trademark rock formations (the Navajo Twins), ***Twin Rocks Trading Post*** (435-672-2341 or 800-526-3448; twinrocks.com) carries an excellent supply of Navajo baskets, rugs, sand paintings, fetishes, pots, and jewelry. The Simpson family, owners of Twin Rocks, has aided in the proliferation of weaving and basket-making within the Navajo reservation. Artists are valued overall, and their pictures accompany the sale of their baskets or rugs. Open seven days a week, 8 a.m. to sunset. While you're there, grab a bite at the cafe. You'll find Twin Rocks at the mouth of Cow Canyon, just off Highway 191 at 913 East Navajo Twins Drive, Bluff.

Around AD 900 a group of Ancestral Puebloans Indians left Mesa Verde and settled 100 miles west at what is now called ***Hovenweep National Monument***. A Ute word meaning "deserted valley," Hovenweep is the site of six separate pueblo settlements and probably more, considering that most of the 784 acres at Hovenweep have yet to be excavated. The Ancestral Puebloans built the towers, one of which is called ***Hovenweep Castle***, around the same time Europeans began erecting their castles. But the purpose and square design of the towers baffle archaeologists, who are still trying to decide whom they were defending themselves against. Archaeologists figure they may have left because of a drought. Tree rings indicate that the ground began to dry up around 1274. By 1300 the site was deserted, and they moved to other sites in northwestern New Mexico or northeastern Arizona.

The best preserved, most impressive, and most easily accessed of the six villages is ***Square Tower Ruins***. Like most cliff dwellings in the area, the ruins at Square Tower sit at the head of a canyon, which gave the inhabitants an unobstructed view of any oncoming threat. The placement of the village also allowed them to dam water from the long draws draining into the canyon and to irrigate their crops growing on the canyon floor. The structures at Square Tower Ruins, which represent every design found at Hovenweep, are excellent examples of pre-Columbian Pueblo masonry. Pick up the guide to the ruins at the visitor center. Along the 2-mile trail watch out for prairie rattlesnakes, which are active during spring and autumn days and summer nights.

There are a couple of approaches you can take to Hovenweep. From Blanding or Bluff, head east on Highway 262, which branches off Highway 191 between these towns. Then follow the signs 31 miles to Hovenweep. The road is unpaved in sections, so inquire at **Hatch Trading Post** (15 miles from the Highway 262/191 junction) about road conditions if the weather has been stormy. A 40-mile scenic approach from Bluff is to head east on Highway 163 to Aneth, and then follow signs from there to Hovenweep (paved roads all the way).

The monument, open year-round, maintains a campground near the ranger station. The closest supplies are at Hatch Trading Post, 16 miles west, or at **Ismay Trading Post**, 14 miles southeast in Colorado.

Places to Stay in Southeastern Utah

BLANDING

Best Western Gateway Motel
88 E. Center St.
(435) 678-2278
Standard

BLUFF

Recapture Lodge
220 E. Main St.
(435) 672-2281
Inexpensive

BOULDER

Boulder Mountain Lodge
20 N. Hwy 12
(435) 335-7460 or
(800) 556-3446
Moderate

FILLMORE

Best Western Paradise Inn of Fillmore
905 N. Main St.
(435) 743-6895
Standard

MOAB

Apache Motel
166 S. 400 East
(435) 259-5727
Standard

Archway Inn
1551 N. Hwy 191
(435) 259-2599
Standard

Best Western Canyonlands
16 S. Main St.
(435) 259-2300
Moderate

Red Stone Inn
535 S. Main St.
(435) 259-3500
Standard

MONTICELLO

Best Western Wayside Inn
197 E. Central
(435) 587-2261
Moderate

OLD LA SAL

Mt. Peale Inn & Spa
1415 E. Hwy 46
(435) 686-2284 or
(888) 687-3253
mtpeale.com
Moderate

TEASDALE

Lodge at Red River Ranch
2900 W. Hwy 24
(435) 425-3322 or
(800) 205-6343
redriverranch.com
Deluxe

TORREY

Broken Spur Inn
Hwys 12 and 24
(435) 425-3775
Inexpensive

Capitol Reef Resort
2600 E. Hwy 24
(435) 425-3761
Moderate

SkyRidge Bed and Breakfast Inn
950 E. Hwy 24
(435) 425-3222 or
(800) 448-6990
skyridgeinn.com
Deluxe

Places to Eat in Southeastern Utah

BOULDER

Burr Trail Grill
10 N. Hwy 12
(435) 335-7511
Moderate

Hell's Backbone Grill
20 N. Hwy 12
(435) 335-7464
Expensive

MOAB

Arches Pancake Haus
196 S. Main St.
(435) 259-7141
Inexpensive

Center Café
60 N. 100 West
(435) 259-4295
centercafemoab.com
Very expensive

Eddie McStiff's
57 S. Main St.
(435) 259-2337
Moderate

Moab Diner
189 S. Main St.
(435) 259-4006
Inexpensive

MONTICELLO

Doug's Steak and BBQ
496 N. Main St.
(435) 587-2255
Moderate

FOR MORE INFORMATION ABOUT SOUTHEASTERN UTAH

TRAVEL COUNCILS

Color Country Travel Region
P.O. Box 1550
St. George 84771
(435) 628-4171 or
(800) 233-8824
Fax (435) 673-3540

Road Conditions
(800) 492-2400

TOP ANNUAL EVENTS IN SOUTHEASTERN UTAH

MARCH-APRIL

Utah Jeep Safari
Moab
(435) 259-7625

AUGUST

San Juan County Fair and Blue
Mountain Roundup Rodeo
Monticello
(435) 587-3225

Grandma's Kitchen
133 E. Central
(435) 587-3017
Inexpensive

Wagon Wheel Pizza
164 S. Main St.
(435) 587-2766
Inexpensive

TORREY

Broken Spur Steakhouse
Hwys 12 and 24
(435) 425-3775

Cafe Diablo
599 W. Main St.
(435) 425-3070
Very expensive

Rim Rock Restaurant
2523 E. Hwy 23
(435) 425-3388
Very expensive

Appendix

State Campgrounds

Antelope Island State Park
4528 W. 1700 South
Syracuse 84075
(801) 773-2941

Bear Lake State Park
1030 N. Bear Lake Blvd.
P.O. Box 184
Garden City 84028
(435) 946-3343

Camp Floyd/Stagecoach Inn State Park
18035 W. 1540 North
Fairfield 84013
(801) 768-8932

Coral Pink Sand Dunes State Park
P.O. Box 95
Kanab 84741
(435) 648-2800

Dead Horse Point State Park
P.O. Box 609
Moab 84532
(435) 259-2614

Deer Creek State Park
P.O. Box 257
Midway 84049
(435) 654-0171

East Canyon State Park
5535 S. Hwy 66
Morgan 84050
(801) 829-6866

Edge of the Cedars State Park
660 W. 400 North
Blanding 84511
(435) 678-2238

Escalante State Park
710 N. Reservoir Rd.
Escalante 84726
(435) 826-4466

Fort Buenaventura State Park
2450 A Ave.
Ogden 84401
(801) 621-4808

Fremont Indian State Park
3820 W. Clear Creek Canyon Rd.
Sevier 84766
(435) 527-4631

Goblin Valley State Park
P.O. Box 637
Green River 84525
(435) 564-3633

Goosenecks State Park
660 W. 400 North
P.O. Box 788
Blanding 84511
(435) 678-2238

Great Salt Lake State Park
P.O. Box 16658
Salt Lake City 84116
(801) 250-1898

Green River State Park
P.O. Box 637
Green River 84525
(435) 564-3633

Gunlock State Park
P.O. Box 140
Santa Clara 84765
(435) 628-2255

Historic Union Pacific Rail Trail State Park
P.O. Box 754
Park City 84060
(435) 649-6839

Huntington State Park
P.O. Box 1343
Huntington 84528
(435) 687-2491

Hyrum State Park
405 W. 300 South
Hyrum 84319
(435) 245-6866

Iron Mission State Park
635 N. Main St.
Cedar City 84720
(435) 586-9290

Jordan River State Park
1084 N. Redwood Rd.
Salt Lake City 84116
(801) 533-4496

Jordanelle State Park
SR 319 #515 Box 4
Heber City 84032
(435) 649-9540

Kodachrome Basin State Park
P.O. Box 180069
Cannonville 84718
(435) 679-8562

Lost Creek State Park
5535 S. Hwy 66
Morgan 84050
(801) 538-7220

Millsite State Park
P.O. Box 1343
Huntington 84528
(435) 687-2491

Minersville State Park
P.O. Box 1531
Beaver 84713
(435) 438-5472

Otter Creek State Park
P.O. Box 43
Antimony 84712
(435) 624-3268

Palisade State Park
2200 Palisade Rd.
P.O. Box 650070
Sterling 84665
(435) 835-7275

Piute State Park
P.O. Box 43
Antimony 84712
(435) 624-3268

Quail Creek State Park
P.O. Box 1943
St. George 84770
(435) 879-2378

Red Fleet State Park
8750 N. Hwy 191
Vernal 84078
(435) 789-4432

Rockport State Park
9040 N. State Hwy 302
Peoa 84061
(435) 336-2241

Sand Hollow State Park
P.O. Box 1435
St. George 84771
(435) 879-2378

Scofield State Park
P.O. Box 166
Price 84501
(435) 448-9449

Snow Canyon State Park
1002 N. Snow Canyon Dr.
Ivins 84738
(435) 628-2255

Starvation State Park
P.O. Box 584
Duchesne 84021
(435) 738-2326

Steinaker State Park
4435 N. Hwy 191
Vernal 84078
(435) 789-4432

Territorial Statehouse State Park
50 W. Capitol Ave.
Fillmore 84631
(435) 743-5316

Utah Lake State Park
4400 W. Center St.
Provo 84601
(801) 375-0731

Wasatch Mountain State Park
P.O. Box 10
Midway 84049
(435) 654-1791

Willard Bay State Park
900 W. 650 North #A
Willard 84340
(435) 734-9494

Yuba State Park
P.O. Box 159
Levan 84639
(435) 758-2611

Public and Private Information Resources

Arts Council
617 E. South Temple
Salt Lake City 84102
(801) 236-7555
arts.utah.gov/index.html

Bed & Breakfast Inns of Utah, Inc.
(a nonprofit trade organization promoting bed-and-breakfast experiences throughout the state)
P.O. Box 3066
Park City 84060
(435) 645-8068
bbiu.org

Bicycle Utah
P.O. Box 738
Park City 84060
(435) 649-5806
bicycleutah.com

Film Commission
324 S. State St., Ste. 500
Salt Lake City 84111
(800) 453-8824 or (801) 538-8740
film.utah.gov/index.html

The Foremost West
(a multistate marketer with information, tours, itinerary planning, and reservation services for international visitors)
770 E. South Temple, Ste. B
Salt Lake City 84102
(801) 532-6666
Fax (801) 532-1921
foremostw@aol.com

Guides and Outfitters
153 E. 7200 South
Midvale 84047
(801) 566-2662
utahguidesandoutfitter.com

Heritage Foundation
P.O. Box 28
485 Canyon Rd.
Salt Lake City 84110-0028
(801) 533-0858
utahheritagefoundation.com

Historical Society
300 Rio Grande St.
Salt Lake City 84101
(801) 533-3500
history.utah.gov

Hotel and Lodging Association
9 Exchange Pl., Ste. 812
Salt Lake City 84111
(801) 359-0104
uhta.org

Museum Service
324 S. State St., Ste. 500
Salt Lake City 84114
(801) 533-3247

National Weather Service
(8 a.m. to 4 p.m., live; recorded information after-hours)
(801) 524-5133

Parks & Recreation
1594 W. North Temple, Ste. 116
P.O. Box 146001
Salt Lake City 84114
(801) 538-7220
statepark.utah.gov

Public Safety
(Utah Highway Patrol)
4501 S. 2700 West
P.O. Box 141775
Salt Lake City 84114
(801) 965-4461 for administration
(801) 965-4518 or *11 (for cellular phones) for Utah Highway Patrol (24 hours a day)

Ski Utah Association
150 W. 500 South
Salt Lake City 84101
(801) 534-1779
skiutah.com

Transportation

U.S. Bureau of Land Management (BLM)
324 S. State St., Ste. 401
P.O. Box 45155
Salt Lake City 84145-0155
(801) 539-4001
ut.blm.gov

U.S. Forest Service Regional Office
324 25th St.
Ogden 84401
(801) 625-5306
fs.fed.us/r4/

U.S. Geological Survey
(to obtain Utah topographic maps)
2300 S. 2222 West
West Valley City 84117
(801) 975-3742
ugs.state.ut.us

Utah Private Child Care Association
1800 S. West Temple, Ste. 201
Salt Lake City 85115
(801) 466-5937

Utah Travel Center
4501 S. 2700 West
Salt Lake City 84119
(801) 964-6000 (Salt Lake area road report)
(800) 492-2400 (within Utah)
utahtravelcenter.com

Utah Travel Council
300 N. State St.
P.O. Box 147420
Salt Lake City 84114
(801) 538-1030 or (800) 200-1160
utah.com

Wildlife Resources
(Utah hunting and fishing information)
1596 W. North Temple
Salt Lake City 84116
(801) 538-4700
wildlife.utah.gov

Nearby National Parks

Arches National Park
P.O. Box 907
Moab 84532
(435) 259-8161

Bryce Canyon National Park
Bryce Canyon 84717
(435) 834-5322

Canyonlands National Park
Moab 84532
(435) 259-7164

Capitol Reef National Park
HC–70 Box 15
Torrey 84775
(435) 425-3791

Cedar Breaks National Monument
82 N. 100 East
Cedar City 84720
(435) 586-9451

Dinosaur National Monument
4545 Hwy 40
Dinosaur, CO 81610
Headquarters (303) 374-3000
Quarry Visitor Center (435) 789-2115

**Flaming Gorge National
Recreation Area**
P.O. Box 279
Manila 84046
(435) 784-3445

**Golden Spike National
Historic Site**
P.O. Box 897
Brigham City 84302
(435) 471-2209

Hovenweep National Monument
McElmo Route
Cortez, CO 81321
(303) 749-0510 or

Mesa Verde National Park
CO 81330
(303) 529-4461

**Natural Bridges National
Monument**
P.O. Box 1
Lake Powell 84533
(435) 692-1234

**Rainbow Bridge National
Monument**
P.O. Box 1507
Page, AZ 86040
(520) 608-6404

**Timpanogos Cave National
Monument**
Route 3, Box 200
American Fork 84003
(801) 756-3238

Zion National Park
P.O. Box 1099
Springdale 84767
(435) 772-3256

Index

About the Author

Michael Rutter is a writer/photographer who has published fifty books and hundreds of articles for magazines, journals, and newspapers. Writing about his home state of Utah is one of his favorite topics.

He is a recipient of the Ben Franklin Book Award for Excellence and the Rocky Mountain Book Publishers' Award. An "addicted" fly fisherman, his outdoor essays have been widely published (from Yale University to *Outdoor Life*). Michael has worked with American Experience on "The Wild West Series" and is interviewed in the A&E documentary *Butch Cassidy and the Sundance Kid* (Netflix, PBS). He has been a Christa McAuliffe Fellow and an AT&T Scholar. He has worked in advertising and as a consultant. He has been a key contractor with Qualtrics, specializing in executive corporate communications and management training.

His book titles include: *Myths and Mysteries of the Old West* (TwoDot Books), *Boudoirs to Brothels: The Intimate World of Wild West Women*; *Wild Bunch Women* (TwoDot Books); *Upstairs Girls: Prostitution in the American West*; *Outlaw Tales of Utah* (TwoDot Books); *Bedside Book of Bad Girls: Outlaw Women of the American West*; *Fly Fishing Made Easy* (Globe Pequot); and *Basic Essentials Fly Fishing* (Falcon Guides). He is currently researching nineteenth-century women of Colorado for a new project. Michael has also co-written twenty-four textbooks on business, marketing, and technical communication for Cengage (South-Western), McGraw-Hill, Pearson, and Thompson.

He spends summers wandering, searching for stories and images—researching, digging into documents, photographing, tracking animals, and throwing copious amounts of fly line. He teaches advanced writing at Brigham Young University and lives in Orem, Utah, with his wife, Shari, three cats, and a large, spoiled dog, a Turkish Akbash named Star.